Siegfried Kracauer

Key Contemporary Thinkers

Siegfried Kracauer

Our Companion in Misfortune

Graeme Gilloch

polity

First published in 2015 by Polity Press

Polity Press
65 Bridge Street
Cambridge CB2 1UR, UK

Polity Press
350 Main Street
Malden, MA 02148, USA

ISBN-13: 978-0-7456-2961-2
ISBN-13: 978-0-7456-2962-9(pb)

A catalogue record for this book is available from the British Library.

Library of Congress Cataloging-in-Publication Data
Gilloch, Graeme.
  Siegfried Kracauer : our companion in misfortune / Graeme Gilloch.
    pages cm
  ISBN 978-0-7456-2961-2 (hardback : alk. paper) – ISBN 978-0-7456-2962-9 (pbk. : alk. paper)   1. Kracauer, Siegfried, 1889-1966–Criticism and interpretation.   I. Title.
  PT2621.R135Z67 2015
  834'.912–dc23

2014022838

Typeset in 10/11.5 Palatino
by Toppan Best-set Premedia Limited
Printed and bound in the United Kingdom by CPI Group (UK) Ltd, Croydon, CRO 4YY

For further information on Polity, visit our website:
politybooks.com

For Peter

There are a lot of people these days who, although unaware of each other, are nevertheless linked by a common fate. ... [T]hey are overcome by a profound sadness which arises from the recognition of their confinement in a particular spiritual/intellectual *[geistige]* situation, a sadness that ultimately overruns all layers of their being. It is this metaphysical suffering from the lack of a higher meaning in the world, a suffering due to an existence in an empty space, which makes these people companions in misfortune.

Siegfried Kracauer, 'Those Who Wait' (1922), in *The Mass Ornament*

Contents

Acknowledgements

The metaphor of the journey runs through this book. Writing it has indeed proved a long (much longer than anticipated) and sometimes daunting adventure. I am grateful to so many people who have shared the road awhile as guides, as well-wishers and, most of all, as constant companions. You have all brought me such good fortune.

My publisher, Polity Press, and, in particular John B. Thompson and Jonathan Skerrett, have been supportive throughout and I am deeply grateful for their kind help and, above all, their perseverance and patience. Thank you for standing by me and by the project.

I would like to thank the Alexander von Humboldt Foundation and the Leverhulme Trust for their kind and generous fellowship awards which enabled me to undertake archive research in Germany. I am very grateful to the Archivzentrum of the Stadt- und Universitätsbibliothek (Johann Wolfgang Goethe Universität, Frankfurt am Main) and the Deutsches Literaturarchiv (Marbach am Neckar) for permission to access and use materials in the Max Horkheimer, Leo Löwenthal and Siegfried Kracauer archives. I would like to thank the archive staff who were always most welcoming, helpful and generous with their time. In particular, I would like to express my sincere gratitude to Herr Jochen Stollberg in Frankfurt and wish him every happiness in his retirement.

This book could not have come into being without the help and support of so many students, colleagues and friends along the way ... indeed, students who have now become colleagues, and colleagues who have now become friends. I have benefited in myriad ways from conversations and exchanges with Ross Abbinnett, Erkan Ali, Andrew Benjamin, Matthias Benzer, Bülent Diken, Nigel Dodd, Karen Engle, Jonathan Fletcher, Adam Fish, Tara Forrest, Emma Fraser, Gunter Gassner, Stefano Giacchetti, Craig Hammond, Christian Hermansen

Cordua, Jeesoon Hong, Noah Isemberg, Troels Degn Johansson, Jane Kilby, Sungdo Kim, Claus Krogholm Kristiansen, Fabio La Rocca, Dee Leahy, Changnam Lee, Esther Leslie, Jack Nye, Ulrich Oevermann, Deborah Parsons, David Pinder, Antonio Rafaele, Jiseok Ryu, Erik Steinskøg, Phillipe Simay, Greg Smith, Paul Taylor, Zoe Thompson, Imogen Tyler and Gül Yassturk. My sincere thanks to all of you.

I would like to thank two writers whose works on Kracauer remain inspirational, two wonderful scholars whose recent passing has been a huge loss to Critical Theory: David Frisby and Miriam Bratu Hansen.

The contribution of some people over the years has been particularly profound: Tim Dant, Jaeho Kang, Allen Shelton and Charles Turner. It is a privilege to know you and to work with you. Your insights and ideas have enriched everything I have written; our enduring friendships everything I have yet to write.

This book would not have been possible without Bernadette Boyle. Translator, proofreader, corrector, discussant, critic. *Bricoleuse extraordinaire*. For everything you have done: thank you.

And lastly, my special thanks to Thomas and Roisín for all the many wonderful distractions which you have provided over the years. You have grown up in the time it has taken me to write this book. I cannot believe how quickly the years have gone by in your joyous company.

This book is dedicated to my father, Peter, with all my love.

*****

Some of the material contained in this book has been published in earlier versions as detailed below. I am grateful to the editors and publishers for their kind permission to publish such materials in revised form.

Sections of chapter 2 were first published under the title 'The Faces of Amsterdam: Rembrandt, Simmel and the Painting of Modern Lives' in *Episteme* [journal of the Centre for Applied Cultural Studies, Korea University, Seoul], No. 4, 2010, pp. 233–56.

Some sections of chapter 4 first appeared in '"Seen from the Window": Rhythm, Improvisation and the City', in Laura Colini and Frank Eckhardt (eds), *Bauhaus and the City* (Würzburg: Königshaus & Neumann, 2001), pp. 185–202.

Other sections of chapter 4 appeared as 'Impromptus of a Great City: Siegfried Kracauer's *Strassen in Berlin und anderswo*', in *Tracing Modernity*, ed. Mari Hvattum and Christian Hermansen (London: Routledge, 2004), pp. 291–306.

Sections of chapter 5 are adapted and reprinted by permission of the publishers from 'The Word on the Street: Charles Baudelaire, Jacques Offenbach and the Paris of their Time', in *Manifestoes and*

Transformations in the Early Modernist City, ed. Christian Hermansen Cordua (Farnham: Ashgate, 2010), pp. 59–75. Copyright © 2010

An earlier version of chapter 6 appeared as 'Orpheus in Hollywood: Siegfried Kracauer's Offenbach Film', in *Tracing Modernity*, ed. Mari Hvatttum and Christian Hermansen (London: Routledge, 2004), pp. 307–23.

The first half of chapter 8 appeared as 'Below the Surface: Anti-Semitism, Prejudice and Siegfried Kracauer's "Test Film" Project', in *New Formations*, 61 (2007) pp. 149–60 [special issue on Siegfried Kracauer]. I am grateful to my co-author, Dr Jaeho Kang, of SOAS, London, for permission to revise this work for publication here.

Parts of chapter 9 were first published under the title 'Ad Lib: Improvisation, Imagination and Enchantment in Siegfried Kracauer', in *Sociétés: Revue des Sciences Humaines et Sociales* No. 110, 4 / 2010, pp. 29–46.

Sections of chapter 10 were first published in 'Urban Optics: Film, Phantasmagoria and the City in Benjamin and Kracauer', in *New Formations*, 61 (2007) pp. 115–31 [special issue on Siegfried Kracauer].

I am grateful to the Max Horkheimer (Frankfurt am Main) and Siegfried Kracauer (Marbach am Neckar) archives for kindly allowing publication of hitherto unpublished archive materials.

The author and publishers are grateful to Princeton University Press for permission to reproduce material from *From Caligari to Hitler*; to Oxford University Press for permission to reproduce material from *Theory of Film* (© 1960 by Oxford University Press, Inc. By permission of Oxford University Press, USA); and to Harvard University Press for permission to reproduce material from *The Mass Ornament: Weiner Essays* (Copyright © 1995 by the President and Fellows of Harvard College).

Our Companion Introduced:
An Intellectual Schwejk

1 The Path to Be Followed

I imagine the critical theorist Siegfried Kracauer standing at a cross-roads, the kind of junction envisaged by the French sociologist Henri Lefebvre in his study *Everyday Life in the Modern World* when he reflects:

> We have now reached a junction, a kind of crossroads, and we could do worse than to examine the lie of the land before we proceed any further. Behind us, as we stand at their point of intersection, are the way of philosophy and the road of everyday life. They are divided by a mountain range, but the path of philosophy keeps to the heights, thus overlooking that of everyday life; ahead the track winds, barely visible, through thickets, thorn bushes and swamps. (2000: 17)

There would be those among us who, fearful of the meandering path ahead and what might be lurking unseen in its undergrowth, would turn tail and head for the security and prospects of the high ground. Others, wrinkling their noses in distaste, would seek to preserve their dignity and distance by treading with disdain as they seek to circum-navigate the difficult terrain ahead, all the while bemoaning their lot and the foolishness of their guide.

There are those rare talents who have come thus far by old smug-glers' routes, and who have the arcane wisdom to find yet more long forgotten and forbidden tracks through the mire (Walter Benjamin is one such perhaps). And there are those, like Kracauer, for whom, with pipe clenched between the teeth, nothing could be more intriguing, enticing and, indeed, important than the overgrown wilderness ahead.

The concrete world of the everyday was his terrain of choice. This is not to say that he was unfamiliar with the high ground of philosophy – after all, he was Theodor W. Adorno's first unofficial tutor in Kantian thought[1] – or that his works lacked philosophical themes, insights and profundity. Far from it – these are all present and correct though often in curious guise. But he was drawn unerringly to those uninviting 'thickets, thorn bushes and swamps' of everyday life. This is the true landscape, not only of his own thinking, but of film, his most beloved medium and the dominant motif of his later writings. 'Landscape', though, is perhaps not the right word here: *cityscape* is more appropriate. For Kracauer remains one of the most sensitive and subtle analysts of the experience and culture of metropolitan modernity – its teeming crowds and noisy traffic; its brilliant lights and sparkling surfaces; its streets and architecture; its manifold distractions and diversions; its dismal leavings and left-overs. He had an acute eye for all those seemingly insignificant and ephemeral phenomena of the city that others blithely overlook and undervalue.[2] As a radical 'ragpicker at daybreak'[3] he recognized their profound potential for the critical unmasking and debunking of prevailing capitalist power and its central mythology of rational technological progress. All such myriad and momentary figures and forms of quotidian life fascinated Kracauer and found exquisite expression in writings penned in five great cities – Frankfurt am Main, Berlin, Paris, Marseilles and New York – and spanning the calamitous events and catastrophes of the first half of the twentieth century.

For me, three things distinguish Kracauer's works and make them so enjoyable and exciting for the reader today, nearly fifty years after his death. Firstly, there is the sheer variety of his writings in terms of their *form*, let alone their thematic and conceptual range: long unpublished treatises dating from the years of the Great War, steeped in the tenets and traditions of *Lebensphilosophie*;[4] feuilleton fragments of all kinds written as journalist, reviewer and editor for the *Frankfurter Zeitung* and attesting to the daily life of Frankfurt and Berlin during the Weimar years; assorted fictional writings, including a novella, a short story or two, and two full-length quasi-autobiographical novels; 'biographical' studies of a peculiar and pioneering kind; sketches of screenplays and film 'treatments'; scripts and questionnaires for a psychological experiment; articles for both academic journals and popular magazines; confidential reports for government agencies; essay collections; three books written in his adopted English language in 'permanent exile' in post-war New York; and even a few adolescent poems. Kracauer was a prolific and hugely adaptable writer who managed to live through the most turbulent and traumatic of times by means of his typewriter.

Secondly, despite this heterogeneity of textual production and the most varied of circumstances across many years, Kracauer's works exhibit a characteristic style and exude a particular tone. Doubtless because they were so often intended to appeal to a wide public, his writings tend to eschew the technical language and tropes of scholarly writing in favour of the vernacular and the everyday. Unlike so much scholarship, then and now, Kracauer's texts are both accessible and readable.[5] And this is true in some measure even of his earliest philosophical texts where the most intricate of ideas are presented with an enviable clarity of expression and precision in phrasing. This is complexity of thought without convolution, sophistication of argument without showiness. For me, the very ease and directness of his writing belies the skill of his textual strategies. It would be easy to underestimate the powerful work of his prose, especially when it might seem a touch pedestrian. Time and again it winds its way through seemingly commonplace examples and turns of phrase to arrive suddenly at an extraordinary and unexpected insight. Looking back at the pages already turned, one realizes that what had hitherto seemed detours and digressions were in fact the only paths to this point. Not a word has been wasted en route: this is what one might term writing *recaptured*.

And then there is Kracauer's distinctive tone, one that is both enlivened and enlightened by wit and humour and yet, at the same time, imbued with a sense of melancholy. *Ginster*, in many ways Kracauer's comic masterpiece,[6] whose eponymous protagonist is a Chaplinesque[7] everyman and would-be good soldier, like Jaroslav Hašek's unforgettable Schwejk,[8] does not compel the reader to laugh out loud but, rather, to smile ruefully at the idiocy of characters and irony of social conditions against the apocalyptic backdrop of the Great War. And then there is the scorn which, years later, Kracauer heaps upon the incipient world of human resources and aptitude tests investigated in his 1929 ethnography of Berlin's white-collar workers, *Die Angestellten* (chapter 3). It is in the unlikely figure of the composer Jacques Offenbach (chapters 5 and 6) that Kracauer finds his kindred spirit: on the one hand, a delightful 'mocking bird' whose operettas parroted and parodied Parisian life under the Second Empire; on the other, a musician with an ear for the sorrowful condition of humanity, the sufferings attendant upon love and loss, and the hope of redemption embodied in the figure of Orpheus.[9] His own proposals for films were for comedies – not just the Offenbach motion picture (chapter 6) but also his suggestions for an adaptation of a Tartarin adventure (based on novels by Leon Daudet) and *Dimanche* (chapter 10). Indeed, American slapstick film comedies (*Grotesk*) and Hollywood musical romances constituted for him exemplary cinematic forms (chapter 9). Although there are high jinks to be had at high altitudes – as Tartarin, Charlie Chaplin, Harold Lloyd and others certainly demonstrate – Kracauer's own way lay through the lowlands and not for fear of falling: for him, this was where the real fun was to be had.

This gravitation towards the comic has its serious side: as we will see in chapters 9 and 10, there is a profound utopian aspect here. And, significantly, it draws Kracauer to popular culture, not only the madcap capers of slapstick film comedy but also the clowning of acrobats and others in theatrical revues, even the drunken reveries of washed-up piano players. My third point then is this: Kracauer had a genuine penchant for popular culture. Indeed, of all those who might have some claim to the title of critical theorist, Kracauer was the only one to treat popular modern culture both seriously as an object of analysis and in a spirit of openness and critical appreciation. He was not immune to the high cultural aesthetics vaunted by bourgeois *Bildung* and embodied in German *Kultur*; nor was he blind to the ideological functions and commodification processes inherent in the capitalist culture industries, as is evident in his more Marxist moments. But his writings point both to the search for a more sociological engagement with metropolitan mass culture and to the formation of a radically new set of criteria for evaluating the role and significance of the emergent mass media. His comments on the 'mass ornament' and his early response to photography, for example, are for the most part critical, but there is also a significant degree of ambivalence: as he makes clear in each case, these are wholly *legitimate* expressions of the modern condition and important in that they exemplify its tensions and contradictions in acute form (chapters 2 and 3). And his endless critical reviews of the banal products of the film industry were always tempered by, and in tension with, a more phenomenological vision of the radical potential of the film medium itself, a view which eventually comes to the fore in his post-war *Theory of Film*. Indeed, the very normative purpose of the latter is to explore and establish definite and distinctive criteria for the appreciation of the unique qualities of the cinematic medium, criteria which run directly counter to the conventions and pretensions of art, both traditional and modernist.

Kracauer's writings do not elide, erase or ignore the catastrophes that beset his generation: a mechanized, bureaucratized and disenchanted modern world, utterly enamoured of its own claims to scientific progress yet prone to industrialized wars of mass slaughter; convinced of its own rationality yet blind to its lapse into a new mythology; fragile in its supposedly democratic structures and susceptible to tyranny and totalitarianism; so complacent in its claims to civilization that the Holocaust is simply unimaginable. Nor is he overwhelmed by them. With the means, with the media, at our disposal, with what is to hand, we can cunningly, courageously challenge these terrors and overcome them. This resoluteness, albeit not resolution, is the final message of Kracauer's 'Film in our Time', the polemical culmination of his writings on the cinematic medium, when the screen is transformed into Athena's shield so that we, the spectators, may behold that which would otherwise turn us to stone and defiantly strike it down. Trenches and muddy no-man's-land; dictators saluting mass rallies; 'total war'; deportations; extermination camps; secret police; show-trials; barbed wire and watchtowers – these are the images which play before the Perseus of modern times, and which Kracauer confronts directly in his writings on his own military conscription, on fascist propaganda and Nazi newsreels, and on Soviet 'satellite mentalities'.

Indeed, film is not only our wise protector, Athena, but also our quick-witted guide, Ariadne. Kracauer writes: 'Guided by film, then, we approach, if at all, ideas no longer on highways leading through the void but on paths that wind through the thicket of things' (TOF: 309). With dogged determination, and with hope, Kracauer accompanies us on this risky journey across inhospitable terrain to an unpromised land. Loyal to the creaturely world of things, loyal to us, yet indulgent of those more haughty and high flown than himself, a 'plain man' blessed with resilience and unerring common sense: Kracauer is our very own Sancho Panza.[10] Eclectic in his interests, accessible in style, as well versed in popular culture as in philosophy, a scholar without pomposity and a wit without cruelty, he will prove the most agreeable of companions amid all our misfortunes.

2   A Sketch of Our Companion

Kracauer was fascinated by the various conceptions and possibilities of the biographical, understood here in its literal sense of how 'to write' (*graphikos, graphein*, Greek) a 'life' (*bios*, Greek). Initially grounded, as we will see, in the principles of *Lebensphilosophie*, Kracauer's concern is twofold: how the 'inner life' of an individual can come to find expression in the work of art, or on screen; and, at the same time, how the life of an individual may contain within it, in miniature, the tendencies and tensions of the wider society of which they are a member. In reconstructing the life of the individual, of certain *exemplary* individuals in particular although in principle *anyone* would do, one might discern his/her society in monadological form. Such ideas inform a number of Kracauer's writings: an essay on the popularity of the biography as part of the prevailing literary landscape; his own two semi-autobiographical novels, *Ginster* and *Georg*; and, perhaps most importantly, his reconfiguration of the biographical mode as 'societal biography' (*Gesellschaftsbiographie*), as a symptomatic reading of prevailing social conditions in his analyses of Simmel and Offenbach. Of course, Kracauer's own life story might lend itself to such a reading, but that is not my intention here. What follows in this study is a series of interconnected essays on a selection of Kracauer's key writings and preoccupations. It is *not* an 'intellectual biography' – whatever that might mean, however that might be different from the biography of an intellectual, or simply a biography. Accordingly, the conventional biographical details that follow here are intended as a contextual frame.[11]

Siegfried Kracauer was born on 8 February 1889, the only child of a middle-class Jewish couple of modest means resident on Elkenbach-strasse in the Nordend-Ost district of Frankfurt am Main. His father, Adolf (1849–1918), a dealer in fabrics, and his mother, Rosette (1867–1942, *née* Oppenheim), had married the previous year. His uncle Isidor Kracauer (1852–1923) was a noted historian of the city's Jewish community[12] and taught at the widely respected Jewish middle school (*Reformrealgymnasium*), the Philanthropin, where Siegfried started as a pupil in 1898, before moving to the Klinger senior high school (*Ober-realschule*) in 1904. With his father often travelling on business, Kracauer spent much of his time with his Uncle Isidor and Aunt Hedwig (1862–1942), and they feature large in the pages of *Ginster*.

Siegfried began his training in architecture at the Grossherzogliche Technische Hochschule in Darmstadt in the summer semester of 1907 before relocating in the October to the Königliche Technische Hochschule zu Berlin, where he would attend lectures in philosophy and aesthetics by, among others, the sociologist Georg Simmel (1858–1918), a figure who was to exert a lifelong influence. In 1909, Kracauer relocated to the Königliche Bayerische Technische Hochschule in Munich for the summer semester and stayed there to complete his final studies with a dissertation on the theme of decorative ironwork in Berlin and the Brandenburg area (eventually published in 1915). Newly qualified as an architect, he began work for an architectural practice in a studio in Munich in January 1912. Kracauer's fascination with both philosophy and writing intensified as his interest in architecture waned. It was in Munich towards the end of 1912 that he met the young student Otto Hainebach (1892–1916), and a close friendship developed, one cut short by Hainebach's death at Verdun but whose echoes reverberate through many of Kracauer's later texts.

The year 1913 saw the composition of his unpublished novella 'The Mercy' ('Die Gnade'), our point of departure in chapter 1. The months preceding the outbreak of war saw an unsettled Kracauer moving back and forth between Munich and Frankfurt working for different architecture practices. If the account in *Ginster* of this moment is accurate, Kracauer was among the many thousands who, caught up in the initial enthusiasm occasioned by the declaration of war in August 1914, immediately volunteered for military service before being stood down for medical reasons. From 1915 Kracauer worked in Frankfurt at the offices of the architect Max Seckbach until the inevitable call-up as the increasing casualties of war required even the physically unfit to be pressed into service for Kaiser and country. Kracauer joined the Mainz Foot Artillery and had the double good fortune to avoid all active service (peeling potatoes seems to have been his main contribution to the war effort) and to be stood down again in early 1918, redeployed to a post in the town planning department (Stadtbauamt) in Osnabrück. During the war years, Simmel's own gravitation towards *Lebensphilosophie* proved influential for a number of Kracauer's substantial, though unpublished works exploring the prevailing state of the inner life of the subject and, in particular, the paralysis of the human soul in the disenchanted modern world of abstractness and rationalism. For Kracauer, such conditions lay behind a longing for both decisive action – one co-opted by the warmongers and propagandists – and unbridled self-expression, as manifest in the ecstatic works of the Expressionist movement (see chapter 2).

Two deaths in 1918, neither connected with the dog days of the war, impacted upon Kracauer. After his father died in July 1918, Kracauer returned to Frankfurt, where his mother, Rosette, Uncle Isidor and Aunt Hedwig then decided, partially as an economy measure, to share an apartment together on Sternstrasse, Frankfurt-Nord. And in September 1918 Georg Simmel died, prompting Kracauer's monograph to his former tutor a year later, a study which, as we will see in chapters 1 and 2, turns Simmel's own approach, as demonstrated in his 1916 study of Rembrandt, back upon the life and work of the sociologist to produce what Kracauer terms a 'topography of being' (*Wesenstopographie*).[13]

Back in Frankfurt, Kracauer was soon to make the acquaintance of two young men who would become his lifelong friends, although these cordial relations were repeatedly strained almost to breaking point: a teenage Theodor W. Adorno (1903–69), with whom Kracauer spent numerous afternoons reading Kant's *Critique of Pure Reason*, and Leo Löwenthal (1900–90), who, in the years to come, was to prove without doubt Kracauer's closest friend at the Frankfurt Institut für Sozialforschung and whose role as the editor of its house journal[14] was to involve some severely divided loyalties. And these contacts led to yet more: Löwenthal was closely associated with the Freie Jüdische Lehrhaus in Frankfurt and the circle around the charismatic teacher Rabbi Nehemia Anton Nobel, among whom two – Franz Rosenzweig and Martin Buber – would become key scholars exploring Judaic mystical traditions and folkways. But, unlike Löwenthal, Ernst Bloch and Walter Benjamin, Kracauer was to remain sceptical of, and always at a distance from, those two alluring chimera: theological speculations of the messianic variety and revolutionary politics of the communistic kind.

Perhaps it is no wonder that, given the impetus of all these new acquaintances, Kracauer's increasing enthusiasm for philosophy and writing would lead him finally to renounce his incipient architectural career and to immerse himself instead in scholarship. His epistemological reflections distinguishing sociology as a phenomenological enterprise (*Soziologie als Wissenschaft*) was published in 1922 and his *Der Detektiv-Roman: Ein philosophischer Traktat* was composed between 1922 and 1925. However, it was not the production of such weighty tomes for the academy that was to be his new profession – as one who suffered from a chronic nervous stammer, Kracauer always felt debarred from giving university lectures – but another form and practice of writing altogether and one much more in keeping with his metropolitan sensibility and milieu: journalism.[15]

Kracauer began writing for the politically liberal *Frankfurter Zeitung* in early 1921, initially as a local reporter and then as a salaried member of the journalist staff before finally becoming a full editor in 1924, when Benno Reifenberg took over the feuilleton section. Kracauer was a prolific writer,[16] producing nearly two thousand pieces[17] for the paper dealing with the widest possible array of subject matter: observations on the everyday street life of both Frankfurt and Berlin; tales recounting particular occurrences and memorable encounters; pen portraits of eccentric and otherwise remarkable street figures; discussions of urban architecture, planning and design; film and literary reviews; reports from exhibitions, shows and premieres; and occasional dispatches from abroad providing for reflections on conditions 'elsewhere'. Kracauer was not afraid to upset his close associates and new friends: his 1922 review 'Prophetentum' of Bloch's study of the revolutionary theologian Thomas Münzer led to a prolonged break in relations;[18] and his biting 1926 review of the first volume of Buber and Rosenzweig's new German translation of the Bible put a peremptory end to their acquaintances.[19] As the two subsequent collections of his feuilleton pieces amply demonstrate, the newspaper was the publication site of many of Kracauer's seminal essays, 'The Mass Ornament' piece of 1927 being perhaps his most famous single contribution. And one should not forget that two of his most critically acclaimed writings – his satirical novel *Ginster* (1928) and his study of white-collar workers, *Die Angestellten: Aus dem neuesten Deutschland* (1929–30) – both first appeared in the newspaper's pages in serialized form.[20]

The mid-1920s saw two other important developments in Kracauer's life: firstly, an increasing interest in historical materialism fuelled by intensive reading of Karl Marx and by the 1926 publication of Georg Lukács's seminal *History and Class Consciousness*;[21] secondly, in late 1925 or early 1926, Kracauer met Elisabeth (Lili) Ehrenreich (1893–1971), who had been working as a librarian at the Frankfurt Institut since its opening in 1924. Their relationship developed, and *Ginster* bears a dedication to her and their time in Marseilles together in 1926. They married on 5 March 1930. By this time, and following a ten-week initial visit to the city in the late spring and early summer of 1929 to collect the materials for the *Angestellten* study, Kracauer had moved to Berlin permanently to assume the editorship of the feuilleton section and the various film reviews and literary features forming the paper's city pages.[22] The Kracauers were to spend the next three years in the German capital before wisely fleeing to France on 28 February 1933, just one day after the Reichstag Fire.[23]

Kracauer left Germany for Paris at the behest of the *Frankfurter Zeitung* with the understanding that he was to become their correspondent there, following in the footsteps of Joseph Roth and Benno Reifenberg. But his position with the paper was terminated four weeks later, leaving the couple to eke out an impecunious existence in the French capital funded by whatever freelance writing Kracauer could manage. This first period of exile was most notable for two studies sparking acrimonious exchanges with Adorno. In 1937, Kracauer published his delightful 'societal biography' *Jacques Offenbach and the Paris of his Time*, a study of the life and works of another, earlier German émigré in the French capital and one whose music became the very signature of the Second Empire. Even though it was laced with ample analogies with the Third Reich, this wittily subversive account of the facile, superficial 'joy and glamour' of Napoleon III's farcical regime was castigated by Adorno and by Benjamin, himself an exile in Paris and in the throes of archival work as part of his famous, unfinished *Arcades Project*. If this were not bad enough, Kracauer's study of totalitarian propaganda, written the following year at Max Horkheimer's suggestion for publication in the *Zeitschrift*, was to be so radically edited and abbreviated by Adorno that Kracauer refused to authorize publication under his name of the final 'version'.

All such disputes were overtaken by more serious events and exigencies: the outbreak of war and the invasion of France. After a brief period of internment, Kracauer left Paris with Lili in the middle of June 1940 and, like Benjamin, who was to follow a few days later, relocated to Marseilles awaiting an escape route through Spain. Now trapped in the very city which had, fourteen years earlier, been a place of such love and happiness that *Ginster* was both dedicated to it and concludes on the Canebière, Kracauer used his time to good effect, working on two rather different film projects. The first, and the more important, was a proposal for a film history of German cinema to be undertaken with the Film Library at the Museum of Modern Art in New York; the other involved working on notes and sketches for a planned volume on film aesthetics, the famous 'Marseilles notebooks' that Miriam Bratu Hansen emphasizes in her account of *Theory of Film*. The Kracauers were lucky. The proposed film history project met with approval and funding in New York. While the role of the now exiled Frankfurt Institut members in Manhattan in bringing about this successful outcome remains a matter of dispute, the guarantee of paid employment in America was the key that enabled the Kracauers to travel across Spain and Portugal to Lisbon, whence, despite a few last-minute financial and bureaucratic hitches, they set sail for New York on 15 April 1941.[24]

For the next twenty-five years, the Kracauers were to live in Manhattan, becoming American citizens and permitting themselves occasional visits to Europe, especially Switzerland, for which they had a particular penchant. Working now exclusively in the unfamiliar English language,[25] something Adorno saw in itself as a betrayal of his true vocation and literary prowess,[26] Kracauer devoted his time and intellectual energies in two main directions. On the one hand, and underwritten by a string of various grants and stipends from the Rockefeller (1942), Guggenheim (1943), Bollingen (1949), Old Dominion (1952) and Chapelbrook (1955) foundations, he pursued work on his adopted medium of film, work resulting in the publication of the two books for which he remains best known in the Anglophone academy – *From Caligari to Hitler: A Psychological History of the German Film* (1947) and *Theory of Film: The Redemption of Physical Reality* (1960). We will explore these in chapters 7, 9 and 10. At the same time, Kracauer was repeatedly engaged on a number of shorter-term empirical projects with various government agencies and non-government organizations, producing reports, evaluations and assessments for, among others, the Scientific Research Department of the American Jewish Committee, UNESCO and the Voice of America broadcasting service. And in 1952 he became senior staff member, and subsequently research director, at the Bureau of Applied Social Research of Columbia University. This second group of writings has been largely ignored by commentators, an omission that this book seeks to alleviate in an initial way at least. And so, chapter 8 examines two of these neglected *Brotarbeit* studies as part of what I term the 'Caligari complex': Kracauer's work during the mid-1940s on a social-psychological 'test film', *Below the Surface*, investigating anti-Semitic attitudes; and his collaboration with the social psychologist Paul L. Berkmann on a study of attitudes among refugees fleeing Soviet oppression in the Eastern bloc, the substantial 1956 report *Satellite Mentalities*. In pioneering work on such materials, I hope not only to demonstrate the variety of Kracauer's post-war writings but also to suggest their thematic and conceptual interlacings.

Theory of Film was the last substantial text Kracauer was to publish in his lifetime. In the early 1960s Suhrkamp Verlag began the rehabilitation of his earlier writings with the publication of two seminal collections of feuilleton pieces chosen by Kracauer himself: *Das Ornament der Masse* in 1963 and then *Strassen in Berlin und Anderswo* the following year, some thirty years after its original conception (see chapter 4). By this time, Kracauer was fully embarked on another project, a study of the philosophy of history deeply imbued with cinematic reflections and analogies, which he would not live to complete but which was published posthumously as *History: Last Things before the Last* in 1969. Siegfried Kracauer died in New York of a lung infection on 26 November 1966 at the age of seventy-seven.

3 Encounters En Route

The rest of this Introduction provides an initial overview of the main themes of Kracauer's work and indicates how these are to be explored in the subsequent chapters. While it is impossible to do justice to such a heterogeneous corpus of work produced across such a chequered lifetime, I would suggest the following as among his abiding preoccupations.

1 A phenomenological concern with the everyday material world and lived experience as materials for illumination through construction and reconstruction. This encounter with the mundane world of bodies and things is chosen in preference to the lofty abstractions of high theory and the grand schemes and pretensions of philosophical musing. In the fields in which Kracauer is working, one must be content to deal with penultimate things, not expect to encounter eternal truths and the Absolute.

2 The critique of the modern capitalist condition understood as a state of 'spiritual shelterlessness' and marked by the pre-eminence of the *Ratio*. Kracauer provides a pessimistic and thoroughgoing interrogation of the disenchanted world. His critical vision of the predominance of instrumental reason in the mid-1920s prefigures that of Adorno and Horkheimer in their 'dialectic of enlightenment' thesis from 1947.

3 A fascination with the times, spaces and possibilities of countervailing modes of practice in interpersonal relations and artistic/cultural life: the marginal and liminal; the accidental and fortuitous; the derided and neglected; love and friendship; improvisation; slapstick comedy; the fairy tale; the renaissance of the human senses; and the redemption of the quotidian by means of film. All these forms of alterity are mobilized against the spiritual impoverishment promulgated by modern capitalist rationality.

4 The identification of the radical promise and possibilities of popular culture.[27] From operetta to detective fiction; from Hollywood musicals and Mancunian dance troupes to circus acrobats; from popular biographies to inebriated pianists – Kracauer's attraction to such commonplace figures and lowly forms was in contrast to his suspicion of the various strands of modernism and the avant-garde, whose artistic experimentations flinched from the task of exploring and representing material life.

5 'Interdisciplinary' and 'transdisciplinary' are terms used all too
   often today in the social sciences and humanities, but they are an
   apt description of the wide scope of Kracauer's oeuvre. Not only
   do his writings take a plethora of different textual forms – from
   feuilletons to film scripts, from novellas to classified reports for
   government agencies – but they also range freely over numerous
   academic fields: philosophy, sociology, ethnography, psychology,
   history, aesthetics, film studies, urban studies and cultural studies.
   Although interested in the demarcations of disciplinary boundaries
   and the specifications of subject matter, as an outsider to the
   academy and intellectual vagabond, he observed no scholarly
   borders. Kracauer was a literary *bricoleur* criss-crossing all these
   different literary forms and genres, an intellectual trespasser in
   scholarly fields which made scarcely any attempt to make him
   welcome.

Written primarily in an essayistic style, this book will seek where
possible to read such diverse texts in combination: philosophical reflections introduced via a novella or novel; a biographical book by means
of a screenplay; his study of film through the lens of sketches for
unmade movies. And, furthermore, this is congruent with Kracauer's
own preoccupation with the role of construction, the presentation of
truth through mosaics of, in themselves, illegible fragments.

My goal in this book is to foreground two essential motifs which run
through the text and for me encapsulate Kracauer's unique work and
contribution to critical social and cultural thought. The first of these is
the notion of 'imagination': by this I mean that Kracauer was above all
a thinker of the visual and *a thinker in visual terms*.[28] Indeed, I would
suggest that he is the unrivalled exponent of the dialectical imagination. The most obvious example of this is, of course, his longstanding
preoccupation with the media of photography and film. But my understanding of this term is both more literal and more general: for me,
Kracauer is ever drawn to how the objects, processes, practices of everyday life – indeed, mundane lives themselves – are manifest in, and/or
can be given, visual representation: 'imagination', then, as the turning
of things into images. And then such visual manifestations are available for reading: as expressions of inner life, as spatial hieroglyphs, as
mosaics, as dreams, as films and photographs, as faces. *Kracauer is the
great physiognomist of the quotidian.*

The second key motif is that of 'improvisation'. This again has to do
with the act of seeing or, more specifically, involves different *temporali-
ties of seeing*: the 'at first sight', the 'at last sight', the glimpsed *en passant*
– above all, *the unforeseen*. By 'improvisation' and the 'improvisional',
I want to suggest Kracauer's fascination with and appreciation of the
'flow of life' – all that is uncertain and indefinite, all that is unpredictable and contingent, all those penultimate things. And, as we will see

in chapter 10, improvisation – as mode of practical activity exemplified in slapstick comedy and the fairy tale – involves a critical appreciation of what is to hand and a spontaneous creativity in response to fear and danger, power and domination. Improvisation involves both a reconfigured sense of time (chronology) and a renewed relationship with objects and Nature (technology), transformations that run counter to and challenge the abstractions and rationalities of modernity. Improvisation as the re-enchantment of the disenchanted lifeworld constitutes a redemptive practice – we must rediscover what has gone *unseen* – and a utopian anticipation. Improvisation is an intimation of emancipation.

In focusing on these themes and motifs, and in bringing together different essays into one volume, I will have to beg the reader's indulgence on at least three counts.

Firstly, even when dealing with writings that are now, in one case, a hundred years old, I forgo making explicit correlations between his ideas then and our reality today, my feeling here being that it is wisest to leave the making of such connections to the reader. Suffice to say, such correspondences are both profound and manifold. Taking just one example, Kracauer's moving reflections on friendship in the wake of the Great War might prove a fascinating point of departure for thinking critically about our world of online dating, of Facebook followers, of enumerated 'friends' and 'likes' on Twitter and the brief encounters afforded by other social media. Indeed, if Kracauer's writings do have resonance today, if he is indeed a *key thinker of the contemporary* (his and ours), then it is because the world that he explored then – dominated by abstractness and quantification; subservient to bureaucratic logics and control; riven by intolerance and violence; peopled by anxious, bored individuals fascinated and distracted by mass media – is a world clearly recognizable as the predecessor of our own today. The spiritlessness of his times is not so very different from that of ours. Again, the reader will be the best judge of this.

Secondly, certain themes and concepts may be returned to more than once. Kracauer himself was not averse to this – the antics of the 'drunken pianist' being a classic example of the replaying of a particular example in a new context. Nevertheless, I have sought, where possible, to eliminate any unnecessary repetitions.

Finally, I confess that this book is guilty of several omissions, some of them substantial. There is another book – many of course! – that could and should be written on Kracauer constituting the negative or doppelgänger of this one, foregrounding all those texts that I have not explored here: the substantial early essays instead of the 'Simmel' and 'Expressionism' studies; 'Sociology as Science' and the treatise on the 'Detective Story' rather than the essays on photography and the mass ornament; the writings on propaganda from the 1930s instead of the *Offenbach* book; the various UNESCO and Voice of America studies rather than *Satellite Mentalities*; and, in the background, *Georg* rather than *Ginster*. When I first embarked upon this journey, I hoped that it might lead to a comprehensive overview of Kracauer's works. The journey has taught me to be more modest in my ambitions. At its end, I feel I have only scratched the surface.

4 Our Itinerary

What follows is divided into five main parts, each containing two chapters. Parts I and II examine a selection of key themes and texts in the early, formative stages of Kracauer's chequered career: his writings inspired by *Lebensphilosophie* focusing on the contemporary condition of the spirit and inner life; his experience of the Great War and as a budding architect (as documented in his semi-autobiographical novel *Ginster*); and his work as an editor, journalist and feuilletonist with the *Frankfurter Zeitung*, first in Frankfurt during the 1920s and then in Berlin in the early 1930s.

Taking Kracauer's unpublished 1913 novella 'The Mercy' ('Die Gnade') as its starting point, the first chapter examines his vision of the struggle between the inner life of the modern individual and the disenchanted society of *Zivilisation*. The subject of numerous and sometimes substantial unpublished (at the time) writings, this contemporary world of abstract thought and cold calculation appears most forcefully in the writings of his former tutor Georg Simmel, to whom he dedicates a major study. It also reflects one form of experience that Kracauer identifies as contesting or counteracting such a bleak world: friendship.

Chapter 2 continues to explore Kracauer's relationship with Simmelian thought, here with respect to what will become an increasingly dominant concern: the theme of visual representation. Kracauer's 1927 'Photography' essay provides an opportunity to work back to a text of profound significance for him: Simmel's philosophical treatise on the great Dutch painter Rembrandt. I seek to show how this study, Simmel's last major work, underpins Kracauer's reading of an art movement of his own time: Expressionism.

Developing these themes, Part II explores Kracauer's journalistic writings in the 1920s and 1930s. Chapter 3 takes *Ginster* as an entry point and considers how the novel repeatedly presents motifs of the de-individualization of the subject and the fragmentation of the human body, ones which find their fullest articulation in the key study from this period: his discussion of the Tiller Girls and the *Ratio* in 'The Mass Ornament'. This chapter also examines Kracauer's 1929 ethnography of the *terra incognita* of Berlin's office workers, *The Salaried Masses* (*Die Angestellten*), increasingly the dominant class in metropolitan modernity.

Chapter 4 considers some of Kracauer's feuilleton fragments from his 'Strassenbuch', *Streets of Berlin and Elsewhere*. We see here how Kracauer, in various texts, identifies and privileges the notion of 'improvisation' in contrast to the mechanized world of the mass ornament. We also look at some of his reflections on the key concept of 'distraction' in relation to the sense of being 'elsewhere'.

Part III is composed of two chapters exploring, from different vantage points, Kracauer's most significant work during his exile in Paris: his 1937 study of the composer Jacques Offenbach, a 'societal biography' that was to provide an account of Paris during the Second Empire as an 'operetta world', a fantasy of arcades, boulevards, commodities, dandies, imperial pomp and ceremony constructed on the fragile foundations of financial speculation, colonial expansion and, in the final instance, self-delusion on a grand scale. Kracauer's study shared many of these motifs with Benjamin, whose own Parisian exile was similarly spent in sustained researches on the Second Empire. Central to Benjamin's ill-fated *Arcades Project* was the analysis of the life and writings of the poet Charles Baudelaire. It is remarkable that Kracauer's Offenbach and Benjamin's Baudelaire studies have so rarely been compared, a project that is, accordingly, sketched here in chapter 5. This looks in particular at the contrasting historiographical methods that each theorist employs in their different attempts to read Paris through the works of particular artists.

Chapter 6 takes a different perspective on the Offenbach book: it is now seen through the lens of Kracauer's subsequent unrealized hopes for a film version of the book. His twenty-page 'film treatment' provides key insights into the main themes of the book, emphasizes the deft wit of the operetta spirit and foregrounds precisely that which Adorno lamented as lacking in the book itself: Offenbach's music. Exemplifying rather than contradicting Kracauer's own cinematic principles, the unmade Offenbach film would have constituted a model instance of the 'recapturing' of music through digression.

The two chapters composing Part IV examine Kracauer's work in American exile during the 1940s and early 1950s under the rubric of 'monstrous states, mental images'. The focus here is on three contrasting studies: Kracauer's celebrated exploration of Weimar cinema and its audiences; a forgotten social psychological experiment testing American students; and a qualitative analysis of accounts given by escapees from the Soviet bloc in the chilliest years of the Cold War.

Chapter 7 provides an account of Kracauer's famous *From Caligari to Hitler*. This 'psychological history' of German cinema during the Weimar years is premised upon the simple yet compelling thesis that, as collective enterprises appealing to mass tastes, the films produced at a particular time and place serve to express on screen the prevailing sentiments of their producers and audiences. Films are social-psychological hieroglyphs which may be deciphered and read to reveal the changing preconceptions, predispositions and predilections of a society, its habitus. Kracauer thus seeks to provide insight into the rise of National Socialism in Germany by tracing the increasing appeal of authoritarian themes and motifs in Weimar cinema between 1918 and 1933, beginning with the eponymous *Dr Caligari's Cabinet*, supposedly a pacifist and anti-establishment story transformed by means of a framing device into an endorsement of benign paternalistic authority.

The psychological aspects of film were explored in another way by Kracauer during the mid-1940s. While the *Caligari* book sought to read mental states from cinematic images, an earlier so-called test film project was designed by Kracauer to explore latent anti-Semitic attitudes among American students. Part of the 'studies in authoritarianism' series of projects undertaken by various Frankfurt School members, *Below the Surface* was a screenplay for a film (never made) which would be shown to selected test audiences in conjunction with various questionnaires. Drawing on archive materials, chapter 8 reconstructs and explores Kracauer's failed experimental project in terms of both the wider themes of his work and a series of motifs drawn from Critical Theory.

Of all the various projects on international communications and propaganda undertaken by Kracauer in the earlier post-war period for UNESCO and the Voice of America, by far the most substantial was a co-authored report from 1956 examining transcripts of interviews with refugees from Soviet-occupied Poland, Hungary and Czechoslovakia. Chapter 8 provides the first sustained account of Kracauer and Berkman's *Satellite Mentality* and argues that, rather than a one-dimensional denunciation of Soviet totalitarianism, the study provides a subtle critique of American politics and propaganda.

Chapters 9 and 10 tease out and then develop different thematic complexes in Kracauer's much maligned 1960 *Theory of Film*: slapstick comedy and the street. Chapter 9 introduces his study of film through his earlier film criticism published in the *Frankfurter Zeitung* and through a consideration of three of his suggestions for film comedies. Through engaging in various techniques of de-familiarization, these highlight what Kracauer comes to see as the promise of film: the redemption of the material world from forgetfulness and the restoration of our faculties and senses by means of the camera. This theme is traced back not only to the 'Marseilles notebooks' of 1941 but also, importantly, to distinctions and tensions already identified in the essay on Expressionism between representing the external world and venting the inner life of the artist. The chapter then pursues the theme of comedy by comparing the writings of Kracauer and Benjamin on slapstick comedy in general and the figure of Chaplin in particular.

Here, once again, the significance of improvisation is explored and emphasized.

The importance of the photographic qualities of film and of 'camera reality' are further examined in chapter 10 in relation to the elective affinity Kracauer sees between film and the 'flow of life' on the metropolitan street. Once again, there is a comparative dimension to this as we explore the writings of Benjamin and Kracauer on the cinematic character of the city and the urban qualities of cinematic experience with reference to the notions of collective dreaming and phantasmagoria.

My inconclusive conclusion highlights and reflects upon some of the principal motifs found in Kracauer's drafts for his eventually unfinished book on historiography, *History: Last Things before the Last*. This, his last work, was concerned with the practice and possibilities of writing history and representing/recapturing the past for the present. Critical of grand historical narratives and teleological notions of progress, Kracauer sets limits to the possibilities of historical understanding and emphasizes the constructedness of 'history' from numerous sources and turbulent temporal currents. We will also see how he takes the opportunity to reflect upon his own work as the exploration of that which has yet to be named, forms of life which still remain *terra incognita*.

Lili Kracauer died in 1971. Her husband's papers were acquired by the German Literature Archive (*Deutsches Literaturarchiv* – DLA) based in Marbach am Neckar just outside Stuttgart, where scholars today can access a vast range of materials on microfiche and paper copy aided by Thomas Y. Levin's incomparable bibliographical volume. The estate itself passed to the New York Association for New Americans (NYANA), a charitable organization set up in 1949 to help settle newly arrived immigrants to the USA, mainly Jewish refugees from Eastern Europe and the Soviet Union. With its work essentially at an end with the demise of communism, the organization was eventually dissolved in the summer of 2008, leaving the issue of copyright ownership in the air, a circumstance that has hampered further translation and publication of Kracauer's writings. Much remains to be done. Despite the hopes attending the 1989 centenary of Kracauer's birth and the enormous revival of interest in the works of other critical theorists, most notably of course Walter Benjamin, Kracauer's work is still relatively neglected. There are some positive signs. The recent publication by Suhrkamp Verlag of new volumes of the *Werke*, and in particular the *Frühe Schriften aus dem Nachlaß* in volumes 9.1 and 9.2 (2004) and the 2012 issuing of volume 2.2 (*Studien zu Massenmedien und Propaganda*) is hugely encouraging. And the appearance of new collections of correspondence,[29] of commentary[30] and of Kracauer's own scattered writings[31] may be early signs of a renewed interest. However, the recent

sad loss of two of Kracauer's most avid readers and astute commentators, David Frisby and Miriam Bratu Hansen, has robbed the academy
of their future insights and enthusiasm for his work. And so my hope
is that this book will contribute in some small way to encouraging new
readers and fresh readings of Kracauer's works; that he will be increasingly recognized as someone with whom it is well worth 'breaking
bread'; and that his works will enjoy good fortune in the coming years
in your safe custody, in your cheerful company.

Part I

FROM INNER LIFE:
SOCIOLOGICAL EXPRESSIONISM

1

Small Mercies: The Spirit of our Times

1   A View from the Bridge

A despondent, drunken young bank employee, Ludwig Loos, aban-
dons his fickle friends in a Munich bar one night and, after wandering
aimlessly through the nocturnal city streets, eventually finds himself
standing on a bridge over the river. Into the swirling waters below he
throws the small flask of poison he has been carrying around with him.
Chance has brought him here and now suggests a better way to put an
end to it all: 'Then he wanted to go down and slowly make his way
into the river, as if to bathe, and wanted to swim bold and brave for as
long as he had strength. And then – he would grow faint and would
be united at last with the elements from which he had issued at that
unhappy hour' (WK 7: 568). But he is not alone. He spots a young
woman who is obviously there with the same desperate purpose. She
begins to climb the railings of the bridge, but Ludwig, startled into
action, is able to grab her before she can jump. They struggle; he refuses
to let her go; exhausted, she collapses to the ground. It is then that he
recognizes in her a mysterious female figure that has haunted him in
strange prophetic dreams. As she weeps, he coaxes her into relating
her sad story: 'the age-old tale of misspent youth and life on the streets
he had often read about in newspapers' (WK 7: 570).

As he tries to console and cheer her, a mutual tenderness grows
between them. They go to her room. And there she realizes that he was
on the bridge for the very same morbid purpose. So, she gently insists
on hearing *his* tale. As Ludwig begins to speak: 'It was as if he was
finally stepping out of the false world of shadows into the dazzling
light of the sun. And he spoke words in which was contained his being,
this poor tormented, helplessly fearful self [*Ich*] in all its need' (WK 7:
572–3).

They kiss. They sleep together. He awakes to find her gone, but there is a note: she has taken the money he wished to give her and gone out to look for a job, to make a new start. 'She thanks him from the bottom of her heart. But he should leave and not wait for her: it would be better for her if she were not to see him again' (WK 7: 574).

And so Ludwig leaves and ventures back to the river but in a wholly different mood. There, imbued with a quiet joy:

> He grasped what delusion his longing, his passion for life and his despair had been. How he had been dreaming away, awkward and only ever injurious to himself, and thus how distorted the reflections of all things had been for him. But he also became keenly aware of the sources of such a sorrowful way of being. He recognized them in the mistrust of his own body, in that dull fear of the new, of the real, which he had borne with him from his childhood days. (WK 7: 575)

And then, in this sudden epiphany of self-realization: 'Spontaneously, he joined his hands as if to give thanks for the mercy which had so transformed him, for the new zest for life, which seemed to him as lasting and definite' (ibid.).

The curious events outlined above constitute the climax of 'The Mercy' ('Die Gnade'), Kracauer's novella, a text planned in 1911–12 and written 'between Easter and Whit' 1913. It would be all too easy to dismiss this tale as a banal piece of literary juvenilia,[1] peopled as it is with stock characters and clichéd figures[2] and steeped in sentimentality and angst-ridden male narcissism. But such an uncharitable reading would overlook how the key motifs of the novella encapsulate and express some of the wider critical themes which preoccupy Kracauer's earliest philosophical and sociological writings and which thereafter take on more direct and pithy form during his journalistic career with the *Frankfurter Zeitung* in the 1920s.[3]

Firstly, there is the fundamental perception of the emerging modern world, exemplified here by the last years of imperial Germany, as the time and space of cultural and spiritual 'disenchantment' (*Entzauberung*), to borrow Max Weber's famous characterization.[4] It was a capitalistic world increasingly marked by the abstraction of modern scientific knowledge and the instrumentalism of technocratic rationality, a world then increasingly shorn of profound spiritual and transcendent values and experiences and geared ever more to calculation, quantification and monetary accumulation. In a number of sometimes substantial unpublished studies from 1917 onwards, Kracauer gives voice to his painful preoccupation with the fate of the modern human subject and the 'inner life' of the individual as she/he struggles to find meaningful modes of self-expression and self-realization in this bleak and dispirited world bereft of religious faith and existential consolation.

According to such a view, we moderns endure an overwhelming sense of collective frustration and disappointment, of immersion in a quotidian realm imbued with an intense anxiety coupled with the interminable boredom of waiting. The fate of our young protagonist, Ludwig Loos, is unmistakably representative of these conditions and afflictions, for they are typically endured most intensely and acutely by a fresh generation and a newly ascendant class (the emerging urban petty bourgeoisie of white-collar workers – clerks, bank employees, secretaries, office staff). Inspired by philosophical reflections and reveries, aspiring to bohemian and artistic circles, Loos is nevertheless condemned by parental injunctions, despite his entreaties, to a secure job and conventional career with the Versicherungsbank – in short, to a life more ordinary. The notion of *Beruf* as a passionate, compelling inner calling to use one's God-given talents has here been transformed into mere bureaucratic advancement and petty promotion in the world of pen-pushing and paperwork. For Kracauer, this is a world best captured not so much by Weberian thought as by the *Lebensphilosophie* which came to imbue the writings of his former tutor in Berlin, Georg Simmel: indeed, it is Simmel who, as we will see, both analyses and embodies the distinctive features of the modern 'personality' and the diminished 'spirit' of modern times.[5]

Secondly, in the context of this rather gloomy *Weltanschauung*, one can appreciate Kracauer's fascination with particular forms of experience which promise to go beyond the tedium of mundane modern existence, moments which still seem capable of imbuing life with profound meaning and vital purpose. One of these is the possibility of an ever greater disclosure and convergence of individual inner selves that constitutes and defines genuine friendship. Central to the novella is the inner loneliness experienced by Loos as he feels himself betrayed by 'friends' who no longer share his views and values, who would now rather devote their time and energies to new-found lovers and other acquaintances. It is the very failure of friendship that leads Loos to the bridge. As we will see later in this chapter, Kracauer distinguishes different levels and forms of intimacy in interpersonal relations in a trilogy of essays on the theme of friendship written between 1917 and 1923, works clearly influenced by the experience of solidarity and camaraderie forged in the face of death by those serving in the trenches during the Great War. The promise and possibilities of true friendship take on a particular significance in the modern epoch as a source of inspiration, consolation and, most importantly, mutual self-actualization.

And there is also another domain of life and activity which, like genuine friendship, points beyond the bitter emptiness of everyday routine and convention: the aesthetic, the realm of art. It is in works of art that the otherwise unfulfilled yearnings and desires of the individual may find a conduit or channel of expression, something of which young Loos is only too well aware as he looks to cultivate his connections with artistic and musical circles. For Kracauer, the very task of contemporary art is to give colour and shape to the modern condition itself – that is to say, to the very struggle of individual inner life with the vast overarching apparatus of industrial technologies, teeming cities and impersonal bureaucratized systems. And the artistic or rather cultural movement which brings such irreconcilable conflicts and intense contestations into sharpest relief for Kracauer visually, dramatically and poetically is that of Expressionism, an aesthetic avant-garde to which he accordingly devotes a critical eighty-page treatise in 1918 (discussed in chapter 2).

Far from being a mere marginal work which can be passed over as immature fiction, Kracauer's little novella, then, not only seeks to encapsulate the spirit of the times but also points to forms of experience and moments which may transcend the stultified modern bourgeois world. Friendship and art are the small mercies which compensate and console us in our disenchantment.

2   Georg Simmel and the Berlin of His Time

The contradictions and conflicts between the precious 'inner life' of the (youthful) individual – that manifold of human aspirations, desires, impulses, interests and yearnings, passions and potentialities, strivings and sufferings – and the exacting external world of capitalist modernity provide the central theme of a number of criss-crossing studies penned in the course and aftermath of the Great War but first gathered together and published only recently as volume 9 of the *Works* (*Werke*) under the collective rubric of *Early Writings from the Archive* (*Frühe Schriften aus dem Nachlaß*).[6] In this chapter, I will focus on one of these with its own untimely publication history: 'Georg Simmel: A Contribution to the Meaning of the Spiritual Life of Our Times' ('Georg Simmel: Ein Beitrag zur Deutung des geistigen Lebens unserer Zeit') (1919).[7] This major monograph exploring the writings of the renowned and recently deceased[8] philosopher and sociologist (and Kracauer's erstwhile teacher in Berlin) is profoundly Janus-faced. In many respects it harkens back to the writings of the war years on the sufferings and frustrations of inner life and the fate of the spirit. At the same time, in its identifica-tion of tendencies and tensions of a particular time and place – the contemporary city of Berlin – as they manifest themselves in the life and (most significantly) works of one particular representative indi-vidual, the Simmel study not only anticipates the semi-autobiograph-ical novels (*Ginster* and *Georg*) but, perhaps most importantly, prefigures the intriguing notion of a 'societal biography' (*Gesellschaftsbiographie*), the key to Kracauer's 1937 *Jacques Offenbach and the Paris of his Time*.

Kracauer's Simmel study is even less like a conventional biography than the later Offenbach book. There is practically nothing detailing Simmel's actual life course, no chronological narration of his personal history and idiosyncratic experiences. And yet, conceived as nothing less than an exploration of the deepest levels of Simmel's 'personality', his enduring intellectual and spiritual principles and qualities, his very 'inner life', it remains biographical in the most profound sense. And Kracauer's ambition is to demonstrate the relationship between this core of Simmel's very individuality, his essence, so to speak, and the prevailing conditions of the modern metropolitan world of capitalist exchange, an environment itself scrutinized and rendered intelligible in Simmel's key writings.

The title of Kracauer's study suggests the dialectic at play here. On the one hand, as a sociologist, Simmel was preoccupied with critically capturing and characterizing 'everything relating to the life of the individual as such', with revealing 'matters of soul [*das Seelische*] in all forms' (MOR: 227). Kracauer observes:

> Equipped with unusually discriminating powers of observation and unparalleled sensitivity, he immerses himself in the depths of human existence and sheds light on the processes that take place within us, often below the surface of consciousness. With gentle fingers he carefully probes the soul, laying bare what was previously hidden, exposing the most secret impulses, and untying the tightly knit weave of our feelings, yearnings and desires. (Ibid.)

In his studies of economic conditions and social formations, and in his various epistemological and aesthetic writings, Simmel sought to disclose the prevailing 'spiritual condition' of the present, of modernity.

On the other hand, and at the same time, Simmel's own intellectual/ spiritual life, as this is disclosed by his writings, is exemplary of the very features he himself identifies. Such a conception can be read in two ways: Simmel – albeit unintentionally – projects his own experiences and qualities onto the world around him, and thereby discloses his own inner life; or – and this seems Kracauer's fundamental contention – Simmel is the very embodiment of, or representative figure for, the hallmarks of modernity. He bears its scars, its traces, its misfortunes, its stigmata within himself. Simmel's diagnosis of modernity is a self-diagnosis; he is his own patient. In accounting for the social world, Simmel unwittingly accounts for himself, too, for these two realms – the personal experience of Simmel the individual and the external, intersubjective life of the social world that he analyses – correspond and/or converge within him. Simmel's inner life hence becomes a lens through which one may discern the spirit of the times. Kracauer writes:

There are creative people who, through their achievements, elevate to consciousness the typical contents of their time. Just as scattered light converges in a burning mirror to be reflected back as a unified beam, so the overall spiritual constitution of the age is condensed in them and takes shape in their works. Simmel is just such a revelation of an epoch; that is to say, I understand him as the philosopher of *West European civilization* [*Zivilisation*] *in its most mature state*. This time speaks through all his works; his fundamental perspectives are wholly that of the time, the essence of which is not interpreted through him but is certainly expressed. (WK 9.2: 242)

The reference to *works* is important here. For Kracauer, it is the analysis of Simmel's texts in their multiplicity *and* consistency that provides the key to understanding his 'inner life'.[9] Appropriately this is an approach that Kracauer adopts and adapts from Simmel. As we will see in the next chapter, Simmel's 1916 study of the painter Rembrandt does not constitute a biography of the artist but, rather, details how the very concept of 'life' (*Leben*) – both the creative inner life of Rembrandt and the inner life of the sitter that manifests itself in their physiognomy – coalesces in portraiture. And, in so doing, Simmel provides Kracauer with an exemplary instance and methodological model for biographical analysis. Kracauer seeks to read Simmel in the same way that Simmel treats Rembrandt – that is to say, to trace his inner life by way of its manifestation in the works. And this Kracauer terms not *biography* as such but rather what he delineates in his 'Suffering under Knowledge' treatise under the rubric 'topography of being' (*Wesenstopographie*).[10] Kracauer explains that, guided by a philosopher's interest in patterns rather than a historian's preoccupation with chronology, the task is not to 'present the biography of the person in question, busy oneself with their statements and achievements in chronological order, but to glean from them the being [*Wesensbeschaffenheit*], the final conditions of the soul, from which they radiate. What kind of mind [*Geist*] produces these or those pieces of work?' (WK 9.1: 191–2). Kracauer continues:

Such a topography of any one person's being [*Wesenstopographie*] explains the life and work of that person as experienced empirically in such a way that it reveals through which structure of the person's inner self they are determined. In it one has, so to speak, a formula for the person in question which teaches us to recognize the conditions, connections and interdependencies of the thoughts, feelings, values, etc., of the person. But with it one arrives at a peculiar and deep understanding for that which we call – in a narrower sense of the word – the history of the person, that is how she/he became who she/he is ... an understanding which fundamentally cannot be obtained through purely empirical observations or generalizations, however precise. ... While one, caught in the usual perspectives, mainly appreciates the sequence of events, tracing their timeline, such a way of looking ruptures the whole sphere and reveals the relationships between what was happening and the being [Wesen] of the person. (WK 9.1: 192–3)

Notwithstanding this break with linearity, Kracauer's topography of Simmel's being (*Wesen*) supplements a 'cross-section' (*Durchschnitt*) of his philosophical and sociological ideas with a longitudinal section (*Querschnitt*) foregrounding their continuity and development.[11] Indeed, it is the remarkable consistency of Simmel's thought that is most striking for Kracauer.[12] While exploring the most diverse and disparate social and cultural phenomena – from central concerns such as the money economy, forms and patterns of sociability, consumption and social differentiation/imitation, to more tangential phenomena such as ruins, door handles, bridges, and marginal figures such as prostitutes, adventurers and strangers – Simmel's fundamental principles remain. For Kracauer these are, firstly, an intense sensitivity and continual devotion to the exploration of social phenomena such that the hidden but fundamental connections between (even) the most remote or seemingly isolated things are made manifest.[13] The full meaning of the object can only be understood when it is truly recognized as a fragment of the totality, the manifold of human life. And secondly, a preoccupation, derived from his reading of Kant,[14] with understanding the relationship between the perceiving human subject and the perceived object and with the consequences of this for the possibilities, limits and certitude of knowledge.[15] For Simmel, the act of observation is neither wholly subjective (a mere idiosyncratic quirk of the observer) nor objective (the thing itself independent of the observer and the act of observation). Rather it involves the meeting and mediation of the inner life of the viewer and the external appearance of the viewed, with the aspiration to distil from this appearance the (always partially elusive) inner meaning of the phenomenon itself.[16]

We cannot know things objectively in their entirety, nor can we come upon them as anything other than as fragments of a totality *that itself is never graspable as a totality* – this has important consequences for Simmel. Claims to definitive, exhaustive knowledge are forbidden to us. The truth, the absolute, the manifold that is 'life' – in short, that for which we strive – is inevitably and always unavailable to us. We must content ourselves with what is possible: the partial, the provisional, the relative. Accordingly, although inevitably permeated by values and value judgements, Simmel's works eschew the 'fundamental convictions' (*Grundüberzeugungen*) (WK 9.2: 183–4) underpinning and guiding other thinkers. And here we see the contours of Simmel as a representative figure of modernity taking shape: immersed in the chaotic phenomenal world whose ultimate principles are ever elusive; preoccupied with fragments, accumulating parts of a puzzle whose completion is nevertheless impossible and whose full image will never be realized; of necessity relativistic[17] and pluralistic;[18] reduced to ethical neutrality[19] and only ever hostile to claims to the transcendental, the Absolute; secure only in one's own insecurity, convinced merely of one's own lack of convictions; a true disciple of 'cosmopolitanism' (*Allerwelts-menschentum*), that is to say, at home everywhere, anywhere, and nowhere in particular;[20] a melancholy witness to a God-forsaken contemporary epoch – Simmel is here revealed as a tragic figure not because he is in any sense untimely, but conversely and precisely because of his timeliness.

3   Simmel and *Zivilisation*

It is in 'Zivilisation', the fifth chapter of Kracauer's study, that the full thrust of his argument becomes apparent. Drawing on the classic dichotomy posited by Ferdinand Tönnies (1887), Kracauer invokes the characteristically German distinction between two models of social solidarity: on the one hand, the traditional community (*Gemeinschaft*), that full and longstanding coming together of likeminded souls, a form rooted in enduring values, beliefs and faith, with a clear sense of its relationship to the absolute (God) – the familiar home to the *Kultur-mensch*, as Kracauer puts it, the fully rounded, mature, complete and coherent subject, the 'personality' (*Persönlichkeit*). On the other, there is that which is increasingly displacing this condition: modern society or association (*Gesellschaft*), 'civilization' (*Zivilisation*).[21] This is character-ized by calculation, quantification and abstraction (exemplified by clock time and the triumph of the money economy); by an emphasis on intellectualism, instrumental reason and relativism; by a privileg-ing of individualism, privacy (isolation) and independence (freedom here corresponding to anonymity and dispassionate detachment, a freedom *from*, not a freedom *with*); by indifference, nomadism and cosmopolitanism.

For Tönnies, as indeed for Simmel in his famous 1903 essay 'The Metropolis and Mental Life', these are the very hallmarks of metropoli-tan living, in the German context, of being a Berliner. They are, of course, Simmel's own attributes, too. In other words, Simmel is himself a figure of *Zivilisation*; indeed, he is the civilized man par excellence.[22] As such, he remains an 'individual', not a 'personality'.[23] Kracauer endeavours to capture this by way of one particular metaphor that becomes a leitmotif of his own writings: the intellectual vagabond. Simmel is the 'wanderer', the nomad, a figure whose curiosity compels him to set out upon countless itineraries and investigations into the character of things.[24] Without a definite point of departure, and with no prospect of final arrival, he is a figure perpetually *unterwegs*, a peripatetic philosopher, a thinker of no fixed abode, a stranger every-where. In a memorable passage Kracauer writes:

> A man moves through dark alleys. Lights shine out from the many windows and beckon to him. He hastens inside and tarries in all the bright rooms, sharing for a short time the life in them. What reveals itself to him is something which is not and will not be revealed to the inhabitants; his soul touches unspoken contexts and the secret that lies beneath. Since, as a stranger, he is not caught up in the toings and froings of those who are at home in these settings, he is granted the freedom and power to voice the unsayable wherever he goes. But he is also *only* a stranger, one who stops by only to leave again soon after. And so: however much he knows of the life of those banished to this place, he has never experienced their very own good fortune. He is a thousand times richer than them because he passes over them, close to each at one time and trusted; and he is a thousand times poorer than them because he has no home [*Heimat*] as they do. This man is Simmel: a guest, a wanderer. (WK 9.2: 270–1)

Without any secure anchorage, he is adrift, with no home port, no safe haven. Simmel is a figure longing for home, an individual afflicted by an existential homesickness, by *Heimweh*, by nostalgia. Simmel is spiritually homeless. And, although he is lonely,[25] he is not alone, in the sense that Simmel is not the only one who suffers this fate. For we all do. This, for Kracauer, is the modern condition itself, one which none of us can escape: 'The human being has become a detached individual, their consciousness unfettered and free, their soul a chaos which threatens to devour them. Loneliness surrounds them' (WK 9.2: 262).

And this is why understanding Simmel's inner life is of such signifi-cance for Kracauer. As a modern, as a metropolitan, a cosmopolitan; as a relativist, a pluralist, a doubter, a sceptic; as a wanderer, a stranger, a melancholic, a nostalgic; as an itinerant God-forsaken individual, he is very much one of us. His tragedy is ours. He is more than just Kracauer's 'companion in misfortune'; he is his guiding spirit.

4 Friends Indeed

Perhaps surprisingly, the figure of the companion does not appear in the three short but intensely personal essays Kracauer devotes to the theme of friendship which, chronologically speaking, book-end the Simmel study: 'On Friendship' ('Über die Freundschaft') (1917–18); 'Thoughts on Friendship' ('Gedanken über Freundschaft') (1921) and 'The Nurturing Conversation' ('Das zeugende Gespräch') (1923). In these brief philosophical reflections Kracauer identifies, characteristi-cally by means of a 'combination of analytical categories and phenomenological observations' (Koch 2000: 9), the specific qualities of genuine friendship, such friendship understood here as an enduring communion of the whole person, as something akin to love, a love born of and developed through ever more intense and intimate conversation. Friendship, in these ideal terms, offers respite from, or consolation for, the inner loneliness that is the fate of the civilized individual, though it is hard to imagine that, given our circumstances, we moderns are even still capable of such generosity, honesty and receptivity.

Kracauer's starting point is to distinguish friendship as a particular and privileged type of relationship from three similar but lesser forms of human interpersonal connection and social solidarity by means of, as Koch disparagingly puts it, 'all sorts of clever distinctions' (2000: 9). The first of these other types, that of 'comradeship' (*Kameradschaft*), is understood by Kracauer as a sense of togetherness and loyalty grounded in the common experience of a shared enterprise, purpose or goal, the common overcoming or endurance of extreme conditions and existential threats. Although, fortunately, Kracauer did not see active front-line service in the trenches, his understanding of the Great War profoundly informs such a conception. While he was an early volunteer put on reserve,[26] Kracauer's initial enthusiasm for the war was motivated less by patriotic fervour than by a naïve and romantic enthusiasm as to the possibilities of new and powerful bonds of communal attachment and involvement in a collective endeavour, by the prospect of being at one with others in a common cause. For him as for many young men, the sense of comradeship promised by the war offered an escape from the enervations and ennui of individual isolation and self-absorption. In a brief 1915 article, 'On the Experience of War' ('Vom Erleben des Kriegs'), he writes of the 'good fortune' (*Glück*) of the combatant's soul:

> Finally it is able to live in the moment, suffering and rejoicing in steady community [*Gemeinschaft*] with the others, without having to fear the self-contemplation of reflection. For the immense task of defending the Fatherland, with death always lurking in the background, demands all one's inner strength such that there can be no tormenting consciousness of the isolated self. (Cited in Belke and Renz 1989: 27)

In his later writings on friendship, once both the atrocities of the front line and the idiocies of life among the reservists had become apparent, comradeship is still acknowledged as a powerful and enduring bond,[27] but one produced by an external situation or compulsion rather than the coming together of those with shared inner dispositions and/or inclinations.[28] Comradeship is forged in adversity rather than embraced under conditions of freedom.

The second of Kracauer's types, 'collegiality',[29] is identified as a tie between those who share the same profession or career (*Beruf*) and with it a particular set of work practices, codes, values and sense of expertise. These occupational relations are characteristic of professional, technical and clerical staff, all those white-collar office employees, those salaried masses Kracauer was to examine years later at close quarters in Berlin. While comradeship is a response to the extreme and extraordinary, collegiality is part of the banal and mundane. Comrades are made on the battlefield, found huddled in shell-holes; colleagues are encountered in the office, found grouped around the photocopier.

Thirdly, and finally, there are those many others we encounter and know for whom the term 'acquaintance' (*Bekanntschaft*) suffices, a relationship based on happenstance[30] and involving a sharing of certain aspects of the self but initially, at least, of a relatively superficial kind and/or short duration. Acquaintances may be varied and many, like the circumstances in which they are made, and, while they may be relatively easily formed and painlessly dissolved, it is nevertheless also true that 'this relationship must have its foundation in the soul itself, must spring from a particular inner need' (UFR: 19).[31]

Comradeship, collegiality and acquaintance are all to be distinguished from genuine friendship in terms of both scope and intensity: friendship properly understood is a profound mutual involvement of all aspects of a person's being, an enduring and intimate engagement of the whole personality of otherwise free and independent individuals. Friendship, then, is to be understood as a shared recognition and correspondence of our innermost selves, a harmonious and lasting meeting of hearts and minds, a mutual disclosure and discovery of kindred souls. Passionate and precious, such perfect friendship is akin to love, but bereft of sex and eroticism.[32]

5   In Memoriam

There are three intriguing issues which follow from Kracauer's particular understanding of friendship. The first concerns the prevailing conditions and possibilities of such an experience given that the individuals must possess the highest degree of self-understanding and self-awareness regarding the complex and ever changing manifold that constitutes their own inner life. Only those who can truly claim to know themselves, who appreciate the 'richness of their being [*Wesen*]' (UFR: 38), can come to share this with, and know that of, another. Kracauer notes: 'We call [such] people personalities [*Persönlichkeiten*] ... Only they can be true friends. Ideal friendship is, as we will say for the present, two people finding each other in accordance with their entire essence [*Wesen*] constituted in the consciousness of the self [*Ich-Bewußtsein*]' (UFR: 38). This 'ideal friendship' is, then, strictly speaking, only possible for those who are genuine 'personalities' or, perhaps as in the Simmel study, *Kulturmenschen*. And if this is so, then it is a profound communion of hearts and minds that is sadly forbidden to us since, as we have seen already, we modern 'civilized' individuals can no longer claim to constitute whole interconnected 'personalities'.[33] Today, 'ideal friendship' exists only as a tantalizing vision of perfection. Indeed this would certainly seem to account in part for poor Ludwig Loos's sufferings in 'The Mercy': he is a young man who desperately yearns for those deep joys of genuine friendship only to find his own relationships with others – his companion in misfortune on the bridge excepted – to be insubstantial and intermittent, circumscribed by convention and convenience, hollowed out by bourgeois respectability and reserve. His suicidal resolve is prompted precisely by his realization of the flaws and failings of his fickle friends.

And yet all is not lost. Ludwig lives. True, this 'ideal friendship' may never be ours, or indeed anyone's, but there may be intimations and approximations in our less elevated everyday relationships. And this was certainly not lost upon, or unfamiliar to, Kracauer himself. Indeed, it is perhaps the very reason for his writing on this particular theme in the first place. For while the 'On Friendship' essay bears no dedication, it was written just a year or so after the death of Otto Hainebach, a man three years Kracauer's junior who became very close and dear to him following their first meeting in Munich in the autumn of 1912.[34] Another volunteer in those heady, early days of the great patriotic war, Hainebach had the misfortune to make it to the front line and was killed in action at Verdun on 14 September 1916,[35] a loss for which the supposed comradeship of the barracks of Mainz provided little solace for Kracauer. If the ghost of Hainebach stands over, or indeed is the very wellspring of, the writings on friendship, then the decentring of comradeship and its displacement by a lament for a lost friend constitutes a subtle but insistent testimony to Kracauer's own transformed perception of the conflict still raging around him. Gone are the fantasies of togetherness forged by the great and dangerous task in common; what remains in these essays are the traces of a life and a love cut short. They are not so much 'on friendship' as an epitaph to a fallen friend. These pages are grief-stricken, haunted.

How exactly does such a friendship, however imperfect, come into being? The answer to this question is to be found in Kracauer's 1923 'The Nurturing Conversation'. Here it is made clear that the formation of friendship is inextricably interwoven with communication and interaction – that is to say, with participation in conversation. Indeed, conversation and friendship are mutually productive and constitutive (*zeugend*). On the one hand, genuine friendship only emerges in the course of dialogue, dialogue understood here as a process of increasingly intimate exchanges, as ever greater mutual disclosures. On the other hand, this complete and confident sharing of the self with another, this turning of each to the other, is only ever possible in the context of friendship. Importantly, such conversations do not always rely on agreement or accord: friends share certain aspects of their inner being, but they do not dissolve into one another. The most fecund conversations, and here Kracauer has in mind those turned towards philosophical matters – beauty, virtue, justice, spirit, the Absolute – can be those in which the interlocutors offer radically opposing views with increasing intensity in the common pursuit of an ever elusive truth. The to and fro of irreconcilable arguments – each being open and inviting to the opinions of the other while remaining resolute in their own convictions – unfolds and encompasses ever more aspects of the problem, probes ever more deeply into the matter itself, whose final truth may be ever more closely approached even if never finally attained. Such conversations are neither motivated by childish competition nor oriented to completion or conclusion. Rather, they serve to foster the ever greater involvement of the discussants, to prompt them to ever new discoveries and disclosures, to ever new visions and revisions.

There is one special kind of conversation that Kracauer values above all others: the paradoxical 'silent conversation'. Kracauer understands this curious conception in a number of different ways. There is, of course, that conversation which remains mute because it is between those who are apart, separated by time and space, that communication mediated by letters, the correspondence. And this, he suggests, is perhaps a privileged conversation, for it is often the case that one may write what one cannot or dare not say, disclosing on paper those most intimate aspects of ourselves. Accordingly, as documents of our innermost selves, letters are perhaps the most revealing testimonies and self-portraits. Perhaps such intense and explicit correspondence formed the intimate bond between Kracauer and the ill-fated Hainebach.

The silent conversation need not be that of letters between correspondents, however. Our innermost selves may be committed to paper in the guise of other kinds of inscription – indeed, they may surely take other forms of representation altogether. For example, the work of art, and that of the critic who subsequently engages with it, may be understood as a kind of silent conversation across time and space. Such a conception would gesture in two directions, one returning us to Simmel's study of Rembrandt, the other pointing us towards Walter Benjamin. As we will see in the next chapter, for Simmel the greatest works of portraiture are those in which the expressive longings and strivings at the very core of the painter's being and the whole inner life and intimate history of his subject are brought into the most felicitous and profound union upon the canvas. The painting of a countenance is no mere matter of producing a convincing likeness but, rather, is the act of capturing a unique and entire existence in a lived moment that is the sum of all previous such moments. Such brushwork presupposes a level of mutual involvement between artist and model that is certainly analogous to that between genuine friends. Every masterpiece of portraiture is testimony not just to the skill of the painter and the patience of the sitter but to the fundamental yet fleeting communion of their individual spirits. Such art, the art of Rembrandt, is a *conspiracy*, a 'breathing together', of painter and painted.

At the same time, reading Kracauer's 1923 reflections one cannot but be reminded of the task of immanent criticism formulated by Benjamin in his 1919 doctoral thesis 'The Concept of Art Criticism in German Romanticism' and which he then sought to demonstrate in his 'exemplary critique' of Goethe's novella *Elective Affinities* (*Wahlverwandschaften*) from 1921–2. The task of immanent criticism, Benjamin contends, is the infinite unfolding of the innermost tendencies and meanings of the work of art as part of its ongoing afterlife (*Nachleben*). The work of criticism is the essential counterpart to the work of art, its critical friend or companion, so to speak. Just as, in the case of genuine friendship, the 'nurturing conversation' or correspondence brings with it increasing understanding, appreciation and recognition of both self and other, so immanent criticism refrains from pompous pronouncements and high-handed judgements about the artwork and instead concerns itself with discerning and disclosing its 'truth-content'. For Simmel, the artist brilliantly encapsulates the truth of a life in a painting; for Benjamin, the critic painstakingly unveils the truth of the artwork. Both are dialectical labours of love.

Kracauer concludes his reflections on the paradox of the 'silent' conversation with the contention that it may actually constitute conversation's most profound, most perfect form: its ideal. It is one between those true friends for whom there is such a degree of mutual intimacy and shared understanding that speech is quite simply unnecessary. When each knows the other so well, so completely, when they are able to anticipate every word and thought, each turn of the argument, each remark and riposte, then the conversation between them may unfold in their own heads without need of any utterance, as a dialogue played out as an inner monologue. Perfect friendship, the correspondence of minds, is unspoken, unwritten, unexpressed. We are together, or apart, and lovingly say everything by saying nothing. And, in this way, such perfect friendships leave no material vestiges, no physical traces. They live only and always within us as memories.

Ludwig Loos and his erstwhile lover may never meet again. Kracauer and Hainebach, Ginster and Otto certainly never will. But their mutual memories, each of the other, will sustain them, keep them from death, keep them company – as genuine friends surely do – for the rest of their lives.

2

Portraits of the Age

1 Two Photographs

She, we are told, is a 24-year-old film diva, a 'demonic Diva' (MOR: 47) no less. *He* is a 28-year-old architect, a disaffected designer. *She* is caught by the camera posing in front of the Hotel Excelsior on the Lido in Venice; her face, her hair, her eyelashes (all twelve of them!) are 'flawless' (ibid.). *He* is standing in the middle of the back row, immediately behind the seated officer, looking straight ahead at the camera with a quizzical expression. *She* is, no doubt, dressed for the occasion in the very latest fashions, set off by a string of pearls with perhaps the *perfect* clutch bag in her hand. *He* is scruffily clad in reservist fatigues, a flat field cap sitting squarely upon his head, his raised right hand grasping something (a cigarette? a flask perhaps?) while his surrounding comrades appear to be holding a motley assortment of items – a book, boots, brushes, bread, a garden hoe. Two are smoking. Smiling, her head tilted at just the right jaunty angle to set off her fringe, *she* has just emerged from her boudoir and is snapped busily en route to some engagement. Glum, *they* look like returnees from a raid on a car boot sale, proffering the booty pillaged. *Her* beauty renders her instantly recognizable, even if she is only one of a dozen Tiller Girls, all chosen for their similar looks. *His* curious countenance and puny physique make him unmistakable, even if he is only one-fifteenth of the Mainz Foot Artillery platoon. *For her*, it is September 1927 and she is simply delighted to be on the front cover. *For him*, it is 1917 and he is simply relieved not to be on the front line. 'This is what the film diva looks like' (ibid.). This is what Kracauer looked like.

Two photographic images, two moments of *ekphrasis*:[1] one introduces Kracauer's provocative and perplexing 1927 essay 'Photography'; the other puts him in the picture, literally.[2] Between them, they capture two key themes of Kracauer's early reflections on the photo-graphic image. On the one hand, photography is caught in the same sense of temporal flow[3] as fashion itself,[4] recording every trivial detail of the momentarily modish for a posterity that will treat it with scorn and ridicule. Anticipating Benjamin's remarks on fashion in the *Arcades Project*, Kracauer astutely observes that the inevitable fate of the new and fashionable is, eventually, to become the old-fashioned and out-dated. There is nothing less appealing, less erotic, than the comic cos-tumes of yesteryear.[5] And, on the other hand, Kracauer claims, photography is the visual equivalent of a particular way of conceptual-izing what has been: 'historicism', that form of historical enquiry that claims, following Leopold von Ranke's precepts, to (re)present the past 'just as it was', with an absolute fidelity to everything and an emphasis upon nothing, as a completely faithful inventory and utterly banal stocktaking of the 'there and then'.[6] Similarly, in the photographic image, it is *all there* just as it was.

And so we are treated to the demonic diva *just as she was* that morning in 1927; and the soldiers, too, appear to us now, just as they did on that day a decade before, grouped together before the lens of the camera. In its analogic recording of everything the camera is all-embracing and entirely indiscriminate. As such, Kracauer contends, photography constitutes the very antithesis of that most unreliable, because always and everywhere partial and selective, witness to the past that is memory. The images which we retain in memory are those, and only those, which have meaning and resonance for us. He writes:

> An individual retains memories because they are personally significant. Thus, they are organized according to a principle which is essentially different from the organizing principle of photography. Photography grasps what is given as a spatial (or temporal) continuum; memory images retain what is given only insofar as it has significance. Since what is significant is not reducible to either merely spatial or merely temporal terms, memory images are at odds with photographic representation. From the latter's perspective, memory images appear to be fragments – but only because photography does not encompass the meaning to which they refer and in relation to which they cease to be fragments. Similarly, from the perspective of memory, photography appears as a jumble that consists partly of garbage.
>
> The meaning of memory images is linked to their truth content. (MOR: 50–1)

Memories are precious 'fragments' culled from the plenitude, not the plenitude itself. Photographs proffer the whole harvest of the past; memories are what remain after the winnowing of experience by time, of time by experience.

The diva is recognizable to the magazine readers of the time because she is *of* the time, and her image corresponds to that in the newsreels and the newspapers. Each of these images corroborates the other. No one would know her today; she could be anyone, just as an old photograph of Kracauer's grandmother as a young woman may be a perfect resemblance but bears no relation to the old woman that he knew. The photograph is wholly at odds with his memories. And so it means nothing to him; it could be 'any young girl in 1864' (MOR: 48). Similarly, the soldiers, then identifiably sons, brothers, husbands, lovers, are now great (great) grandfathers/uncles. There are perhaps those today in Germany who have exactly this same photograph of Kracauer's platoon and who, ignoring the curious-looking man behind the officer, point out another figure, the one polishing his boots perhaps, with a 'There he is, our ... your ...' The soldiers are all long dead, Kracauer included, but the image of them on that day remains as sharp as ever, undiminished by time, even if there is no one who remembers them, even if they are now forgotten and unmourned. The photographic image exists and persists even as its significance recedes, even as the faces become, one by one, unrecognizable. Indeed, Kracauer contends that this is precisely the fate of the photograph: whatever meaning it held in the moment in which it was taken drains away with time such that we are left with figures dressed in the now comic costumes and beset by the curious clutter of the past. They are anonymous ghosts among shadows. He observes:

> Once a photograph ages, the immediate reference to the original is no longer possible. The body of a deceased person appears smaller than the living. Likewise, an old photograph presents itself as the reduction of a contemporaneous one. The old photograph has been emptied of the life whose physical presence overlay its merely spatial configuration. In inverse proportion to photographs, memory images enlarge themselves into monograms of remembered life. The photograph is the sediment that has settled from the monogram, and from year to year its semiotic value decreases. The truth content of the original is left behind in its history; the photograph captures only the residuum that history has discharged. (MOR: 54–5)

As time passes, memories become ever fewer. But, instead of meaning draining away from them, this process of reduction is a kind of distillation in which what remains becomes increasingly concentrated. All incidentals evaporate, leaving behind what is most intense and definitive, the very essence of the person, the 'truth content', as it were, of their life. Memory images form one final image in which their existence is encapsulated: the signature of the person. Kracauer terms this the 'monogram' or the 'last image':

The image in which [these] traits appear is distinguished from all other memory images, for unlike the latter it preserves not a multitude of opaque recollections but elements that touch upon what has been recognized as true. All memory images are bound to be reduced to this type of image, which may rightly be called the last image, since it alone preserves the unforgettable. The last image of a person is that person's actual *history*. (MOR: 51)

The 'last image' is a final rendezvous, a vestigial moment of correspondence, between the remembering subject and the remembered.[7] Such images are 'biographical': a depiction of a life, not merely a fragment of that life but the truth of a whole existence. There is a connection here I think between this concept of the 'last image' and Kracauer's earlier reflections on friendship. The persistence of the image of the other in memory is part of an enduring silent conversation, the mark of genuine friendship. The 'last image' is a lasting image, perhaps the afterlife of friendship. One can envisage an example of this in the contrast between Kracauer's own vivid personal recollections of Otto Hainebach and the photograph of a nervous, awkward young soldier, the uniformed volunteer of 1914, an image which Kracauer might have both recognized and failed to recognize as a true likeness of his ill-fated friend. No, this is not how he remembered him. His 'last image' is not to be found on page 27 of the *Marbacher Magazin* of 1988 – for all we know, it could be anyone – but rather in Kracauer's mind's eye as long as he lived. For him, the true friend, Hainebach, was 'unforgettable'.

2   Photography and Physiognomy

We will return to Kracauer's photography essay later in this chapter. Suffice to say now that such a critical view of the camera and its (in)capacities is one that Kracauer will revise and re-evaluate in his writings on the medium of film. Indeed, by the time of *Theory of Film* (1960) it is precisely the exhaustive recording of reality by the camera – photography's 'historicism' – that is the key to its promise of a visual redemption of the world of things in an era beset by indifference and amnesia. Kracauer's sceptical vision of photography in the 1920s and his subsequent privileging of the work of the camera in the context of film are both deeply indebted to his reading of Simmel and, in particular, his 1916 *Rembrandt: An Essay in the Philosophy of Art*. Indeed, Simmel's treatise on the Dutch master is decisive for Kracauer's writings on visual culture in several ways:

a) It informs his thoughts in the 1927 'On Photography' essay regarding not only the relationship between photography and painting but also, and most significantly, how the camera accords with and transforms the modern sense of perception and capacity for cognition.

b) This in turn will become the foundation for his writings in the post-war period on film. While the actual textual origins of *Theory of Film* are, as Miriam Bratu Hansen has rightly observed, to be found in a series of notebooks scribbled in Marseilles in 1940–1, the underpinning ideas clearly derive from an earlier period of existential crisis – the final years of the Great War.

c) This is because the relationship between the strivings of the artist to give form to his/her inner life in relation both to the external world of Nature and the inner lives of others provides Kracauer with the key conceptual framework for his critical interpretation of the pre-eminent artistic/cultural movement of the early twentieth century, namely Expressionism, to which he dedicates an essay of 1918.

d) It is also of the utmost methodological importance, not only as an apprenticeship in framing the relationship between an individual life, a body of work and the society in which she/he exists, but also as an initiation into the dialectics of depth hermeneutics – recognizing and reading surfaces as the essential manifestations of what lies below.

e) Finally, I want to suggest that Kracauer's notion of memory images and, in particular, the idea of the 'last image' may be understood as a particular reconfiguration of Simmel's vision of Rembrandtian portraiture. These pictures, in capturing the whole existence of the sitter in a moment, are distillations of their lives – in short: 'last images'.

What follows in this chapter is an extended reading of Simmel's essay as a necessary prolegomenon to an examination of Kracauer's three great early studies of the visual culture of his time: our old acquaintance the 1927 'Photography' essay; the 1918 'On Expressionism' study; and then, in the next chapter, perhaps the most important of Kracauer's Weimar feuilletons, 'The Mass Ornament'.

Let us begin by returning briefly to the soldiers of the Mainz Foot Artillery in 1917. It is apparent that only the officer seated at the centre of the group exhibits anything like a proper Prussian military bearing. Around him, the lower ranks look awkward, uncomfortable, somewhat dishevelled. Instead of rifles they are armed with a motley assortment of objects which bespeak a life of tedious routine among the reservists: there are boots to be polished, loaves of bread to be sliced and buttered, diaries to be updated, cigarettes to be smoked, even vegetable plots to be tended. On the parade ground, there are salutes to be given, drills to be mastered, marching to be practised. An hour at the firing range may break the monotony. This is the anxious banality of waiting that Kracauer satirically captures in *Ginster*. And perhaps this photograph of him and his reservist comrades is also a wry comment on the strange no-man's-land between the horrors of front-line combat and the *ennui* of mundane civilian existence. It is impossible to know, of course, the photographer's intention or indeed what Kracauer is thinking as he poses thus for this group portrait, but at least this is how he appeared that day, in that moment long ago, standing behind the officer, posing before the camera, with that quizzical look on his face. We know this because the advent of photography brought with it the image as an exact analogue of what was in front of the lens at the instant of the shutter's release, the precise distribution of light and shade at a specific moment. The camera captured a true likeness, a faithful representation, a simple copy of the figures, objects and scenes to which it was directed. Yet whatever the validity of such now long-contested claims to the 'realism' and verisimilitude of photography as a medium, the photographic image is nevertheless, for Kracauer, impoverished in some way. And the same is true for Simmel, as is evident from various asides about the medium in his Rembrandt study. Yes, the camera records the actual appearances of people and the surfaces of things, but there is at the same time, for him, a fundamental flatness to this form of representation, a profound failure to penetrate beneath these exterior manifestations to that which is of most significance: the dynamic 'inner life' of the subject as perceived and rendered by the creative impulse of the genuine artist. The photographic portrait is objective and objectifying, remaining somehow external to the person depicted, limited to the limits, out in the cold, so to speak, allowing for no genuine physiognomical reading of inner contents from outer contours. Such an image is fixed and frozen, bereft of any sense of the flow or movement of lived experience, incapable of any intimation or intuition of what has gone before, of what is to come in the life of the subject, unable to attest to a past or to anticipate a fate. Compared with the painting, the photograph seems devoid of substance; it is hollow, empty, mechanical. The very living warmth of the human subject is lost in the icy exactitude of photographic portraiture. Indeed, it is precisely its technological precision and pristine clarity that ensures the superficial and static qualities of the snapshot. And, curiously, this means that the photograph fails to correspond to our actual lived experience and perception of the 'real'. Simmel compares the works of painter and photographer thus:

> The artist brings movement to its climax ... by knowing how to bind movement into a factually static painting. And only then when we make it clear to ourselves that we, too, vis-à-vis reality do not see things the way they are captured in the photographic moment, but rather movement as continuity and not as composition made up of individual moments that were neither a process nor an activity, so then we realise that the work of art offers much more 'truth' than does the photographic snapshot. In this case we do not need to appeal to the so-called 'higher

truth' at all to which the work of art – in contrast to the mechanical reproduction – is said to be entitled. Rather, with total immediacy and in a completely realistic sense, the painting, whose impression concentrates continuous movement via some means, is closer to reality (here merely meaning the conscious perception of reality) than is the snapshot. (REM: 39)

Ironically, it is through the illusion of movement that the painting appears more 'real' than the photographic image. It is more authentic because it is seemingly more 'alive', the very indistinction between tones of light and shade suggesting seamless merger and flow from one time and space to another. By contrast, the frozen face in the photographic portrait seems inscrutable, inanimate, devoid of life and of death too, death conceived here as an integral part of the life process itself.[8] As such, the flatness of the photograph is fully in accord with the impersonal, indifferent and abstract world of capitalist modernity. Photography is the modern medium par excellence, its most representative mode of representation. But perhaps this is, as Simmel recognizes, to misconstrue the actual relationship between the 'real' (Nature) and the image, as if the latter were merely the dependent, derivative representation of the former. We will return to this.

The capacity for capturing this flow of inner life is not, however, an attribute of painting per se. The painter Simmel has in mind is no ordinary artist: it is Rembrandt Harmenszoon van Rijn (1606–69). Nothing could be more like the 'real' individual living human being, nothing could be less like the inert photographic image, than the Rembrandt portrait. In his painting, even more so in his drawing, Rembrandt's images are everything photographs are *not*: vibrant, vital, imbued with movement and meaning, embodying the ongoing duration of the subject's 'becoming' rather than the particular instant of their 'being', fully expressive of the illumination imparted by an inner spirituality and religiosity consonant with an age of profound inwardness and Protestant piety, haunted by life's faithful companion, death. Rembrandt's works depict not just the individual lives of his sitters, everyday Dutchmen and women, but also the intensity of their resolute faith in the full knowledge of mortality. Rembrandt is nothing less than the painter of the very souls of Amsterdam. This, for Simmel, is Rembrandt's genius.

3 Excursus: Simmel, Rembrandt and the Painter of Inner Life

In the 'preface' to his 'philosophical essay' on the Dutch master, Simmel clarifies his intentions in a phrase that finds an unmistakable echo in

Kracauer's 'Mass Ornament' essay a dozen years later. He writes: 'What has always seemed to me to be the essential task of philosophy – to lower a plumb line through the immediate singular, the simply given, into the depths of ultimate intellectual meanings – will now be attempted on the phenomenon of Rembrandt' (REM: 3). This apparent privileging of that which is at depth needs some qualification: it is only by means of 'surface-level expressions', as Kracauer later terms them (MOR: 75), that such depths are in any way to be discerned or read at all, fathomed by means of a 'plumb line'. What we have here is a kind of philosophical *physiognomy* of the phenomenal world. And this is wholly appropriate as the fundamental principle for a study of Rembrandt, for his great gift, according to Simmel, was his unrivalled ability to regard and render the inner life of the sitter as expressed through their exterior physical form – in particular, their face. Rembrandt, then, was himself the great artist-physiognomist. And more. It is not only this inner life of the subject that makes the Rembrandtian work of art fascinating. This is only one half, so to speak, of what constitutes the artwork: the picture is also equally an expression of the painter's own inner life. The canvas is the *rendezvous* or meeting place of the inner lives of both subject and artist. In the work of art these are brought together and set in tension or reconciled as if in some kind of dialectical synthesis.[9] In taking Rembrandt as his subject, Simmel is concerned with the representation of an individual life dedicated to the representation of 'life' (*Leben*).

My purpose here is not to provide an exhaustive examination of the intricacies and complexities of Simmel's reading of Rembrandt's works and the manifold distinctions between them and Classical and Renaissance artworks. A sketch must suffice. Simmel's argument is set out in three parts: on inner life; on individuality; and on art and religion.

Simmel's point of departure is Rembrandt's distinctive capacity for capturing the inner life of the sitter as manifest in their external appearance, their countenance, at a particular moment in their life. But, it must be remembered that this particular moment is nothing other than the culmination of everything that has gone before.[10] The countenance, the body, bears and discloses to the artist's eye the many traces of the life that the person has led heretofore in the form of coloration, scars, marks, lines and blemishes. These traces are ingrained in, or etched into, the very living face itself. And so, in rendering this with the utmost felicity, Rembrandt comes to depict not simply the inner life of the subject as it is but also the entire past of that inner life, the subject's very own history as a process of unfolding or becoming.[11] In the light of this, Rembrandt's penchant for older subjects becomes clear: for these faces are precisely those most fashioned by the contingencies and exigencies of the past.[12]

Since Rembrandt's works present life as a perpetual process of flow, unfolding and movement, he is to be understood as the painter of 'becoming', not of 'being'.[13] And, importantly, this 'becoming' is always conceived as continuous, never as fragmented into a series of distinct and discrete moments. As Simmel stresses, the dynamism of his pictures is of a wholly different order to that suggested by the depiction of figures artificially frozen midway in the enactment of some gesture or other, by motion reduced to a standstill. What distinguishes Rembrandtian movement is the (miraculous!) manner in which the artist animates the whole image from the moment of its conception and inception.[14] Through composition, colours, tone and texture, movement appears as an indivisible living totality, not as a mechanical sequence of disconnected actions (as in a film strip). It is at once complete (uninterrupted) and incomplete (part of the endless restlessness that is life itself).[15]

In Rembrandt's portraits, Simmel claims, 'the portrayal of a human being is filled with inner life to the highest degree, but is not psychological' (REM: 10). Such paintings, then, provide neither an analytics of ephemeral emotional or mental states nor the 'character' of the individual depicted – for Simmel, 'character' suggests some essential and enduring substratum of the psyche.[16] Rather, Rembrandt's inimitable achievement is in giving expression to the dynamic quality of individual inner life as the continuous constitution of the subject through ever new experiences, the always mutual shaping of subject and external conditions through time. It is this that renders the immediately recognizable individuality of the individual.[17] Eschewing the beautiful figures of classical ideals and archetypes – and especially the 'accentuated' individualism[18] of narcissistic patrons rendered by obsequious Renaissance artists – Rembrandt's art is devoted to the idiosyncratic countenance of the unique human being. For him: 'individualization only means that the presented appearance in question is determined by, and, so to speak, visually understood with respect to, the total stream of life leading toward it that simply is, and can only be, the life of this one person' (REM: 89).

Paradoxically, this attentiveness to the individuality of the sitter constitutes at the same time a disclosure of generality. How is this possible? Put simply, what we share as human beings is precisely our manifold differences and uniqueness. The individual sitter is both a meaningful whole and yet also a fragment of a greater totality, humankind, just as a star is both an entity in itself and part of a wider constellation. In Rembrandt's art, the superficial differences between individuals are scrupulously captured and simultaneously transcended. Indeed, Rembrandt renders that which is *beyond* all individual manifestations but which is only discernible *in* them: 'the generality of this individuality itself, not standing above this or some other, but the unity of life that takes its course in a unique way, of which all its describable particularities are merely products or retrospective fragments' (REM: 92–3). Hence Rembrandt himself may be said, like Simmel, to drop a 'plumb line' through the particular (the individual) to the general (the human).

And it is not only as the profound expression of the inner life of the sitter that this notion of the human is to be found. In Rembrandt's portraits one is also privy to their sense of death – death understood here not as some end point towards which the ever fearful individual is doomed but, rather, as that sense of one's own inevitable mortality that softly and unerringly accompanies each person through life. We know we are to die. The individuals in Rembrandt's paintings know they will die. This absolute certainty of our own human mortality is our constant companion, not as some ominous, omnipresent terror but as that which ultimately and profoundly gives life itself meaning and value.[19] Hence Rembrandt's works do not, as was the tendency of those by earlier painters, present death as some independent power or figure – the grim reaper or a skeleton leading the Dance of Death. Rather, he recognized and gave expression to the 'immanence of death in life' (REM: 73). Life and death are symbiotic, always contrasting, like light emerging fleetingly from and then disappearing back into the darkness of the picture. Hence, Simmel observes, death 'inhabits all Rembrandt portraits' (REM: 70). And this death is both entirely general and wholly individual. Forms, ideals, types endure; individuals do not.[20]

The third and final section of Simmel's study addresses the human response to this quiet certainty of death. What is the substance or quality of the inner lives of the sitters depicted by Rembrandt? Simmel's answer to this is a particular moment of religiosity – not the ostentatious 'objective' public religion characteristic of Catholic pomp and ceremony, but rather the simple yet profound inward faith[21] of the humble 'religious person' (REM: 113), the calm and conviction of Protestant piety.[22] And this inner spirituality or religiosity is represented in light, by the luminosity which seemingly originates from within the human subject in Rembrandt's paintings. Contrary to any naturalistic depiction, his figures are illuminated neither by sunlight flooding through windows nor by burning nocturnal candles. Nor are there any shafts of celestial light from on high or halos crowning holy figures. Rather, it is as if light emanates from deep within the sitter him-/herself such that the countenance alone becomes visible, a radiant visage enshrouded in a fog of darkness and shadow.

This curious beacon of light amid gloom is the human soul. Herein, for Simmel, lies Rembrandt's incomparable achievement and genius: he is the painter of the soul:

Rembrandt has means to realize this constellation beyond human individuality: *light*. This light behaves like the religious expression of being in Rembrandtian figures who bear the thus characterized meaning immediately within themselves, and not as though it was something transcendental – a dogmatic fact that was manifested by them. This light is, so to speak, religious as a natural reality just as those figures are religious as inner reality. Just as, however peasantlike, narrow, thoroughly earthly they are, their religiosity bears in itself metaphysical solemnity and is in and of itself a metaphysical fact, so in his religious etchings and paintings Rembrandtian light is something clearly sensually earthly that points to nothing beyond itself but is as such beyond the empirical. (REM: 135)

In Rembrandt's works one witnesses a double transposition: the profane, the ordinary layman, is shown to possess this inner light of transcendence; at the same time, the holy, the divine, takes on the countenance of the mundane.[23]

When one looks at the Dutch as they appear in peasant and bourgeoisie paintings – with their zest for life, deeply rooted in the soil, inclined in their hearts toward good food and drink – it is a shocking prospect that precisely these people are prepared, without a second thought, to face death, and fates worse than death, for their ideals, for their political freedom, and for their religious salvation. This almost appears to be symbolized in many of Rembrandt's religious paintings and etchings: simple characters lacking any subjective imagination, earthy, gruff – and in themselves already participating in that immanent religiosity they are once more embraced by light in order to bear a totality that manifests the same character of a pure inner transfiguration – an earthiness that is transcendent without reaching beyond itself. ... This light is religious solemnity, the sign of divine origin in the atmosphere, in the spatial world around us, whose pure inner quality alone thereby finds expression. (REM: 136)

This, then, is the 'truth content' of the everyday existence of these humble, pious people. In rendering this intense inner light, Rembrandt is perhaps less the first portraitist of modern life and more the inimitable painter of the 'last images' of early modern souls.

4 The Poverty of Photography

Rich and suggestive in so many ways,[24] Simmel's Rembrandt essay has a threefold significance for Kracauer: as a model of a *Wesenstopographie*; as an exemplary way of reading works of art *of his own time*; and as a characterization of the elective affinity between photography and modernity. The last of these rests on a complex co-existence and co-determination of the 'real' and the representation. All images are illusions of 'reality' (of Nature – if this is what they portray). They cannot be otherwise. To say one image is more or less 'realistic' than another is to miss the point: it is not a question of a pre-existing 'reality' and images that subsequently more or less correspond to it. The way we see Nature is itself parallel to the way we see an image. Privileging reality and consigning the image to some secondary standing is misleading: art is not derivative of reality but another order in and of itself with its own integrity. It is not a question of real and fake. The picture is also 'real', both a material and an optical phenomenon. Simmel clarifies this with respect to a picture of Rembrandt's mother: a fur collar and the same fur collar painted on a canvas are not the same thing but they are equally 'real', both visible and tactile – the hairs and textures of one correspond to the brushstrokes and paint layers of the portrait.[25] Indeed, might it be that our perception of this 'real' is actually conditioned by the way we perceive images? What if, as Simmel suggests:

> in each epoch people see nature in the way their artists have taught them to. We experience our real fates in the way, and with those emotional reactions, that our poets had already anticipated. In the field of vision we glimpse the colours and forms suggested by our respective painters and are completely blind to other inner visual formations, and so on. (REM: 150)

Human perception itself, how and what we see, is not 'given' but rather historically and culturally constructed and conditioned. 'Reality' and 'representation' are mutually constitutive, or set in dialectical interplay. If, in the past, Nature, the 'real', was viewed through the medium of painting and drawing – the images of Rembrandt, for example – then today it is seen through the lens of the camera. Our vision is configured and filtered by the most dominant and ubiquitous modes of representation of the time: in modernity, by photography and film. And if this photographic medium combines a formal flatness with an icy exactitude, then this is how we moderns experience and view the rationalized world of today's *Zivilisation*. If Rembrandt's images are misty windows, shadowy portals, through which one is able to discern the piety and tranquillity before death of our early modern forebears, what do they offer now to us, their disenchanted descendants and spiritually impoverished heirs? Indeed, how can we even comprehend such images today? How can we appreciate Rembrandt's genius when we are condemned to view his works with our modern eyes, eyes conditioned by the banality of the photograph? With the proliferation and preponderance of photographic images, we moderns are witnessing the masterpieces of *Kultur* at last sight.[26]

Kracauer's conceptualization of the relationships between art, photography and modernity develop Simmel's vision here. He, too, points to the elevation of the painting over the photograph in terms of capturing the 'real', the *really* 'real', so to speak. Kracauer cites Goethe's defence of the two sources of sunlight in a Rubens landscape:

> This is how Rubens proves his greatness, and shows to the world that he stands *above* nature with a free spirit, fashioning it according to his higher purposes. The double light is indeed violent, and you could even say that it is contrary to nature. But if it is contrary to nature, I also say that it is *higher* than nature; I say that it is the bold hand of the master, whereby he demonstrates in a brilliant way that art is not entirely subject to natural necessity but rather has laws of its own. (MOR: 52)

Indeed, Kracauer adds: 'A portrait painter who submitted entirely to "natural necessity" would at best create photographs' (MOR: 52); in other words, she/he would serve to record and represent what *appears* or *appears to be*, the superficial exteriority of things and of people. The painter is not bound to the slavish reproduction of simple similarity, mere likeness but, rather, freed from such 'natural necessity', may disclose what lies within. She/he is true to how things *are*, not how they *seem*. Painting, like the work of memory, involves the act of depiction grounded in discrimination, the selection of features guided by criteria of significance. Both are precious and fragile, subject to decay with the passage of time but not to diminution of meaning: Kracauer notes:

> This likeness refers to the look of the object, which does not immediately divulge how it reveals itself to cognition; the artwork, however, conveys nothing but the transparency of the object. In so doing it resembles a magic mirror which reflects those who consult it not as they appear but rather as they wish to be or as they fundamentally are. The artwork, too, disintegrates over time; but its meaning arises out of its crumbled elements, whereas photography merely stockpiles the elements. (Ibid.)

If painting is a revelatory 'magic mirror', then does photography at least provide a 'window' on the world? Such a claim to transparency and 'realism' is deceptive for Kracauer not because, as Roland Barthes famously argues some forty years later, it ingenuously purports to be an innocent image or message 'without a code', effacing its own rhetorical tropes and ideological machinations,[27] but rather because it offers the viewer only 'reified appearances as they manifest themselves in spatial relations' (MOR: 53). Photography captures the 'real' at most and at least: *at most* in its exhaustive detailing and cataloguing of everything and anything that was before the camera; *at least*, because all one can say about these things, shorn of their qualities, meanings and associations, is that they were there in this particular configuration at this specific moment in time. *So they were*, or, in Barthes's terms,[28] 'that has been' [*ça a été*] – this is the defining gesture (*noeme*) of photography.

In taking the world at face value, the photographer as failed physiognomist is very much at home in modern capitalist society. Indeed, Kracauer notes, 'the world itself has taken on a "photographic face"' (MOR: 59). What does this mean? Firstly, Kracauer points to the immense proliferation and sheer ubiquity of the photographic image as part and parcel of the rise of modern mass media, populated by Hollywood stars and 'celebrities' drawn from popular entertainment and professional sports. The example he chooses is telling: a magazine cover featuring a Tiller Girl, a face the reader recognizes from countless other media appearances – no one of his time can be in any doubt as to the identity of our 'demonic diva'. Her image is just one among a 'blizzard of photographs' (MOR: 58) obscuring, indeed obliterating, everyday reality and prompting only 'an indifference toward what things mean' (ibid.).[29] In this avalanche of newsprint, one reads more, sees more, and learns less than ever before. Itself written as a feuilleton piece for the *Frankfurter Zeitung*, Kracauer's 'On Photography' offers a biting indictment of the photographic image as part and parcel of the prevailing mass media and culture industry. 'Never before', he announces, 'has an age been so informed about itself, if being informed means having an image of objects that resembles them in a photographic sense' (ibid.), adding that this paradoxically ensures that 'Never before has a period known so little about itself. In the hands of the ruling society, the invention of illustrated magazines is one of the most powerful means of organizing a strike against understanding' (ibid.). Not only is the photographic image to be distinguished from that of memory, but its commonplace claim to be *a prompt for memory* is unfounded. For Kracauer: 'the flood of photos sweeps away the dam of memory' – indeed, 'The assault of this mass of images is so powerful that it threatens to destroy the potentially existing awareness of crucial traits' (ibid.).[30] Behind the smiling 'photographic face' is a society with no sense of itself, with a memory wiped blank.

Secondly, modernity and photography share a common spirit: the diligent documenting of what is. Through the relentless work of disenchantment, the capitalist imagination transforms the modern perception of the world of things such that the realm of Nature is envisaged no longer as a Book of divine creation, bequeathed by God and named by Adam, but instead as a colour catalogue of raw materials and energies to be harnessed and exploited by the rapacious industrialist; no longer a Fallen paradisiacal Garden but a profitable commercial plantation. Photography, in its indifference to the meanings and the qualities of things beyond/beneath their appearance, corresponds to this utterly disillusioned state of the rationalized secular world.[31] Abstract, quantifying, instrumental, myopic – photography and capitalism for Kracauer share the very *spiritlessness* of the *Ratio* that prevails in modernity.

That this vision of photography as systematic, soulless stocktaking will later be reconfigured and re-evaluated as the very 'redemption of the physical reality' is perhaps less surprising given the closing passages of the 1927 essay. These suggest a more equivocal view of the medium, one very much in keeping with the acute ambivalence and ambiguity of the notion of 'disenchantment'. On the one hand, photography provides the perspective, the way of seeing, that strips and reduces the world of things to the very minimum of significance. Photography is an act of reduction, of diminution. But, on the other, this process of rationalization may enable us for the first time to confront the world unvarnished by the symbolic fancies and the allegorical trappings of past traditions, to encounter it in its raw state, so to speak, and with, as Karl Marx famously puts it in the *Communist Manifesto*, 'sober senses' (1977: 224). What is left, the world laid bare, bereft of consolation, is archived by photography such that we may bear witness to it anew. And so, despite the negative qualities and consequences of the photographic medium, Kracauer deftly changes tack to suggest that it at least saves for posterity 'in effigy the last elements of a nature alienated from meaning' (MOR: 62). Denuded of religious mystifications and romantic sentimentalism, the world retains a plain and cheerless countenance, a 'photographic face' perhaps. And, like the 'demonic diva', we certainly recognize it; we must surely re-cognize it. This urgent task of rethinking is the challenge, the imperative that we moderns confront: how is our new relationship with the world of things to be envisaged – is it to be one of ever greater capitalist instrumentalism and commodification or one in which reason, technology and nature are somehow reconfigured as collaborators, as conspirators who 'breathe together' in an epoch of human self-determination and emancipation? What face is the coming world to have? This is what animates Kracuaer when he claims that 'the turn to photography is the *go-for-broke game* of history' (MOR: 61). He writes:

This warehousing of nature promotes the confrontation of consciousness with nature. Just as consciousness finds itself confronting the unabashedly displayed mechanics of industrial society, it also faces, thanks to photographic technology, the reflection of the reality that has slipped away from it. To have provoked the decisive confrontation in every field: this is precisely the go-for-broke game of the historical process. The images of the stock of nature disintegrated into its elements are offered up to consciousness to deal with as it pleases. Their original order is lost; they no longer cling to the spatial context that linked with them an original out of which the memory image was selected. But if the remnants of nature are not oriented towards the memory image, then the order they assume through the image is necessarily provisional. It is therefore incumbent on consciousness to establish the *provisional status* of all given configurations, and perhaps even to awaken an inkling of the right order of the inventory of nature. (MOR: 62)

What photography has fragmented and frozen, burying and simultaneously preserving beneath a layer of snow, film will recollect and recompose as montage and sequence. Film, Kracauer concludes, 'plays with the pieces' (MOR: 63) it inherits from the God-forsaken world of modernity. This is its calling.

5 Painters of Modern Life

Unpublished in his own lifetime, Kracauer's 83-page typescript 'On Expressionism: Essence and Meaning of a Contemporary Movement: Treatise' ('Über Expressionismus: Wesen und Sinn einer Zeitbewegung: Abhandlung') (1918) is chronologically sandwiched between Simmel's 'philosophical essay' on Rembrandt and his own '*Wesenstopographie*' of Simmel. It is unmistakably indebted to the former, sharing the same fundamental postulate that the work of art is to be understood as a moment of correspondence or coincidence between the 'inner life' of the artist and that of the other or the external world.[32] Starting from this, Kracauer seeks to provide a critical understanding not of the masterpieces of the past but rather of the garish and jarring artworks of his own time. For him, the distorted and disturbing[33] visual images and literary texts[34] of Expressionism were, if not the principal aesthetic achievements of the early twentieth century, then at least the epoch's most distinctive and characteristic cultural manifestations produced by a new generation of artists.[35] Kracauer addresses a number of key questions: What is 'the *essence* [*Wesen*] of this new direction in art?' (WK 9.2: 13). What is its 'meaning' (*Deutung*) and sense (*Sinn*)? Moreover, how might we assess and make a 'judgement' (*Beurteilung*) as to its significance? In short: What exactly does Expressionism *express* and what are the consequences of this movement for an understanding of the present? Echoing Simmel's Rembrandt study, Kracauer's reflections on Expressionism are prompted not so much by an art historical or aesthetic interest as by the possibilities and promise of a *sociological* exploration of the life of the German spirit in the dying days of the Wilhelminian Empire – not exactly the 'newest Germany', as Kracauer will later term it,[36] but perhaps the newest before the new. His conclusions are bold: Expressionism is not so much a painterly response to the rise of photography (and/or the works of Impressionism) as a vital and violent reaction to a society that has adopted a 'photographic face' (MOR: 59). Irreducible to an artistic fashion or trend, it constitutes instead a full-scale 'cultural *movement*' (*Kulturbewegung*) (WK 9.2: 70) extending across a plethora of aesthetic media and forms (visual, cinematic, sculptural, dramatic, poetic, literary), embracing different schools and centres (most notably 'The Bridge' ('Die Brücke') in Dresden and 'The Blue Rider' ('Der Blaue Reiter') in Munich) and galvanized by a common central thematic complex: the desperate yearnings of the youthful *Kulturmensch* in the era of *Zivilisation*, the outcry of the soul in soulless times – in short: the 'Ludwig Loos complex'.

Typically for this period of his writings, Kracauer begins by sketching a classificatory typology to frame his arguments. All works of art – and here it is perhaps best to think in terms of visual representation – involve a certain relationship between the creative impulses and inspirations of the artist (that is to say, part of his or her 'inner life') and the external world (Nature, a model, a sitter, an object) which (or who) constitutes the thing depicted, the subject matter of the artwork. Given this Simmelian premise, Kracauer suggests that such works of art may therefore be usefully divided broadly into three types, types which are obviously really tendencies, points along a continuum, rather than hard and fast categories. While recognizing that *all* art engages in some way with 'reality' (*die Wirklichkeit*),[37] he distinguishes artworks tending to:

a) a harmonious or equal balance between the inner life of the artist and the demands of the object/the life of the sitter. One might take Simmel's Rembrandt as an exemplary instance of this perfect fusion of artist and model in the artwork;[38]

b) a conscious renunciation on the part of the artist of his/her own subjective impressions[39] in favour of either (i) a painstaking attention to the representation of the external world; or (ii) a strict adherence to a set of formal and abstract rules. Kracauer identifies two artistic approaches here:[40] on the one hand, the most precise rendering of the 'real' that defines aesthetic 'realism' and/or 'naturalism' in which the artist hopes to serve as a mere window upon Nature; and, on the other, those pioneering modernist currents preoccupied with the workings of light, purity of colour, use of line, properties of form and rules of composition to produce abstract works. While the resulting artworks themselves are radically different, and indeed are often seen as antithetical, in both cases the inner life of the painter is subordinated and constrained;

c) a disdain for copying Nature and a rejection of the imposition of all formal rules and strictures. Such art is driven exclusively by the inner life of the artist, who must seek again and again to capture and give 'expression' with the utmost fidelity to the manifold and maelstrom of the self.

For Kracauer, Expression is exemplary of the last of these tendencies,[41] the laying bare of inner life and experience (*Erlebnis*) 'wholly naked and pure' (WK 9.2: 32) on the canvas, on paper.[42] But, before moving on to follow his argument further, it is important to tarry a moment to consider the significance of this conceptual scheme as a way of characterizing visual culture. Kracauer's distinction between those images and artworks that strive to accord with and represent the external world, the 'real', and those which insist on departing from it is highly significant. Some forty years later, in *Theory of Film*, he will contrast the 'realistic tendency' (or 'cinematic approach') of films, which rightly devote themselves to the portrayal of the physical world, with the 'formative tendency', those workings of narrative devices, storylines, editing, camerawork and other influences and interferences by the film-maker, which, while an essential part of any film, may erroneously take pride of place and indeed become the *raison d'être* of the film. Far from revealing the everyday world anew, the experimental films of the artistic and cinematic avant-garde, for example, indulge in the technical trickery of the film medium itself and the stylistic whims of the director-as-*auteur*. Kracauer's antipathy towards such pioneering visual experiments as Walter Ruttmann's famous 1927 *Berlin, Symphony of a Great City* is grounded in what he deems the contrived use of montage and sequence editing to make supposedly critical (but actually banal) comments on modern metropolitan existence, coupled with the failure to penetrate beneath the surfaces of everyday phenomena such that they remain as appearances, as mere ornamentation. In pandering principally to the formalist pretensions of its makers instead of genuinely depicting the everyday concrete realities of the city, Ruttmann's film fails to engage with the politics and experiences of the very metropolitan world it presumes to reveal. The genuine promise of film as a medium, Kracauer argues, lies elsewhere: in its 'realist tendency'. As we will see in chapters 9 and 10, his contention is that film discloses what has hitherto gone unseen, redeems what has been forgotten or consigned to oblivion, rejuvenates the human sensorium and revitalizes our experience of the world. Significantly, the categorical distinctions and conceptual tools that are decisive for Kracauer's later cinematic understanding may be traced back to these initial and incipient frameworks devised as early as 1918 in the 'On Expressionism' essay. Accordingly, it is no exaggeration to say that the starting point for Kracauer's theory of film is Simmel's reading of Rembrandt – not, then, the raucous streets of 1940s Marseilles but, surprisingly, the radiant souls of seventeenth-century Amsterdam.

To triumph over the petty restrictions of everyday life, to free the self from the confines and constraints imposed by conventions and customs, to reduce the prevailing external reality to rubble – these, Kracauer acknowledges, are the 'fundamental feelings' (*Grundgefühle*) fuelling the Expressionists (WK 9.2: 33). At the same time, he astutely observes that, while they appear as the medium for the liberation of inner experience, the works of Expressionism should not be understood as representing the actual personal strivings and cravings of the individual artist per se. There are two reasons for this: the collective character of Expressionism and its preoccupation with the unconscious.

Firstly, Expressionism is to be understood more broadly as a wide-ranging *movement* rather than as the output of a single or solitary artistic genius. This *collective* aspect spanning a number of different media means that the works of Expressionism are *more*, rather than *less*, important for Kracauer: the artworks composed by the individual genius – Rembrandt, for example – are idiosyncrasies which have at best an uncertain relationship to the wider society in which they are conceived; like those who produce them, such works are *exceptional* rather than exemplary.[43] Conversely, it is the works of lesser lights, of the many aesthetic journeymen and women working to a common purpose and/or with some shared set of principles (a studio or 'school' perhaps) that are more truly representative of their times.[44] Accordingly, Kracauer states:

> When in history we are concerned not with an outstanding personality ... but with a large movement sweeping many along with it, then we can conclude from the outset: it must be possible to understand this uniformity of direction, this curious conformity of all the people in sensibility, works and ultimate goals ... *inter alia* from the effect of certain general relationships of the time on the souls of those who are subjected to the prevalent external and internal conditions of being [*Daseinsbedingungen*]. (WK 9.2: 12)

The Expressionists, as groupings of more modest talents, are a much more useful indicator of the state of contemporary culture and the life of the spirit. As a youthful protest against the hegemony of *Zivilisation* and the diminution of the personality, the *Kulturmensch*, Expressionism claims and expresses the representative experiences of a new generation rather than those of any particular individual or unique self. With this collective and combative stance, Kracauer sees here the critical and transgressive potential of Expressionism as the most acute and poignant protest of the spirit against the spiritlessness of his times. And so, on one level, the movement cannot but elicit Kracauer's own profound intellectual sympathies and critical inclinations. Indeed, with its protagonist's painful quest for spiritual nourishment and the sexual love of a soulmate against the backdrop of bourgeois boredom and white-collar routine, his own novella, 'The Mercy', would qualify as an exemplary Expressionist drama.

Secondly, in seeking to depict the turbulent and tumultuous inner life of the artist, the adherents of Expressionism were highly selective in their choice of traits and characteristics. What was to be put on canvas was not the full human personality, but only those impulses and inclinations that were seen as most under threat, most subject to control and repression in modernity: the frustrated life of instinctual and irrational drives. And so such works – vented by means of vivid colours, frenzied faces and figures, and nightmarish visions – all manner of primal passions and violent excesses, ecstatic and erotic fantasies, brutality and cruelty, the unrestrained and untrammelled emotional outpourings of the Freudian id. Such primordial pictures and Dionysian imagery were the results of Expressionism's valorization of the unconscious and its penchant for a pantheistic 'primitivism', its quest to strip away the prim and proper pretensions of modern humankind and release our pure 'original' or 'primeval self [*Ur-Ich*]' (WK 9.2: 45 and 46).[45] For Kracauer, this is Expressionism's fundamental failing: it succumbs to a naïve but nevertheless virulent irrationalism, a rabid rejection of rationality and modernity as the illegitimate and unconditional domination of instinctual life. It is not the fate of the individual, the modern subject, that finds expression in Expressionism but, rather, the rudimentary urges of some mythical human ancestor, uncontaminated and unadulterated by any pernicious 'civilising process'[46] – less *Kulturmensch*, more *Urmensch*. For Kracauer, this eruption of the irrational and celebration of the cultic and mythic is dangerous nonsense, forms of regression and atavism rather than any radical demand for genuine freedom. In the final analysis, then, Expressionism may be an acute and legitimate howl of protest emitted by the suffering spirit of the now,[47] but it provides little real insight into the actual conditions of the modern individual and simply remains blindly, hopelessly hopeful of some fantastical future 'victory of the human personality' (WK 9.2: 74) over the emptiness and enervation of contemporary civilization. The future, though, is not Expressionism's strong point. In its celebration of the '*Ur-Ich*' and its concomitant virulent anti-intellectualism,[48] Expressionism ultimately succumbs to the most retrograde delusions of a pagan past.

Such philistinism also ensures that Expressionism lacks reflexivity: it possesses no sense of itself, no capacity for nuance, and absolutely no sense of irony or wit.[49] Intensely introverted and 'monstrously earnest' (WK 9.2: 48), Expressionism is, for Kracauer, the most po-faced protest against what is. The humourless Ludwig Loos would surely have been a disciple if only he could paint or write. Indeed, his scorn for the artist Nyström is sparked by the latter's casual attitude to his aesthetic labours, preferring the cheerful comforts and chatter of café life to the solitary agonies and ecstasies of the atelier. Nyström simply does not bear the requisite stigmata to be a real artist. Certainly, Expressionism was far too serious and censorious for Kracauer's own lightness of touch and deft satirical skills. If 'Die Gnade' was his closest encounter with the Expressionist movement, then the flirtation was short-lived and certainly over by 1918. In Weimar Germany, Expressionism was *passé* and anachronistic; its clarion call for youthful action and energy[50] for the sake of the Teutonic *'Ur-Ich'* against the evil and corrosive values of foreign *Zivilisation* had all too easily been channelled into nationalist fervour and co-opted by the imperial war machine. Franz Marc and August Macke, all too 'derring-do [*tatenfroh*]', all too 'trusting of the inherited human primeval being' (WK 9.2: 50), were among the first to volunteer for and then fall victim to the carnage. And so Kracauer's own literary critique of modernity and of the horrors of the Great War was to be written not in the naïve agonistics of Expressionism but rather in the biting irony of a picaresque tale, the comic story of a hapless everyman who is not thrown into the catastrophic industrialized violence but made to sit (and sit out) among the reserves, practise drills, perfect salutes, and 'peel potatoes against the enemy' (cited in Belke and Renz 1989: 53). And to pose for the occasional group photograph. Innocuously, inconspicuously, he will survive and quietly discover himself as a whole world collapses around him. He will tell of all this in his own simple and prosaic words: *Ginster*, as written by himself.

Part II

FROM OUR WEIMAR CORRESPONDENT: THE 'NEWEST GERMANY' AND ELSEWHERE

3

On the Surface: The Dialectics of Ornament

1 Automaton and Avatar

Out walking one day, the disaffected young architect, known to the reader only as Ginster, chances upon his dear friend Otto, now fully attired in the uniform of the Imperial German Army. Otto candidly admits his utter disenchantment with the war. Now he sees through the grandiloquent rhetoric and patriotic claptrap that inspired him along with countless other young men to abandon their families, their studies and their careers for heroic fantasies of daring deeds and duty in the honourable service and just cause of the Fatherland. Ginster, himself deemed unfit for military service,[1] learns of Otto's newfound scepticism:

> The young people, above all the students, participate because they lan-
> guish under the specialization at the universities and now finally believe
> they discern a goal to which they may devote themselves as whole
> human beings; or because from their aimless freedom they long for dis-
> cipline and obedience. Moreover, this is infectious, and hardly any of
> them know what they are actually fighting for. (WK 7: 52)

But it is not so much Otto's *words* as his *actions* that strike Ginster as remarkable: he recalls the peculiar course of their conversation:

> 'I am very well' – Otto raised one arm in a strange way – 'the constant
> physical activity' – Otto's head twitched suddenly to the right – 'decent
> superiors' – his arm once again – 'once I'm back from the war' – Otto's
> whole body stiffened – 'spend less time with the books' – sharp turn to
> the left.
>   They have turned him into a rectangle, thought Ginster, an automa-
> ton. At every second uniform his arm went into the air. It wasn't swung

into the air by Otto, but flew there automatically. Otto would not have recognized the uniforms. The arm must have been fitted with little cogs in his body. The system was controlled by the uniforms remotely. It could not be disengaged and presumably functioned better without Otto. (WK 7: 50)

From the 'whole men' who volunteered, the German army has already fashioned through its disciplinary regimes an assemblage of compliant human body parts, one which, in many cases, will become a disassemblage of shattered body parts. The imperial war machine has reproduced itself in miniature in the physical being and programmed physiological responses of the common soldier. Even as the effects of propaganda have worn off, Otto has been objectified, reified.[2] He has become doubly reflexive: he has come to realize the error of his ways and indeed the folly of his generation; at the same time, the intense and incessant routines of drill have reduced him to a series of unconscious reflexes. He is a conscious objector trapped in an unconsciously obedient body. He will soon be killed in action. If he is lucky, his body might be recovered and buried in the military cemetery for the heroes of the Fatherland currently being designed by Ginster as part of an architectural competition. Ginster's original idea of a labyrinthine garden with hidden graves is deemed too 'tender [*zart*]' (WK 7: 112) and is superseded by a rectilinear ground plan laid out according to 'strict scientific principles' (WK 7: 113), with serried ranks of the dead each allotted the same, specific amount of space, each grave identical. In death, as in life, the soldiers are to be dutifully organized and uniformly ordered. Transforming Otto into a rectilinear form is the perfect preparation for his final resting place. Perhaps it is such forward thinking that impresses the architectural judges: in any case, Ginster's design wins first prize (WK 7: 114), even though there are concerns it will not prove big enough (WK 7: 109).[3] Death in the trenches; victory at the drawing board: even a simple soul like Ginster grudgingly admits on returning to civilian life: 'earn money, architecture better than war' (WK 7: 204).

But it is not just Otto the doomed volunteer who is reduced to an automaton, to a mechanism functioning independently of any human will, a human then, only in appearance. Ginster visits Otto's grief-stricken mother to offer his condolences, to pay his respects. Robbed of her beloved son, this distraught woman now numbly continues to go through the motions, routines bereft of any meaning, any purpose. She retains the semblance of life but really she no longer lives. She exists. She is there but no longer present, as if she were now somehow forever elsewhere, a now permanent exile from herself.[4]

Ginster's own response to Otto's death is curiously constricted. He confesses to barely shedding a tear for his fallen friend; instead he is simply relieved to be alive himself.[5] And this emptiness or numbness is telling in terms of the whole compositional style of Ginster's narrative. Yes, there is certainly some insight into the inner life of our eponymous everyman – the reader is indeed privy to his thoughts and feelings, his motives and misconceptions, his hopes and fears *such as they are*. Yet even though this is certainly a kind of modern *Bildungsroman*, an unsentimental education relating a coming to knowledge and a growing awareness of one's self and the ways of the world, there is precious little emotional intensity, no profound passions. Ginster is an ingénu who makes his way blithely and benignly through the chaos and catastrophe enveloping him. He escapes seemingly unscathed but remains inscrutable, psychologically inert and innocuous, conspicuously colourless. Ginster's memories bear little resemblance to those precious and ultimately unforgettable 'last images' lauded by Kracauer in the 'Photography' essay. This is no poignant portrait of the architect as a young man. Rather, Ginster appears as a blank canvas or, better still, a walking-talking photograph, a monochrome moving picture, a passing shadow.

There is a double optic at work in *Ginster*, and this is the key to its comic ingenuity. Our Chaplinesque[6] innocent-at-large is the reader's overly trusting and hence wholly untrustworthy guide to the world: we can observe events and characters only through his eyes, but we do not consider him a reliable witness. On the contrary: the reader repeatedly *sees through* what Ginster merely sees. And this discrepancy between how things *appear* (to him) and how they *are* is a continual source of irony and satire, partly at Ginster's expense, but principally to the detriment of others: in their interactions with our well-intentioned albeit not well-informed hero, it is *their* stupidity and selfishness, *their* cruelty and callousness, *their* pretensions and posturing that are disclosed, *not to Ginster* but *through him* to the reader. Ginster is neither a window upon nor a mirror reflecting the world: rather, he is a prism in which all the constituent elements of individuals, organizations and institutions are refracted and separated out, revealed in their true colours.

Ginster is, of course, supposedly an autobiographical work – 'written by himself' (*'von ihm selbst geschrieben'*) – and so it is perplexing that it takes throughout the third-person singular rather than the first. Ginster tells of *himself*, not *myself*, as if viewed from the outside, as if the narrator were not so much recalling his own personal experiences as narrating someone else's life altogether, as if writing from elsewhere.[7] This curiously disembodied voice of the author may playfully accord with the tenets of the then voguish notion of 'New Objectivity' (*Neue Sachlichkeit*), but the effect of such estrangement is to lend this 'autobiography' the sense of an *alibi*. Moreover, this 'autobiography' is, in any case, the semi-autobiography of *Kracauer*: Ginster is only a pseudonym, a fictional persona who writes of his past life in this second-hand dispassionate prose as if Ginster were *his* creation, *his* avatar. And so, corresponding to the novel's double optic, there is also a double displacement or dislocation: from Kracauer to Ginster (as author) and thence to Ginster (as character).[8] In this deceptive disappearing act, Kracauer leaves the reader in the dark as to the veracity of all these encounters and events with respect to his own biography. True, the main contours do seem to accord closely with Kracauer's experiences – born in F. (Frankfurt am Main); studies in M. (Munich); trains and works as an architect; loses a close friend in the war; volunteers in 1914 but is rejected; later conscripted but once again stood down; designs a cemetery for the war dead; sketches a housing project in Q. (Osnabruck) – but this duplicitous double (dis)articulation ensures that we can be sure of nothing beyond these broad outlines. In blankly, blandly recounting it all, Ginster gives nothing away. Indeed, if Ginster remains a mystery, Kracauer is an enigma wrapped in this mystery.

2   From Troop to Troupe

It is no surprise that this sense of disembodiment and of being elsewhere reaches its apotheosis when Ginster eventually joins the army and is subject to those same drills and disciplines which conditioned Otto. The good soldier Ginster learns what is most important: to salute; to stand to attention; to carry his rifle and pack; to march; to sing while marching; to banish all thoughts of death with a simple 'La-la-la-la' (WK 7: 176). In the exhaustion and futility of marching:

> The legs were alone in the world.... Since they only ever marched straight ahead the world was turned according to their requirements. All that was left apart from them were the backs and the necks, which served as buffers. Up and down, up and down, Ginster fell into two parts, right leg, left leg, right and left, head up, going on, nothing going on. When he manages a spring in his step, he gets entangled in his carbine. Like a matchstick man formed of three lines. (WK 7: 174)

This mechanistic repetition of 'left foot, right foot', all set to a dubious rhythmic accompaniment, has a mnemonic effect: 'Ginster remembered the dance lessons which had cost him the same efforts; only there it was the feet that had been at fault' (WK 7: 160). Shortly after his arrival in M. (Munich), he decides to seek out some sociable female company and enrols at a local dance class. But his hopes are quickly disappointed. These lessons are the most *asocial* encounters imaginable – thoroughly depersonalized affairs in which dance partners disdainfully treat each other as more or less awkward bodies to be manoeuvred around the floor. Locked in perfunctory, passionless embrace:

The one pair of legs was magnetically connected to the other: together four legs, in parallel without destination. Later, he [Ginster] had to lead two girls in easy-care blouses, Elli and Paula. ... There was no point talking to the girls since they were only here to learn too. They served as mannequins, all done up in dances instead of modelling beautiful clothes. The dummies used each other ... In the breaks, Ginster leaned against the narrow wall of the ballroom, an orphaned instrument of use. (WK 7: 27–8)

Twinkle-toed footsteps under the watchful eye of the dance teacher and sore-footed slogs on officers' orders are certainly very different, but Ginster's recollections attest to an intriguing connection: dance and drill as forms of corporeal discipline and dressage involving the co-ordination and synchronization of bodily movement. Indeed, the link is more compelling when one thinks not so much of the subdued shuf-flings of Ginster in the ballroom as of that frantic but futile 'mere marking of time' (MOR: 66) which Kracauer sees (in his 1925 piece 'Travel and Dance') as the hallmark of contemporary jazz syncopation and jitterbugging, forms of dance attuned to 'a tempo that is concerned with nothing but itself' (MOR: 67) and in which all hitherto pleasures of 'danced ceremoniousness – pleasant flirtation, a tender encounter in the realm of the senses' (MOR: 66) – are expunged by an individualistic fetishizing of rhythms. Such dancing, distinguished by the 'lack of substantive meaning over and above that of disciplined movement' (MOR: 67), finds its corollary in the mechanization of repetitive bodily reflexes conditioned by the demands of the Taylorized production line, and reaches its apotheosis in the abstract choreography and synchro-nized 'tap and kick' of dance troupes: the Tiller Girls.

3   On the Surface

Fifty years ago, at Adorno's suggestion,[9] Kracauer named the first col-lection of his journalistic writings after his 1927 essay 'The Mass Orna-ment'.[10] This was the clearest acknowledgement that this text was the most important, both methodologically and theoretically, of his feuil-leton writings for the *Frankfurter Zeitung*, rivalled only by the later serialized pieces forming *Ginster* (1928) and *Die Angestellten* (1929).[11] In each of these, the figure of the mass takes centre stage albeit in different guises: on the parade grounds of the imperial army with its disciplined ranks of marching male bodies; as synchronized lines of dancing female forms treading the boards of the revue theatres; and as white-collar employees ensconced behind typewriters in offices or canoodling in the serried banks of seats of Berlin's picture palaces.

Certainly both wartime architect and revue choreographer are masters in the matter of controlling the distribution and arrangement of multiple bodies in time and space for aesthetic effect. Indeed, Ginster's own prize-winning cemetery is exemplary here. Set out in straight lines with equidistant spacing, of standardized shape and size, bereft of any idiosyncratic decoration or personal touches, the soldiers' graves exhibited both martial mass uniformity and the dictates of modernist architectural style and practice. This seemingly Spartan aesthetic is not, however, the absence of ornamentation as such but rather its transformation: the organizational regularity and rigour of austerity itself becomes a source of aesthetic gratification. The rectilinear, the geometrical, the composition of parallel and intersecting lines and planes – these involve a new privileging of and pleasure in precision, exactitude and synchronization. Such abstractions and repetitions – and not the spirals and arabesques doodled in Ginster's sketch book, still less the intricate tracery and filigree of early wrought-iron work that Kracauer studied in his 1915 doctoral thesis in architecture – are the fundamental principles and practices of the modern mass ornament.

It is the living bodies of the young women of the Tiller Girls dance troupe, not the corpses of the fallen, which become for Kracauer symptomatic of mass culture in the mid-1920s. Echoing Simmel's opening to the Rembrandt study, the 'Mass Ornament' essay begins with an articulation of the depth hermeneutic at work not just in this particular feuilleton piece but throughout his entire journalistic *oeuvre*:

> The position that an epoch occupies in the historical process can be determined more strikingly from an analysis of its inconspicuous surface-level expressions than from that epoch's judgements about itself. Since these judgements are expressions of the tendencies of a particular era, they do not offer conclusive testimony about its overall constitution. The surface-level expressions, however, by virtue of their unconscious nature, provide unmediated access to the fundamental substance of the state of things. Conversely, knowledge of this state of things depends on the interpretation of these surface-level expressions. The fundamental substance of an epoch and its unheeded impulses illuminate each other reciprocally. (MOR: 75)

In this dialectical conception of surface and depth, the study of superficial phenomena is not to be conflated with superficial study (journalism, perhaps?). Rather, these apparently trivial and insignificant manifestations are the essential, indeed only, points of access to that which lies below, to the fundamental conditions prevailing in a society at any given time (the proper subject matter of sociology).[12] The Tiller Girls themselves, ostensibly the focus of Kracauer's text, are then only an *alibi* for what principally concerns him. An alibi, perhaps, but certainly not an arbitrary one, for the Tiller Girls embody the fate of the body itself in modernity, exemplify its subordination to new and powerful underlying social and cultural logics – the triumph of a machine aesthetic as emblematic of the rationalized, disenchanted world; the domination of instrumental reason; the hegemony of the *Ratio*.

As several commentators have pointed out, 'The Mass Ornament' starts with a factual error: the Tiller Girls were *not* an American phenomenon.[13] As part of the 'culture industry', the Tiller Girls were, appropriately enough, founded in the birthplace of modern industrialization – Manchester – in 1890 by the theatrical impresario John Tiller. At full strength numbering some thirty-two dancers, the Tiller Girls were initially recruited from young women working in the factories and mills of north-west England – ironically, then, drawn from the very mechanized production lines that their dance routines so resembled. Carefully selected to ensure similarity of colouring, physique and appearance, they were trained to perform specially choreographed and synchronized 'tap and kick' dance numbers to entertain holiday-makers and day-trippers in the nearby seaside resort of Blackpool. From such humble beginnings, the troupe became an international sensation, performing on stages and in revues across Europe and North America, eventually spanning three centuries in the process.[14] The performances themselves were modelled on the chorus lines of variety theatre in which the arms, legs and bodies of the dancers moved rhythmically and in unison, forming patterns and shapes to popular tunes of the time. In these routines, which anticipated the more elaborate and intricate musical film dance sequences of the American choreographer Busby Berkeley in the 1920s and 1930s, the body of the individual dancer was seemingly separated into its distinct constituent parts – ostentatiously costumed heads, torsos and limbs – and then reconfigured and recomposed into a larger functioning and moving entity. Each individual woman was deliberately dissolved into a single collective organism, a colourful and co-ordinated chimera of waving, kicking, twisting, jiggling, smiling elements.

Kracauer's interest in the phenomenon of the Tiller Girls as a relatively novel and extremely popular form of commercial light entertainment is, if nothing else, a prescient early identification of a prototype of what is today an utterly ubiquitous small-scale theatrical and televisual spectacle: the dance routines observed in any number of mainstream music videos, with groups of identically attired background dancers moving in time and as one while, in the foreground, a differently dressed singer dances and lip-synchs to the music. And insightful too: he is aware that such synchronized performances have been extended into much grander events, with casts of hundreds, thousands even, in the rhythmic gymnastics spectacles and choreographed extravaganzas forming those incipient media events of his time,[15] and ultimately the multi-media mega-events of ours.[16] But what exactly do the Tiller Girls as 'surface-level expressions' *express* for Kracauer in the 1920s? The short answer is that they are not simply manifestations of the vacuity of modern culture as mere spectacle and distraction but, more importantly, indications and intimations of the fate of the modern individual under capitalism. There are a number of inter-woven themes here.

Firstly, there is the issue of de-individualization, of 'massification' itself. The young women were carefully selected with an eye to mini-mizing any individual or idiosyncratic bodily features – or, put another way, to maximizing the appearance of uniformity and identity of the troupe. In the performances of the Tiller Girls one observes not unique and distinctive dancers moving spontaneously and independently but rather a series of 'indissoluble girl clusters' (MOR: 76). They form not a group of individuals with a common talent and purpose in dancing but, rather, a thoroughly *de-individualized* totality, a mass, which appeals in its precise functioning to an equally undifferentiated audience. Per-former and spectator mirror each other, admire each other. Through multiplication, the individual as a unique being is deliberately eradi-cated to the delight of the onlooker. This is not Simmelian indifference as such, the metropolitan's blasé attitude, but rather the transformation of indifference itself into a new aesthetic principle: the nothing-new of mass-production and commodity culture experienced as *pleasure in repetition. This is the spectacle of sameness and sameness as spectacular.*

Secondly, there is a fundamental shift from the organic/biological to the mechanical, the automatic. The visual effect and aesthetic principle at work in the Tiller Girls routines is grounded in multiplication and synchronization, in the subjection of the dancing bodies not to innate or natural rhythms but to mechanistic repetition. The body of the dancer does not so much *perform* as *function* with robotic regularity. This has two consequences: de-sexualization and alienation. Kracauer observes how, despite the racy costumes and displays of female flesh, the bodies of the dancers are subject to a process of de-eroticization. There is nothing seductive about these performances, no sensual or sexual energy, because there is precious little of the human, of the human body, left at all. Broken down into their component parts, the Tiller Girls 'can no longer be reassembled into human beings after the fact' (MOR: 78) and become merely a line of 'sexless bodies in bathing suits' (MOR: 76).[17] Moreover, just as, in his famous formula-tions of alienation in the capitalist industrial production process, Marx recognizes how living labour, the body of the worker, is transformed into the mere appendage of industrial machinery, so this subordination to the supremacy of the mechanical now becomes the basis for our entertainment: so-called free time appears as the after-image of the workplace, dancing as 'routine'. Kracauer writes:

> The structure of the mass ornament reflects that of the entire contempo-rary situation. Since the principle of the *capitalist production process* does

not arise out of nature, it must destroy the natural organisms that it regards either as means or as a resistance. Community and personality perish when what is demanded is calculability; it is only as a tiny piece of the mass that the individual can clamber up charts and can service machines without any friction. (MOR: 78)

The mass ornament is, he adds,

conceived according to rational principles which the Taylor system merely pushes to their ultimate conclusion. The hands in the factory correspond to the legs of the Tiller Girls. Going beyond manual capacities, psychotechnical aptitude tests attempt to calculate dispositions of the soul as well. The mass ornament is the aesthetic reflex of the rationality to which the prevailing economic system aspires. (MOR: 78–9)

This leads us to the third key aspect of Kracauer's study: 'The mass ornament is an *end in itself*' (MOR: 76). As the 'aesthetic reflex' of capitalist logic – understood as that part of reason which contents itself with efficiency and efficacy while remaining unconcerned as to ends, in other words, instrumental reason (*Zweckrationalität*), the '*Ratio*', as Kracauer terms it – the performance of the dancers is geared to the production of patterns and formation of figures for their own sake. Their bodies become instruments in the service of pure abstractness. There is no gestural intention, no attempt at representation or communication. Nothing is hidden or concealed: there is no subtle secret message. Like the photograph, everything is visible, everything is available on the surface. Kracauer recognizes both the novelty and the significance of this radical insignificance:

The star formations have no meaning beyond themselves, and the masses above whom they rise are not a moral unit like a company of soldiers. One cannot even describe the figures as the decorative frills of gymnastic discipline. Rather, the girl-units drill in order to produce an immense number of parallel lines, the goal being to train the broadest mass of people in order to create a pattern of undreamed-of dimensions. The end result is the ornament, whose closure is brought about by emptying all the substantial constructs of their contents. (MOR: 77)

The stars created in the mass ornament are even more pointless than military manoeuvres. But such *meaninglessness* is itself the message. Abstractness triumphant; obedient and compliant bodies subordinated to the logics of capitalist production – such a senseless, sexless spectacle affords the most telling insight into the conditions of modern existence. And so, far from mercilessly castigating its vacuity, Kracauer comes to recognize the mass ornament as the most acute aesthetic expression – and expression of the aesthetic – of his time: 'No matter how low one gauges the value of the mass ornament, its degree of reality is still higher than that of artistic productions which cultivate outdated noble sentiments in obsolete forms – even if it means nothing more than that' (MOR: 79).

Finally, Kracauer is concerned with the position and role of the spectators of the mass ornament: they are incorporated into the very spectacle they have congregated to watch. It is almost as if, particularly in the great new sports stadia of the time,[18] the mass has assembled to bear witness *to itself* as much as to the performance. The simple *presence of* the mass becomes the principal *spectacle for* the mass. Indeed, while the patterns of the Tiller Girls are intended to be identifiable by the spectators in the theatre, those attending larger events not only have no proper perspective on, or overview of, the proceedings but are often themselves expected to produce figures recognizable only from a bird's-eye viewpoint.[19] Human beings become mere specks, dots of colour in some giant pointillist image, or points of light swaying in a giddy galaxy. As Kracauer astutely observes, the mass ornament transforms humans into microscopic organisms, a bacterial culture, by means of a camera elevated to the heights of a watchful god. The mass ornament of the stadium is oriented not to those who are physically present but to the camera as eye in the sky, to aerial photography.[20] The mass ornament has a 'photographic face' with the individual reduced to a single pixel. Kracauer writes:

> Although the masses give rise to the ornament, they are not involved in thinking it through. As linear as it may be, there is no line that extends from the small sections of the mass to the entire figure. The ornament resembles aerial photographs of landscapes and cities in that it does not emerge out of the interior of the given conditions, but rather appears above them. (MOR: 77)

This impossibility of oversight by the unwitting participant is then reconnected to the structuring principles of the capitalist industrial system:

> The production process runs its secret course in public. Everyone does his or her task on the conveyor belt, performing a partial function without grasping the totality. Like the pattern in the stadium, the organization stands above the masses, a monstrous figure whose creator withdraws it from the eyes of its bearers, and barely even observes it himself. (MOR: 78)

Ultimately the mass loses sight of itself. And here the self-regard of the mass is transformed into subservience to surveillance. As the spectator is absorbed into the spectacle itself she/he becomes the object of the supervisory and sovereign gaze of the leader. The spectacle of the mass is the ornament of totalitarianism.[21]

4 *Ratio*, Abstractness and Beyond

Spectacle and commodification; disciplined, docile bodies viewed by some lofty eye of power: Kracauer's account of the mass ornament seems to provide us with anticipations of both Guy Debord and Michel Foucault.[22] My concern here, though, is with a connection that is both more direct and demonstrable: Critical Theory. For me, the rhythmically moving limbs of the Tiller Girls keeping time with music and song anticipate an image which stands at the heart of Adorno and Horkheimer's *The Dialectic of Enlightenment* (1947):[23] the oarsmen who, with their ears stopped with wax, are able to row in time, back and forth, back and forth, and so propel the ship bearing their tormented captain, Odysseus, away from the Sirens whose seductive songs would lure them all to destruction on the rocks.

Adorno and Horkheimer's book, arguably *the* foundational document of Critical Theory, comprises a number of essays which most notably introduce the notion of the 'culture industry' and articulate the triumph of instrumental reason in modern capitalism as the very betrayal of the radical emancipatory promise of the Enlightenment project. Rather than questioning and challenging what is, freeing us from superstition, scarcity and want, instrumental reason – in the guise of modern science and technology – now serves the capitalist exploitation of Nature and totalitarian domination of humankind. Critical thought itself, negativity, refusal – these faint traces of otherness and opposition have been all but absorbed, incorporated, extinguished. This is the new world of modern myth.

Kracauer's 'Mass Ornament' essay prefigures such a vision in terms of the transformation of culture into banal commodity, the hegemony of a partial reason (the *Ratio*) and the power and pre-eminence of abstractness. Kracauer distinguishes between the process of *abstraction* as a necessary and legitimate moment of philosophical reflection and rational thought particularly within the idealist tradition and its product: *abstractness*, the failure to engage with the existing material conditions of historical life. Abstractness involves distraction – entertainment, amusement, an orthogonal aesthetic in and for itself. Abstractness leads to subtraction – removal and withdrawal of the organic and living from Nature; of the spontaneous and erotic from the now mechanized and automated human body; of meaning and expression from dance become nervous agitation or purposeless patternings; of beauty and culture transformed into pre-programmed routine; of critical thought and genuine wisdom reduced to affirmative 'information'. Abstractness is at home in metaphysics, philosophical speculation and pseudo-science – forsaking the concrete and particular, the messy and complex everyday world of lived experience and human relations for the supposedly lofty and dispassionate realm of concepts and generalities, of high-flown propositions and principles, in which human beings feature only as data and statistics, never as subjects, individuals or agents.[24] Abstractness is precisely that tempting elevated terrain from which Kracauer turns, guiding us, his companions, down into the tangled thickets of the quotidian which constitute the rightful *topos*, and true subject matter, of sociology.

Abstractness results from both the partial disenchantment and the partial remythologization of the world. But for Kracauer, unlike Adorno and Horkheimer, these are only *partial*. His vision is less bleak, more hopeful.[25] Kracauer sees capitalist modernity not as the final defeat of reason and the promise of Enlightenment by one-dimensional instrumentalism but, rather, as a society in which the 'go-for-broke' game of history is still being played out. In the midst of the Weimar Republic, Kracauer can still insist that the problem of contemporary capitalism is, crudely expressed, not *too much* rationalization but rather *too little* – that is to say, that the critical promise and emancipatory potential of the Enlightenment are still redeemable. As Marx recognized, capitalism has at least required human beings to confront the secularized world with 'sober senses', shorn of the spurious consolations of religious dogma. Capitalism itself must now be subject to disenchantment. In a key passage inflected more by such historical materialist thinking than *Lebensphilosophie*, Kracauer writes:

> the *Ratio* of the capitalist economic system is not reason itself but a murky reason. Once past a certain point, it abandons the truth in which it participates. *It does not encompass man.* The operation of the production process is not regulated according to man's needs, and man does not serve as the foundation for the structure of the socioeconomic organization. Indeed, at no point whatsoever is the system founded on the basis of man. 'The basis of man': this does not mean that capitalist thinking should cultivate man as a historically produced form such that it ought to allow him to go unchallenged as a personality and should satisfy the demands made by his nature. The adherents of this position reproach capitalism's rationalism for raping man, and yearn for the return of a community that would be capable of preserving the allegedly human element much better than capitalism. Leaving aside the stultifying effect of such regressive stances, they fail to grasp capitalism's core defect: it rationalizes not too much but rather *too little*.[26] The thinking promoted by capitalism resists culminating in that reason which arises from the basis of man. (MOR: 81)

Kracauer is unequivocal here: there is certainly no way back to some long lost bucolic idyll of *Gemeinschaft* in which the full human personality is restored and reconnected to the land and soil as extolled by reactionary critics of modernity such as Tönnies and Spengler. What is at stake is the choice of path to be taken forwards. Even now it is not too late. Not quite. We find Kracauer, join him not a moment too soon, at the crossroads.

5 *Terra Incognita*

'But you can find all that in novels', one private employee replied when I asked her to tell me something of her life in the office. I got to know her one Sunday on the train journey to a Berlin suburb. She was returning from a wedding banquet that had lasted the whole day and, as she herself had admitted, she was a bit tipsy. Without prompting she divulged her boss, who was a soap manufacturer; she had already been working for three years as his private secretary. He was a bachelor and admired her lovely eyes. (TSM: 28)

This chance meeting with a stranger on a train opens *Die Angestellten* (*The Salaried Masses*), Kracauer's pioneering and prescient ethnography of Berlin's burgeoning white-collar workforce.[27] Based on observations made and materials accrued during a visit to the German capital between April and July 1929,[28] his text first appeared, like *Ginster*, in instalments in the *Frankfurter Zeitung* in December 1929 before publication in book form the following month. It was greeted with enthusiasm and acclaim.[29] In his review, for example, Benjamin extols Kracauer for his 'important contribution to the physiology of the capital' (TSM: 111) and critical exposition of the transformed class relations and cultural conditions of the Weimar Republic. A 'landmark on the road to the politicization of the intelligentsia' (TSM: 113), Kracauer's study is the most timely inspiration to redeem those untimely fragments which the present has carelessly discarded. Benjamin's vision is both political and poetic:

So by right this author stands there at the end – all alone. A malcontent, not a leader. Not a founder, but a spoilsport. And if we wish to visualize him just for himself, in the solitude of his craft and his endeavour, we see: a ragpicker at daybreak, lancing with his stick scraps of language and tatters of speech in order to throw them into his cart, grumbling, stubbornly, somewhat the worse for drink, and not without now and again letting one or other of these faded calicoes – 'humanity', 'inner nature', 'enrichment' – flutter ironically in the dawn breeze. A ragpicker at daybreak – in the dawn of the day of the revolution. (TSM: 114)

Whether sharp-eyed *chiffonier* or intrepid urban anthropologist, Kracauer undertakes to map the '*terra incognita*'[30] of the increasingly dominant metropolitan class of his (most assuredly *our*) time, one whose habits and dispositions had gone hitherto unobserved precisely because of their apparent visibility, their very proximity and familiarity.[31] 'It is high time', he declares, that 'the light of publicity fell on the public condition of salaried employees, whose situation has been utterly transformed since the pre-war years' (TSM: 29): changes in number,[32] in gender,[33] and in terms of the ever more routinized character of the work itself.[34] Kracauer's study presented Berlin as the 'newest Germany', an environment in which emergent political, social, cultural and economic tendencies and trajectories were most manifest and legible. And his rather flirtatious, seemingly innocuous, and quite possibly apocryphal encounter on the train is indicative of these in many ways.

Firstly, and at the very least, it sets the tone for what follows: writing couched in an informal and conversational style[35] mixing personal anecdotes and other incidental musings with wry insights into the brave new world of office work, with its incipient recruitment procedures, staff training and professional development, and codes of conduct all co-ordinated by ever watchful personnel departments. Eschewing more systematic sociological analysis, Kracauer takes cognizance of the contingent, marginal and ephemeral, combining them with an eclectic array of materials drawn from a variety of official and other sources: interviews with employers and employees of varying degrees of formality; newspaper and magazine stories and advertisements; various government and ministerial reports; the publications of various professional associations and trade organizations; a scattering of statistics borrowed from surveys of various kinds and even more varied reliability. This seemingly casual assemblage does not constitute for Kracauer mere reportage, *good* journalism to be sure, but *journalism none the less*.[36] Such a plethora of fragments culled from the everyday lives of Berliners do not speak for themselves but, rather, as the 'surface expressions' of deep-seated social processes and realities, constitute and serve as the raw material for the critical work of (re)composition and (re)construction. They are the tesserae of his mosaic of metropolitan modernity. Kracauer writes:

> Reportage, as the self-declaration of concrete existence, is counterposed to the abstractness of idealist thought, incapable of approaching reality through any mediation. But existence is not captured by being at best duplicated in reportage. ... For it merely loses its way in the life that idealism cannot find, which is equally unapproachable for both of them. A hundred reports from a factory do not add up to the reality of the factory, but remain for all eternity a hundred views of the factory. Reality is a construction. Certainly life must be observed for it to appear. Yet it is by no means contained in the more or less random observational results of reportage; rather it is to be found solely in the mosaic that is assembled from single observations on the basis of comprehension of their meaning. Reportage photographs life; such a mosaic would be its image. (TSM: 32)

Painstakingly and precisely juxtaposed, the quotidian material that Kracauer collects and collates in *Die Angestellten* bears witness to and critically disenchants the developing structures and identities constituting bureaucratic, 'Fordist' modernity. In so doing, the study brings the central paradox of the white-collar world into sharp focus: the individual is simultaneously eradicated and resurrected in mythic form. The bureaucratized apparatus is premised, as Max Weber astutely recognized, upon impersonality, anonymity and objective criteria of formal, technical expertise. Indeed, the whole principle of such rationalized systems is the dispensability and seamless replacement of individual office holders. And yet, at the same time, ever greater significance is attached by employers to the individual and personal attributes, morals and virtues of the individual employee. Individual traits are valued as desirable and vaunted as decisive in precisely the same moment that genuine idiosyncrasies and characteristics are eradicated. Impression management and the pseudo-psychological aptitude test have arrived: what counts in selection processes is no longer *what you can do*, Weberian technical competence, but *who you seem to be*. Kracauer reports a conversation with an official at a Berlin job centre:

> I try to learn from him what magical properties a person's appearance must possess in order to open the gates of the firm. The terms 'nice' and 'friendly' recur like stock phrases in his reply. Above all employers want to receive a nice impression. People who appear nice – and nice manners are naturally part of the appearance – are taken on even if their references are poor. The official says: 'We have to do things the same way as the Americans do. The man[37] must have a friendly face.' (TSM: 38)

What exactly is the secret of a 'friendly face', or, rather, what does it signify? The exquisite answer proffered by a smug department store personnel officer – 'a morally pink complexion' (TSM: 38) – is both illuminating and infuriating. Kracauer cannot conceal his scorn:

> A morally pink complexion – this combination of concepts at a stroke renders transparent the everyday life that is fleshed out by window displays, salary-earners and illustrated papers. Its morality must have a pink hue, its pink a moral grounding. That is what the people responsible for selection want. They would like to cover life with a varnish concealing its far-from-rosy reality. ... The same system that requires the aptitude test also produces this nice, friendly mixture; and the more rationalization progresses, the more the morally pink appearance gains ground. It is scarcely too hazardous to assert that in Berlin a salaried type is developing, standardized in the direction of the desired complexion. Speech, clothes, gestures and countenances become assimilated and the result of the process is that very same pleasant appearance, which with the help of photographs can be widely reproduced.

A selective breeding that is carried out under the pressure of social relations, and that is necessarily supported by the economy through the
arousal of corresponding consumer needs. (TSM: 38–9)

In this charming, well-groomed, youthful world of the office, salon
and department store filled with fashion accessories and beauty products, we see prefigured the 'wellness' world of today, with its health
spas, fitness centres and obligatory gym membership. A society with a
'photographic face' requires one to be photogenic. And to smile: the
outward show of a 'pleasant personality' suffices in the absence of any
genuine *Persönlichkeit*. Then as now, 'characters', those worn and weary
countenances who sat patiently before Rembrandt's easel for example,
need not apply.

6   Lives More Ordinary

The 'newest Germany' is a realm of surfaces and appearances, of
make-up and make-believe.[38] Indeed, Kracauer's erstwhile travelling
companion, with her 'lovely eyes', would fit the bill perfectly, combining an agreeable appearance with an open and outgoing manner,
although she is so forthcoming only because this is a special trip out
and she has had a drink or two.[39] Clearly, she is not simply on her
regular journey to work – commuters would observe the code of silence
proper to buses, subways and suburban lines. Significant, too, that she
likens her own story of everyday office intrigues to that of a novel, an
intertwining of an actual life with the narratives of popular romantic
fiction. In so doing, she unwittingly anticipates two of Kracauer's
essays on prevailing popular reading trends: 'The Biography as an Art
Form of the New Bourgeoisie' from 1930 (MOR: 101–6) and 'On Best-
sellers and their Audience' published a year later (MOR: 89–98).

As a measure of white-collar tastes, the market success of certain
books constitutes another 'surface expression' of the new cultural life
of Berlin in the Weimar years. Literary merit, according to traditional
bourgeois aesthetics and as embodied in the canonical texts of *Kultur*,
plays little or no role in this.[40] The salaried masses are the new dominant readership to which writers and publishers must pander if popular
renown and financial profit are to be achieved. A bestseller

is the *sign of a successful sociological experiment*, proof that elements have
once again been blended in such a way as to correspond to the taste of
the anonymous mass of readers....The success of a particular book
cannot be explained by the qualities of the work itself – or if so, only to
the extent that they satisfy those needs. And should these qualities per-
chance contain real traces of substance, they secure the book its fame not
in their capacity as contents but rather as responses to widespread social

tendencies. The success of a book as a commodity ultimately depends upon the book's ability to satisfy the demands of a broad social stratum of consumers. These demands are much too general and constant for their direction to be determined by private inclinations or mere suggestion. They must be based on the *social conditions* of the consumers. (MOR: 91–2)[41]

Kracauer's concern here is with popular books, but the points he makes are equally applicable to that other growing form of popular storytelling, film. Indeed, as we will see in chapter 7, it is precisely as a visual rather than a textual repository for the deep-seated fears, frustrations and fantasies of its audience that Weimar cinema provides a fundamental insight into the increasingly authoritarian predispositions, prejudices and proclivities of that historical moment. Such tendencies are not manifest to the feuilletonist of 1931, however. Rather, the common elements of the bestsellers identified by Kracauer are forms of compensation and consolation for what is so desperately lacking in bureaucratized boredom and banality: the struggles of the 'individual who perishes tragically for the sake of an idea' (MOR: 95); the foregrounding of emotion and sentiment;[42] exotic adventures offering escapism and an 'intimate relationship with nature' (MOR: 97); and the avoidance of 'embarrassing questions' (ibid.) about the everyday world. If these seem to indicate a common craving for romantic passions and seductive otherness, then it is only a half-hearted one. In yet another echo of Simmel's vision of the blasé metropolitan personality, Kracauer sees the hallmark of the bestseller and its contemporary readership as '*indifference*' (ibid.), an acquiescence to inertia and apathy.

Kracauer's reflections on the increasing appetite for (auto)biographies (MOR: 101) come to similar conclusions. The living of quiet, quotidian lives clearly stimulates a demand for narratives of extraordinary ones. In a modern world beset by tumultuous political events and industrialized wars, by revolutions and catastrophes in which the individual has so evidently been reduced to a minimum of significance,[43] the biographical form continues to propagate the myth of the potency of the truly exceptional individual. Politicians, sovereigns, generals, artists, scholars – these appear as inspired and inspiring figures who shape history by force of their own will, who change the course of world events through great deeds, who leave behind their indelible mark.[44] The biography then is an anachronism, but a curiously comforting one in its affirmation of the endurance and persistence of the (bourgeois) subject just as she/he exits the historical scene. Kracauer observes:

As the literary form of the new bourgeoisie, the biography is a sign of escape or, to be more precise, of evasion. In order not to expose themselves through insights that question the very existence of the

bourgeoisie, writers of biographies remain, as if up against a wall, at the
threshold to which they have been pushed by world events. Instead of
crossing this threshold, they flee back into the bourgeois hinterlands.
(MOR: 104)

The meaningful life of the individual to which the biography
attests may elicit considerable and continuing popular interest, but
this is akin only to the fascination with a relic of a bygone age, an
archaeological find.[45]

Whether an avid reader of bestselling novels or of popular biographies, the woman on the train is certainly not referring to *Ginster*.
Indeed, the eponymous autobiographical figures of Ginster and Georg,
heroes neither of production nor of consumption, lead lives more ordinary and, in so doing, *express* rather than *escape* from the modern condition of individual obscurity and impotence.

The Weimar version of the 'Ludwig Loos complex', this fascination
with the more exciting lives of others, is typical of the salaried masses
and symptomatic of their structural position. As members of the petite
bourgeoisie they find themselves alarmingly exposed in a hierarchical
no-man's-land between the two warring parties of modern capitalism.
On the one hand, they disclaim any common cause with the proletariat
and lack any sense of class consciousness,[46] solidarity, or socialist/com-
munist struggle.[47] On the other, lacking cultural and social capital, they
find themselves excluded from the traditional haute bourgeoisie with
its emphasis upon individual accomplishment and learning, its confidence in professional expertise and etiquette, its smug and snobbish
stewardship and monopolization of those venerable imposters *Bildung*
and *Kultur*. Disdaining the one, debarred from the other, the white-
collar worker is a stranger to both. She/he is a neither/nor.[48] As a
result, the salaried masses are, as Kracauer puts it, 'spiritually shelterless' (*geistig obdachlos*) (TSM: 88),[49] an echo of Georg Lukács's notion
of 'transcendental homelessness', a condition manifest precisely in the
novel form,[50] although this is surely not what Kracauer's interlocutor
on the train had in mind when she exclaims 'But you can find all that
in novels' (TSM: 28). Nevertheless, it does return us to her once more.
For, most assuredly, Kracauer's transient meeting in transit itself is
suggestive of this overwhelming sense of the dislocation of the modern
individual, of the itinerant and nomadic condition of the contemporary
metropolitan self. For Kracauer, such an individual is increasingly left
to inhabit the in-between spaces, the neither here nor there, all those
'non-places' of contemporary existence.[51] And we are always hastening
'elsewhere'. Our lives are no longer odysseys. Rather, our travels are
tedious, repetitious commutes in which we may roam ever further
afield, but about which there is ever less to remember and be said. After
all, what could be drabber and drearier than a Sunday afternoon outing
to the suburbs?

In a key passage Kracauer writes:

> The mass of salaried employees differ from the worker proletariat in that they are spiritually homeless. For the time being they cannot find their way to their comrades, and the house of bourgeois ideas and feelings in which they used to live has collapsed, its foundations eroded by economic development. They are living at present without a doctrine to look up at or a goal they might ascertain. So they live in fear of looking up and asking their way to the destination.
>
> Nothing is more characteristic of this life, which only in a restricted sense can be called a life, than its view of higher things. Not as substance but as glamour. Yielded not through concentration but in distraction. (TSM: 88)

The salaried masses as the 'spiritually shelterless' are the enthusiastic spectators of the mass ornament, the avid readership of the best-sellers, the crowds who, 'little shop girls' among them, fill the cheap seats of the city's cinemas. In *Die Angestellten*, Kracauer's principal point is neither to lambast white-collar bad taste nor to lament the demise of bourgeois high culture – even if many of his comments seem to do one or the other, sometimes both. Rather, it is to recognize these sociologically as the tell-tale 'surface expressions' and legitimate manifestations of the 'newest Germany', which is itself a mere way-station, Kracauer hopes, on the path of reason along which we have advanced not too far, but as yet too little.

4

Berlin Impromptus

The worth of cities is determined by the number of places in them
devoted to improvisation. (SBA: 51)

1   Strassenbuch

He has a child's face, we are told, and its changing expression confirms
our suspicion that, although he is here, seated at the grand piano in a
fashionable Berlin bar, he is utterly lost in his thoughts, his dreams, his
memories. Playing the merest 'murmur' (SBA: 105) of music to accompany the hum of conversation, shifting seamlessly from one melody to
the next, his hands and fingers move effortlessly over the keyboard as
if they have a life of their own, as if wholly independent of the man's
middle-aged, rather corpulent body. The pianist plays absent-mind-
edly. Yes, he is certainly here, but he is also, unmistakably, 'elsewhere'
(*anderswo*).

Our musician is one of the motley assortment of characters found in
the 'Figures' section of Kracauer's *Streets in Berlin and Elsewhere* (*Strassen
in Berlin und Anderswo*). Published by Suhrkamp Verlag in 1964, this
was his second collection of feuilleton pieces from the *Frankfurter
Zeitung* dating from the Weimar years.[1] While he was fully aware that
the vast majority of these miniatures would experience the usual fate
of newspaper articles – penned one day, read and forgotten the next
– Kracauer nevertheless harboured hopes that some of them might
prove of more lasting significance than mere 'journalism', a term, as
we have seen, he considered to be pejorative. He was – so he claims
– incapable of treating such texts as mere *Brotarbeit*, as matters of financial expediency, and instead composed them with the same spirit and
meticulous care as his more substantial literary, sociological and

philosophical writings.[2] The reason for this attentiveness is clear: Kracauer recognized the felicity with which textual miniatures were able to capture exemplary and decisive moments culled from the concrete reality of quotidian metropolitan existence, raw material shot through with social, political and, indeed, existential significance. For Kracauer, as for Benjamin and Bloch, the inconsequential manifestations of the cityscape were 'surface expressions', 'hieroglyphs', 'dreams'[3] to be recovered and deciphered by the critical theorist. For them, such fleeting traces were the very stuff from which modernity was made and the very basis of its legibility.[4]

It is not surprising, therefore, that, following the success of *Die Angestellten* around 1930, the idea of collecting some of his specifically metropolitan writings into a single volume appealed to Kracauer. Another literary 'mosaic' would further capture the kaleidoscopic city and penetrate its reality in a way forbidden to mere 'reportage'. Kracauer might have modelled his proposed 'street book' (*Strassenbuch*)[5] on Benjamin's 1928 *One-Way Street*, a seemingly exemplary instance of fragmentary composition for the 'profane illumination' of contemporary culture and metropolitan modernity. Here, amid aphorisms, dreams, jokes and anecdotes, the nomenclature of the cityscape provided points of departure for philosophical/metaphysical speculations and political enunciations. Kracauer, however, envisaged his *Strassenbuch* rather differently: its building blocks are not fragments as such but rather self-contained literary miniatures – much more akin to Benjamin's *Denkbilder* – and these texts, although certainly not bereft of wider philosophical and sociological import, display a greater loyalty to the material itself, to the concrete particulars and specific moments of the urban environment. Kracauer's collection was intended to give voice to this cityscape rather than simply to utilize its signage as captions for the presentation of abstractions. Accordingly, there was to be precious little, if any, reworking of the forty-one feuilleton pieces Kracauer selected for inclusion and certainly no overarching commentary. The thematic and conceptual repertoire would emerge from the material itself through the precise juxtaposition of texts. These were to be divided into three sections based on spatial, rather than chronological considerations: 'On the Street' (*Auf der Strasse*), 'Beside the Street' (*Neben der Strasse*) and 'Figures' (*Figuren*).

Kracauer's hopes for the publication of his *Strassenbuch* remained unrealized for thirty years, however. It would be easy to overlook what is most remarkable about *Strassen in Berlin und Anderswo*. Despite the most traumatic intervening years imaginable, it is remarkably similar in structure and content to Kracauer's original conception: most of the earlier selection is retained, there are a few additions, and the texts are now divided into four sections under a new rubric: 'Streets' (*Strassen*), 'Localities/Bars' (*Lokale*), 'Things' (*Dinge*) and 'People' (*Leute*).[6]

In short, the writings Kracauer deemed most significant in the 1930s have, in his view at least, maintained their relevance through the war years and into the post-war period. The question arises: How are these texts, newspaper pieces addressed to a contemporary readership, supposed to speak to a subsequent generation?[7] Seemingly, Kracauer saw no need to address this issue. The 1964 volume contains no foreword or introduction elucidating how, for example, these texts penned during the Weimar Republic might be read as intimations of the catastrophic events to follow, as analyses perhaps of a class soon to swap its white collars for brown shirts. Indeed, there is no revision, no attempt to give the pieces a new inflection or orientation. This is especially puzzling given Kracauer's abiding sense that his work had never received proper scholarly recognition. Here was an opportunity to bring his writings to the attention of a new and highly receptive generation of German readers, one already schooled in Critical Theory. It is surprising how little he chose to make of it.[8]

The new title is the only concession – the inclusion of the name of the city: Berlin. That this needed to be specified at all is perhaps indicative of Kracauer's own distance from the city in spatial, temporal and intellectual terms and that of the book's potential readership. *Strassenbuch*: in 1930s Germany, this would surely have sufficed as a title. Where else, when else could this be other than the here and now of contemporary Berlin? The titular reference to Berlin serves to specify the focus of the book, one which otherwise might not be so obvious given that no fewer than fourteen of the thirty-three pieces[9] actually date from the period 1925–9, when Kracauer was still resident in Frankfurt. The reader is left in no doubt: Berlin is what matters, Berlin rather than 'elsewhere', an 'elsewhere' that is always defined in relation to Berlin, an 'elsewhere' which Berliners might nevertheless chance upon in the course of their travels – whether real, physical journeys or spiritual/intellectual wanderings. Everywhere else – even Paris, the subject of several texts[10] – is simply *anderswo*.

2 *Terra incognita* – Revisited

This is instructive: as we have seen in the previous chapter, for Kracauer, Berlin came to constitute the definitive modern metropolis, the 'newest Germany' with a newly ascendant class crowding its streets and squares, frequenting its myriad shops, enjoying its diverse attractions: the white-collar employees. Kracauer astutely recognized that Berlin was *their* city. Accordingly, in seeking to survey the '*terra incognita*' of these office employees, his writings for the *Frankfurter Zeitung* in the 1930s encompass not only their experience of the occupational structure but also their fundamental role as customers, clientele, spectators, audiences and readers. The countless distractions spawned by the modern metropolis – the glistening display windows of department stores and fashionable boutiques, the showrooms and exhibition halls presenting the latest gadgets and devices for modern living, the glossy magazines, brochures and catalogues, the dazzling neon signs illuminating the nocturnal boulevard, the brilliant interiors of polite cafés and the moody half-light of less reputable bars and dancehalls, the splendour of picture palaces and variety theatres, the rides and attractions of the early amusement parks such as the Lunarpark – all these elements of the modern cityscape and mediascape vied for the attention of these salaried masses, all sought to separate the masses from their salaries.

And, indeed, it was not long before many of these petty bourgeois employees were to be parted from their earnings. The *Strassen in Berlin* collection presents images of these socio-economic strata subject to the economic and political crises of the early 1930s. The growing numbers of unemployed come to constitute an atomized mass,[11] one which must endure petty indignities in the crowded labour exchange and negotiate its labyrinthine corridors leading, not back to the world of work, but only to the back of beyond.[12] The sombre gloom of the welfare centres providing temporary refuge for the penniless contrasts with the spectacular illumination of the cityscape of consumption.[13] Anxious investors queue forlornly outside banks in the vain hope of recovering their precious savings and assets.[14] Patrons assemble at dismal morning and matinee cinema performances in search of cheap respite from the boredom of useless days.[15] Even the Tiller Girls, the exemplary mass ornament spawned by the distraction industry, have had their day – nothing could be more out of kilter with the paralysed industrial production system than their upbeat, dynamic, rhythmic routines.[16]

In Berlin, the figures of poverty and destitution, unwanted reminders of a collective bad conscience, stalk the cityscape and imbue it with a sinister atmosphere even where the lights shine brightest and the mood seems most convivial.[17] For Kracauer, the city is haunted, and not just by the shadows of economic misery, or just by the growing spectre of political terror, but also by something far less tangible. Berlin is haunted by the alienated modern condition itself, by our inner emptiness and loneliness, by the absence of social solidarity, community and consolation, by the evacuation of meaning and hope for which no upturn in the stock market can compensate. Such a bleak vision of metropolitan modernity finds repeated expression in Kracauer's early writings and imbues the Berlin studies.[18] And no wonder: the salaried masses are the 'spiritually shelterless' par excellence. As those who serve as the impersonal functionaries of this bureaucratized world, they now find themselves the main bearers of its stigmata: melancholy, frustration, resentment, repression, boredom, fatalism. Perhaps this explains why Kracauer saw so little need to revisit and transform the material from the original *Strassenbuch* scheme. Yes, these feuilleton pieces certainly bear witness to the particular crises and convulsions of the 1930s – how could they not? But as a mosaic they also seek to disclose what is more enduring from the ephemera: the disenchanted cityscape of Kracauer's time as the fully recognizable precursor of our own; an urban environment and existence beset by abstractness and alienation, by reification and ruination; modernity as myth, progress as catastrophe.

3 Distraction and the Cinematic Cityscape

The *unsalaried* masses would not have figured among the well-heeled and well-connected clientele entertained by our pianist, but, for me, 'The Pianist' ('Der Klavierspieler') serves as a point of conjuncture for a number of central themes in Kracauer's *Strassenbuch*: distraction; transition and transience; asynchronicity and improvisation. The first of these, distraction (*Zerstreuung*), is most apparent here and plays a double role: the pianist, as a professional musician, is a provider of distraction for others; moreover, he is himself presented as a distracted figure, one inattentive both to his musical labours and to his otherwise engaged audience. The pianist plays in a state of distraction to an audience that is equally distracted: he is elsewhere and so are they. This is music to be heard and not listened to. In fact, it is scarcely to be heard at all. This music is to serve as acoustic décor covering over any unsightly cracks in the conversation. The pianist's non-audience have other, more enticing distractions: gossip and chatter.[19] The music must not distract them from these more serious, more salacious delights. Accordingly, there is little pleasure to be found in this music – indeed, perhaps this is why no one listens, not even the pianist himself. For him, of course, it is work. And the merger of the spheres of entertainment and labour is central to Kracauer's studies. He perceives the proliferation of 'entertainment' as the extension of capitalist domination with the rhythms and logic of the industrial work process transposed into the cultural domain. 'Leisure' involves the systematic orchestration and arrangement of 'free time' into a mass phenomenon spuriously experienced as individual lifestyle. Rationalized, alienated labour finds its after-image in the mechanized synchronicity of the mass ornament and in the 'organized happiness' of the amusement park.[20] Kracauer's miniatures attest to the dutiful character of distraction: at weekends, the Berliners decamp and head off in search of pleasures elsewhere, leaving behind an eerily deserted Sunday cityscape;[21] hordes of day-trippers venture into the country to sample the pseudo-rustic delights of the *Mittelgebirge*;[22] fatalistic crowds flock to performances of clairvoyants and mesmerists;[23] in the cinema, they laugh in the right places.[24] Autonomy, spontaneity and distinction have no place in the modern world of heteronomous and homogeneous entertainment. The Berlin variety theatres, providing for all tastes and none, present banal popular singers and chorus-line routines on the same bill as classical virtuosos and talented but impecunious soloists, a mingling of commercial entertainers and serious artists that squeezes out any genuine cultural variety.[25] Such 'motley [*kunterbunt*] offerings' (BEN: 31) fail to disguise the fact that the white-collar world of distraction lacks contrast and colour. And our pianist, a figure who, like his music, fades imperceptibly into the background, and his listless audience are symptomatic of this grey indifference, this dull insensitivity to the unique qualities of things, of an underwhelming but inescapable boredom.[26]

Kracauer's critique of mass culture and distraction unmistakably prefigures Adorno and Horkheimer's 'culture industry' thesis. Indeed, the all too easy on the ear music of our pianist is precisely that which Adorno was to decry in his writings on Tin Pan Alley jazz.[27] Moreover, the corresponding inattention of the audience provides clear evidence of their diminishing capacity for concentration, of a pernicious and pervasive 'regression of listening'. Kracauer's response is more equivocal than this, however, and more sensitive to positive moments in popular cultural forms and the experience of distraction.[28] His work involves what one might term a 'dialectics of distraction', one which anticipates Benjamin's 'Work of Art' essay. Benjamin's principal argument, namely that the advent of photography and film leads to the withering of the 'aura' of the unique, original, authentic work of art, needs little repetition here. His attempt, convoluted at best, to develop a positive understanding of distraction is of relevance, though. Film and photography, he claims, involve reception in a state of distraction. These new media neither demand intense concentration nor permit leisurely contemplation. Rather, the distracted cinema audience is, Benjamin contends, relaxed and receptive, at ease and aware of its own expertise, conscious of itself and critical of what is presented on screen.[29] This is because the inattentive apprehension of aesthetic objects – Benjamin's model is the ordinary architecture of the cityscape – provides for a familiarity and an intimacy that is the very antithesis of the fetishistic adoration of the auratic artwork.[30] Habitual acquaintance integrates the work of art into everyday life, fostering confidence and composure and affording a sense of mastery – not of the object and the environment but, rather, of one's *relationship with* them.[31] While habit may threaten to dull the senses, to produce amnesia and indifference, distraction points in the direction of a new sensitivity to the world, of new forms of recognition and receptivity. Distraction is not simply inattention, a failure to give due consideration to what is at hand;

rather, it is a *paying attention elsewhere*, the *diversion* of one's perceptual faculties to that which is not of immediate importance, to what is commonly overlooked or neglected. Distraction is, then, an attentiveness to that which lies at the edge of our conventional field of vision and/ or which fleetingly crosses it. Distraction involves a particular openness to the marginal, the liminal and the transient, to that which escapes the everyday perceptual realm. It is here that film emerges as the medium of distraction par excellence. For it is film that focuses our attention on the hitherto inconspicuous, that identifies and penetrates the 'optical unconscious',[32] that discloses the *terra incognita* of the modern cityscape. Film promises distraction for the distracted: it engenders a heightened appreciation of the urban environment for an accomplished, expert audience.

In his 1926 essay 'Cult of Distraction: On Berlin's Picture Palaces', Kracauer both prefigures and pre-empts Benjamin's attempt to develop a radical vision of cinematic *Zerstreuung*, offering a perhaps more cautious and politically equivocal understanding of distraction's tensions and tendencies. For Kracauer, the sense of distraction experienced by the audiences flocking to the capital's cinemas is not so much a form of mastery modelled on familiarity with the cityscape as an accurate and necessary index of the complete collapse and obsolescence of traditional cultural values and concepts, of a fundamental evacuation of meaning in everyday urban life, of a forlorn preoccupation with all that is left: externality and surface. In the proliferating cinemas of the city, the producers and purveyors of the culture industries leave nothing to chance:

> A correct instinct will see to it that the need for entertainment is satisfied. The interior design of movie theatres serves one sole purpose: to rivet the viewers' attention to the peripheral, so that they will not sink into the abyss. The stimulations of the senses succeed one another with such rapidity that there is no room left between them for even the slightest contemplation. Like *life buoys*, the refractions of the spotlights and the musical accompaniment keep the spectator above water. The penchant for distraction demands and finds an answer in the display of pure externality. (MOR: 325–6)[33]

Yet, for Kracauer, things could be otherwise. It is not the phoney amelioration of modern existence but its critical intensification that is film's promise. The disappearance of the time and space for aesthetic contemplation is not a cause for lamentation. Contemplation is, as for Benjamin, simply obsolete, inappropriate to the temporal-spatial compressions and collisions of modern metropolitan existence. And the possibilities of critique lie not in any nostalgic longing for the lost leisure of contemplation, but rather in the development of forms of distraction which correspond to and correlate with the attenuation and alienation of everyday urban existence. As the metropolitan experiential form par excellence, distraction threatens to make manifest the real prevailing conditions of existence – this is precisely what the film studios strive against. Hence, for Kracauer, as for Benjamin, it may contain a critical, indeed explosive, *potential*:

> But this is the case only if distraction is not an end in itself. Indeed, the very fact that the shows aiming at distraction are composed of the very same mixture of the externalities as the world of the urban masses; the fact that these shows lack any authentic and materially motivated coherence, except possibly the glue of sentimentality, which covers up this lack but only in order to make it all the more visible; the fact that these shows convey precisely and openly to thousands of eyes and ears the *disorder* of society – this is precisely what would enable them to evoke and maintain the tension that must precede the inevitable and radical change. In the streets of Berlin, one is often struck by the momentary insight that someday all this will suddenly burst apart. The entertainment to which the general public throngs ought to produce the same effect. (MOR: 326–7)[34]

Distraction both mirrors the alienation and 'uncontrolled anarchy' (MOR: 327) of the metropolitan lifeworld and has the potential to disturb and destabilize it radically by way of a new experiential and aesthetic mode: 'improvisation' (ibid.).[35] And it is here that Benjamin and Kracauer part company. For, while Benjamin advocates both film and architecture as media of distraction, Kracauer posits a radical disjunction between them. Given Kracauer's architectural training and the numerous pieces on particular buildings, architectural exhibitions and design competitions he wrote for the *FZ*, the absence of architecture in the Berlin collection is noticeable and instructive.[36] In the *Strassenbuch*, Kracauer was interested less in architecture as the formal organization of space and matter than in the myriad, unforeseen and fleeting constellations appearing and vanishing amid the currents and eddies of metropolitan existence, the 'architectures of the instant' (*Architekturen des Augenblicks*), as Franz Hessel once termed it.[37] Kracauer's 1931 fragment 'Seen from the Window' ('Aus dem Fenster gesehen') (originally entitled 'Berlin Landscape' ('Berliner Landschaft')) contrasts the cityscape as monumental composition and as vital contingency:

> One can distinguish between two types of cityscape: those which are consciously fashioned and those which come about unintentionally. The former spring from the artistic will which is realized in those squares, vistas, building ensembles and perspectives which Baedecker generally sees fit to highlight with a star. In contrast, the latter come into being without prior plan. They are not, like the Pariser Platz or the Place de la Concorde, compositions which owe their existence to some unifying

building ethos. Rather, they are creations of chance and as such cannot be called to account. Such a cityscape, itself never the object of any particular interest, occurs wherever masses of stone and streets meet, the elements of which emerge from quite disparate interests. It is as unfashioned as Nature itself, and can be likened to a landscape in that it asserts itself unconsciously. Unconcerned about its visage, it bides its time. (SBA: 40)

Chance configurations of traffic and crowds in motion, fleeting constellations and conjunctures, the physical fabric of the cityscape in perpetual transformation, Berlin subject to time – these spatio-temporal, *cinematic* aspects of modernity fascinate Kracauer. In the city 'Everything moves, everything stirs [*Alles regt sich, alles bewegt sich*]' (SBA: 31). And only film is adequate to this sense of motion. His collection of miniatures is like a cinematic odyssey around the metropolis, a series of filmic vignettes, cut and juxtaposed to create a montage of images setting up a series of tensions, bringing the 'surface-level expressions' of the city into sharp and critical focus.[38] Kracauer's book is conceived as cinematic images of the city[39] – not as moving pictures, of course, but as pictures of movement – for those urbanites for whom the cinema had become the pre-eminent form of modern mass media: the little shop girls and boys who went to the movies. The texts in *Strassen in Berlin* are cinematically inspired offerings for cinematically inclined and experienced audiences, distractions for the distracted.

4 Extempore

Berlin is a rich hunting ground for those in search of sites of transition, of objects in transit and of transient forms. And Kracauer devotes himself to these 'non-places' of the modern metropolis. On the one hand, his texts focus on those in-between spaces (*Zwischenräume*) that we habitually navigate yet fail to notice, the loci of the optical unconscious: anonymous squares hurriedly criss-crossed by busy commuters and shoppers; tramline junctions; the subterranean world of the underpass; the railway bridges affording driver and passengers a fleeting initial impression or last parting glimpse of the city centre; the beige corridors of the labour exchange. And, on the other, he is fascinated by thresholds, spaces of waiting, hangouts where one must dutifully hang around: cinema foyers and hotel lobbies, cafés and bars, the welfare refuge. And some sites, such as Berlin's Lindenpassage (actually the Kaisergalerie), are there to pass through and to pass the time. A passageway connecting streets, it invites dawdling, encourages us to tarry a while. But time has passed it by. The luxurious and fashionable goods which filled the arcade during its heyday[40] are long gone, and it serves now only as a temporary refuge for the remnants of a long-vanished world of commodities. Like Benjamin and the surrealist Louis Aragon before him, Kracauer observes the metropolitan shopping arcade as a ruin on the point of demolition, at last sight. Indeed, in *Strassen in Berlin*, one finds not only a dialectics of distraction but also a complex dialectics of disappearance. Spaces, things and people are captured only as they are about to vanish or are remembered only after they have already gone. This tension is made explicit in an intriguing text from 1932 – 'Street without Memory' ('Strasse ohne Erinnerung') – in which Kracauer recalls how, before catching a train, he strolled along to one of his favourite cafés on the Kurfürstendamm only to discover with surprise that it had closed. He has to make do with another bar nearby, one far too garish for his taste. A year or so later, Kracauer is suddenly struck by the disappearance of this second café – a sign in the window merely informing passers-by that the premises are now available to rent. He reflects upon this seemingly commonplace experience:

> Elsewhere, the past clings to the places where it resided during its life-time; on the Kurfürstendamm it departs without leaving so much as a trace. Since I have known it, it has changed fundamentally again and again in no time at all. The new businesses are always brand new and those they expel are always wholly obliterated. (SBA: 17)

The fate of the cafés is suggestive of how, in the city, 'perpetual change erases memory' (SBA: 17); how the past is consigned to oblivion by the present and how it may fleetingly reappear as a disturbance that gives a shock to today's passer-by. Paradoxically, the very act of oblit-eration – the present absence of the former cafés – calls them so vividly to mind. Demolition and erasure bring with them a sudden apprecia-tion of what is no longer there.[41] The Kurfürstendamm is without memories, but Kracauer is not.

The peculiarly memorable character of the transient and of the in-between – Kracauer provides an exquisite illustration of this drawn from the distraction industry: the 'number girl' (*Nummernmädchen*) at the Scala variety theatre.[42] Between each act, it is her task to walk across the stage in front of the lowered curtain carrying aloft a number cor-responding to the programme number of the next turn. Her perform-ance, such as it is, is a brief interlude between the performances. However charmingly she executes her 'delicate mission' (SBA: 113) – and for Kracauer her every appearance is nothing less than 'a genuine solo' (ibid.) – she herself does not figure in the programme; she has been allotted no number. But we ignore the number girl at our peril. For who is to say what will prove significant and what will prove trivial in later years? After all, Kracauer observes, warming to his theme, dates may acquire an importance for later historians long after the actual events of those years themselves have faded into the background or become obscure. The numbers may be all that is left to us. And, as if to exemplify this, all that remains of Kracauer's evening in the Scala are his memories of their smiling bearer. Of the acts to which they referred, not a whisper.

Our pianist is also a complex figure of memory: firstly, his playing involves a particular combination of memory and improvisation as well-rehearsed melodies are connected and embellished with a few new accents and flourishes; secondly, freed from the need to concentrate on his music, the pianist is preoccupied with his own memories;[43] and, finally, the pianist prompts and sets in train Kracauer's remembrances. Indeed, he interrupts his account of the Berlin bar and its pianist to recall another piano player, one whose task it was to accompany the silent films shown in the local cinema many years before, and one so remarkable and memorable that he figures again twenty-five years later in Kracauer's *Theory of Film* under the rubric of 'The drunken pianist'.[44] This musician was, so it was said, a genius who once trained at the conservatoire and whose talents had now gone to waste. Seated at the piano in the cinema in various states of inebriation, this pianist could see little – his hazy view of the screen was completely obstructed by the instrument itself. Unable then, even with the best of intentions, to match his music to the events unfolding on screen, he contented himself instead by playing music at random: old melodies and familiar songs played time and again; improvised passages and flights of fancy; military marches and popular dance tunes; whatever occurred, or gave expression, to his own stupefied senses. Film image and impromptu music accordingly bore no particular relation to one another. And it was precisely this asynchronicity which charmed Kracauer: 'This lack of relation between the musical themes and the action they were supposed to sustain seemed very delightful indeed to me, for it made me see the story in a new and unexpected light or, more important, challenged me to lose myself in an unchartered wilderness opened up by allusive shots' (TOF: 137). Of course, by coincidence, on odd occasions the music *did* correspond in some way to the film scenes on screen, and these occurrences gave the impression that some sublime, secret connection might indeed exist all along: 'a relationship which I considered perfect because of its accidental nature and its indeterminacy. I never heard more fitting accompaniment' (TOF: 138).

Kracauer's comic anecdote is highly suggestive. It privileges the spontaneous, the improvised and the contingent in opposition to the predictable, the predetermined and the routinized – in short, those features characteristic of modern mass metropolitan culture. There could be no greater contrast between the idiosyncratic music of the drunken pianist and the precision-engineered film soundtracks produced by the distraction industry, with their formulaic, standard-ized themes and calculated emotional manipulation. Out of time, out of step, out of kilter – what could be less like the mass ornament, indeed, what could debunk the mass ornament more completely than this piano-playing? The asynchronous music of the pianist becomes a wry comment upon and destabilizes the meaning of events on screen: melancholy music transforms comedies into solemn occasions, just as serious drama is subverted by frivolous tunes. This is important because Kracauer extols the comic and critical powers inherent in things out of time, by asynchronous or, more precisely, anachronistic objects. He writes satirically of certain objects of the recent past which once attested to the orderly world of the upstanding, independent, self-assured bourgeois, objects whose contemporary fate serves as an index of the present crisis: a three-page 'historical study' chronicles how the dignified fashion of wearing braces has waned in a period of belt-tightening;[45] an essay ponders the sociological significance of the umbrella's apparent fall from favour;[46] and another recounts the mis-adventures of an upright piano, an instrument increasingly out of tune with the times and one of the first things sold to the second-hand shop when economies become necessary.[47]

The last of these narratives is perhaps the most interesting and pro-vides a counterpart to the figure of the pianist. Kracauer's anthropo-morphic tale of the upright piano is an allegorical story ridiculing the social and cultural pretensions of the lower middle classes, the white-collar workers. The upright piano, symbol of familial musicality and *Bildung*, stands cramped and rarely played in a corner of a typical petit bourgeois home. It aspires to cultural elevation, considering itself the very equal of a grand piano, only less showy. The piano dreams of being elsewhere, of taking its proper place in the order of things, of being the object of attention and admiration. Its special qualities and capacities are unused and unappreciated. Preferring solitude to any alliance or acquaintance with the other objects of the interior, it has no wish to be part of the furniture. Such snobbery is cruelly exposed, however, when the piano finally ventures into a nearby bar – a far less sophisticated establishment than that of our piano player, indeed, more the haunt of the drunken pianist – and finds itself playing together with a number of other instruments in an impromptu band. But things go awry – the music is banal and inferior, the democratic spirit is not to the piano's liking, and conflict ensues. Its lid is slammed shut and it is sent packing. In 'The Piano', Kracauer presents a far from subtle satire of the individualistic sensibility and snobbery which ensures the failure of the salaried masses to develop any sense of class consciousness. They pin everything on their personal upward mobility and are left dumbfounded when real-life circumstances catapult them in the oppo-site direction. They are a 'lonely crowd' searching in vain for solace, for satisfaction, for compensation and consolation in the remaining pleasures of the cityscape. In the streets of Berlin and elsewhere, the metropolitan multitudes fail to find companionship in misfortune.

It is no coincidence that 'The Piano' is followed immediately by the 1927 piece 'The Little Typewriter' ('Das Schreibmaschinchen'), for there is another figure who, like the pianist, sits lost in thought as his fingers move swiftly and lightly over the keys in front of him: the writer. It should come as no great surprise that our piano players – both sober and sozzled – should serve as opportunities to reflect upon the position and practice of the contemporary writer, the journalist and the critic. These musicians are highly ambiguous, highly ambivalent allegorical figures. On the one hand, they offer a kind of utopian vision of textual production: to be able to write as they play – effortlessly summoning from the keyboard a smooth, endless flow of words – would be, as Benjamin once observed, nothing less than to be in the 'Arcadia' of one's writing.[48] In the ease and expertise of the pianist, the painfully staccato rhythm of writing has been transcended. This positive inflection is particularly evident in the case of the intoxicated musician – his creative spirit and unpredictable output run directly counter to and debunk reality. The drunken pianist acts as a kind of intemperate, unintentional critic. He is an accidental theorist. But he is also an absurd and ridiculous figure, who, having frittered away any real talent, is reduced to eking out a living in a miserable movie-house. And the café pianist has fared little better. He is the very centre of inattention, a distracted daydreamer whose principal aspiration is to be elsewhere. He is a non-entity whose mediocre music falls on deaf ears. Our baby-faced piano player corresponds to a writer without readers, a contemporary Cassandra whose voice goes unheard amid the chatter and gossip. And perhaps it is the scream of this Cassandra that echoes through the streets of Berlin and elsewhere and makes Kracauer's blood run cold.

Part III

FROM THE BOULEVARDS: PARIS OF
THE SECOND EMPIRE IN KRACAUER

5

Offenbach in Paris

1 Introduction

Que le lecteur ne se scandalize pas de cette gravité dans le frivole. . . .

There is a certain irony in the fact that Kracauer chose to open his 1937 book *Jacques Offenbach and the Paris of his Time*[1] with an epigram from the poet Charles Baudelaire. For, just as Kracauer's monograph was being published,[2] his friend and fellow exile in 1930s Paris, Walter Benjamin, was embarking on a major study of Baudelaire, one which, like the wider ongoing *Arcades Project* from whence it emerged,[3] was never to be completed.[4] Benjamin's labours were to result in some characteristically dazzling literary miniatures which have subsequently far outshone Kracauer's much more substantial text. Indeed, the Offenbach book suffered the most hostile and humiliating reception imaginable from his colleagues at the Frankfurt Institute for Social Research: Adorno, Benjamin and even Löwenthal, Kracauer's closest and most enduring friend, were unanimous and unequivocal in their critical condemnation.[5]

'It has far exceeded my worst expectations' (ABC: 183), Adorno confesses, freely if not gleefully, in his letter to Benjamin of 4 May 1937. He then proceeds to denounce the cursory treatment of Offenbach's music itself as 'crassly erroneous'; the preface and the idea of a 'societal biography' (*Gesellschaftsbiographie*) as 'shameless and idiotic'; and the book's supposed 'social observations' as nothing more than 'old wives' tales, the foolishness and superficiality of which find their only equivalent in that blinking petty bourgeois look with which, half admiringly and half resentfully, he squints at "society" and indeed the demimonde' (ABC: 184). Adorno concludes scornfully: 'if Kracauer really does identify with this book, then he has definitely erased himself from the list of writers to be taken at all seriously' (ibid.), a list indeed which was doubtless extremely short and not necessarily always featuring Benjamin.

For his part, Benjamin, clearly a not disinterested figure, was quick to endorse Adorno's damning verdict – 'I cannot believe that our judgements about the book diverge in any way' – and equally forthright in his critique of Kracauer's exemplary failure.[6] The book's naïve and apologetic stance forbade any insight whatsoever: 'Lovely as many of the things in his sources are', Benjamin laments, 'they only appear shabby and mean in the text itself. And hardly any of the numerous anecdotes make a proper effect when they are reproduced' (ABC: 186). Benjamin then makes perhaps the most telling comment, one whose spirit Adorno was only too keen to communicate to Kracauer in his letter of 13 May 1937.[7] Interpreting the book as a desperate act of financial expediency, Benjamin opines: 'With this book Kracauer has essentially resigned himself. He has composed a text that only a few years ago would have found its most ruthless critic in the author himself' (ABC: 185). In short, with the Offenbach book Kracauer had betrayed not only Adorno and Benjamin but, most significantly, *himself*. Kracauer must be rescued from his own folly.[8] By 1937, Adorno certainly knew best. He was fast outgrowing his erstwhile philosophical mentor and, dare one say it, his own boots too. He would soon take it upon himself to rewrite Kracauer's work for him.

The Offenbach book failed to find a defender even in Löwenthal, who, as editor of the Institut's house journal, the *Zeitschrift für Sozialforschung*, not only readily agreed to the publication of Adorno's – albeit more muted – critical review[9] but also suggested a less ambivalent, more strident critical conclusion. Indeed, for Löwenthal, the very fact that Kracauer's book was reviewed at all in the *Zeitschrift* did the study an undeserved honour.[10] It is little wonder then that subsequent scholars have paid little attention to Kracauer's Offenbach writings.[11] Even so sympathetic a critic as Martin Jay passes quickly over the Offenbach book, noting Adorno's 'mixed review' and acknowledging the greater 'conceptual daring and breadth of vision' of Benjamin's *Passagenarbeit* (Jay 1986: 166), praise indeed for a text that was never actually finished.

Benjamin's unconcealed distaste for Kracauer's 'messy box of chocolates' (ABC: 186) must have given his own work an added sense of urgency and purpose, with the need for a genuine critical exposition of the origins of capitalist modernity in the cultural forms and commodified spaces of Paris during the Second Empire ever more acute. But Benjamin's own initial text on Baudelaire was also to fall foul of Adorno. Conceived as the central section of a tripartite book-length study[12] and completed in 1938, 'Paris of the Second Empire in Baudelaire' became the object of a critical correspondence between

Benjamin and Adorno[13] in the light of which the text was substantially redrafted and finally published, under the new title 'On Some Motifs in Baudelaire', in the *Zeitschrift* in 1939.

Given the potential parallels[14] between the Offenbach and Baudelaire studies, it is remarkable how little attention has been paid to points of correspondence, comparison and contrast.[15] In this chapter I seek to juxtapose Kracauer's Offenbach and Benjamin's Baudelaire in the hope that they might prove mutually illuminating. This is intended not as a systematic inventory or definitive mapping of shared concepts and motifs but rather, more modestly, as an initial identification and elaboration of three common thematic complexes:

a) the work and character of mediation: How do the works of the poet/composer communicate or give voice to the society in which they were composed?
b) the circumstances and contingencies of reception: To whom were these poems and musical compositions addressed at the time?
c) the politics and task of present-day redemption: How might these works speak to the critical theorist writing in the 1930s (and indeed to us today)?

The brooding, bohemian author of the scandalous *Les Fleurs du mal* and the eccentric composer of briefly fashionable but always frivolous operettas may appear an unlikely pair of subjects for Marxist cultural theorists writing as impoverished exiles amid the political turmoil of the 1930s. But, by exploring how Kracauer and Benjamin themselves come to pose and respond to the questions above, it should become evident that their choice of subject matter was anything but innocent or arcane. On the contrary, both theorists were preoccupied with what they saw as the pressing task of developing the principles and practices of a materialist cultural-historical analysis, one which would facilitate the critical redemption and disclose the contemporary resonance of artworks from the recent past at a time of chaos and crisis.

2   Mediation: Biography and Expressivity

Both Kracauer and Benjamin are concerned with the possibilities and problems of reading or deciphering a particular place and time – Paris during the Second Empire – from and through the life and (especially) work of an individual artist. There are two aspects to this: firstly, how might artworks (be they cycles of poems, literary reviews or essays, be they musical scores, libretti or theatrical compositions) identify, capture and articulate wider social patterns and processes?; secondly, how

might the artist him-/herself be understood in terms of the constellation of prevailing socio-economic and political forces, as a representative or exemplary figure of a milieu or class position, interest, experience
and attitude? Both the Offenbach and Baudelaire studies engage with
these fundamental concerns, ones which clearly lie at the heart of *any*
attempt to provide a historical materialist account of artistic and cultural production. In short: how do the works of the poet/composer
mediate the society in which they first appear?

Kracauer's book addresses this issue from the outset: the book's title
itself alerts the reader to the fact that its subject matter is not just Offenbach but also 'the Paris of his time', and the preface then clarifies the
distinctive principle of a 'social' or 'societal biography' (*Gesellschaftsbiographie*): 'It is a biography of a society in that along with portraying
the figure of Offenbach, it allows the figure of the society that he moved
and by which he was moved to arise, thereby emphasizing the relationship between the artist and a social world' (JOF: 23). While conventional biographies, in chronicling the life of a particular individual,
typically present prevailing social conditions and circumstances merely
as 'a blurry background' (ibid.), Kracauer insists upon a different,
indeed a double (or dialectical) optic. Offenbach is to be the focus of
his study in so far as the composer provides a lens through which mid-
nineteenth-century Paris may be descried and described. Hence, Offenbach *is* the focus to the extent that he *brings the Second Empire into focus*.

If Offenbach is, then, a kind of alibi, he is still a necessary one. The
composer of operettas is certainly no arbitrary choice. He made himself
very much at home in the fashionable spaces and social circles of his
time. Kracauer observes:

> Many great artists have been comparatively independent of the times in
> which they lived; not so Offenbach. He had to be in perpetual contact
> with the world about him in order to be creative at all. All who knew
> him bear witness to the fact that he was the very personification of socia-
> bility. He plunged into social life because it alone supplied him with the
> necessary tensions. He lived in the instant, reacting delicately to social
> changes and constantly adapting himself to them. The speed with which
> he made a name for himself was largely due to the fact that at the
> moment of his debut a society was crystallizing that satisfied the cravings
> of his being. He had only to be himself for success to be there for the
> asking. (JOF: 90)

Offenbach's compositions drew their life from these settings: the
fashions of the arcades and imperial pomp of the World Exhibitions;
the boulevards with their motley cast of bohemian characters (fops and
dandies, flâneurs, artists, journalists, courtesans, actors, swindlers);[16]
and the bourgeois salons, with their superficial propriety and politesse
and their undercurrents of intrigue, scandalous gossip and idle

tittle-tattle.[17] These milieus were necessary for Offenbach: his artistic energy and productivity were indebted to their vitality and exuberance; and the witty repartee, *bons mots* and silly chatter provided him with the very words for his musical libretti. These spaces, these times, speak, or rather sing, through him. Indeed, for Kracauer, it seems Offenbach is a kind of conduit for that which envelops him. The operetta is nothing other than the *self-expression* of the boulevards[18] and the salons which Offenbach frequented and to which he has simply given aesthetic, musical form. His music becomes the very signature, the theme music, so to speak, of an age of superficiality, spectacle and speculation.

Offenbach's operettas do not merely give form to the social spheres from which they emanate; they also satirize them. Kracauer stresses that Offenbach 'is a mocking bird' (JOF: 25), a metaphor aptly capturing the lightness and levity of his music. Puncturing pretension, parodying conceit, parading self-deception, his compositions are comical musical mirrors *of* their times *for* their times. Here the work of art is conceived as a reflection of, or rather, to be more precise, as a *mode of reflection for*, the society in which it appears. Offenbach's theatrical works re-presented, restaged, the 'joy and glamour' (JOF: 151) of the Second Empire for the amusement of the Second Empire. The social spheres which inspired him were also those from whence his audiences came. Offenbach's compositions expressed his times, comically reflected them, and pandered to them as well. Many of his works met with enduring adulation; others met with ephemeral enthusiasm; a few were yawned off stage (but only a few, and these towards the end of his life). For what distinguished Offenbach, and what makes him the perfect exemplar of his times, is his possession of 'an exceptional sensitivity to his society. His rise only begins when all the conditions for the ascent of the operetta are in place ... [T]hose conditions are inseparable from the longevity of the dictatorship, the domination of finance capital, the eruption of the international economy, and the Boulevards and their fashionable Bohemianism' (JOF: 24).

More than any other composer, indeed, any other artist or cultural figure of the time, Offenbach and his works form 'a precision instrument' (JOF: 25) for calibrating the changing tastes, predilections and nuances of life under the Second Empire. A double movement is involved here: Offenbach and his work are exemplary of the prevailing social, economic and political environment;[19] and, at the same moment, Kracauer presents his own study of Offenbach as a veritable model or 'test-case' of historical materialist cultural analysis.[20] The 'societal biography' becomes for Kracauer *the* Marxist method for reading the relationship between artist, artwork and society.[21]

And nothing could be more infuriating for Adorno. Far from providing a definitive method for critical cultural-historical enquiry, the idea

of a *Gesellschaftsbiographie* is the principal target of Adorno's scornful
letter of 13 May 1937:

> This can certainly only mean that Offenbach's work and his history are
> examined in connection with the societal history of the epoch. If the
> epoch is really to be assembled out of the work, then this can only happen
> where both are truly interwoven: namely, in the musical form, more
> precisely, in technical analysis. To do without them is nothing less than
> to posit analogies or vague relations instead of conclusive determination.
> (AKB: 354)

Adorno's complaint here is compelling: any serious attempt to
gauge the course of the Second Empire through Offenbach's compositions and their reception would, at the very least, have to explore
technically and systematically the actual music itself, an undertaking
which Kracauer explicitly avoids and of which he was almost certainly
incapable. The focus instead on Offenbach's libretti is inadequate.
Indeed, one might question whether this was an account of Offenbach
and his times or of Ludovic Halévy and Henri Meilhac, the wordsmiths
of the operetta.

So much for Offenbach. And the 'Paris of his time'? Warming to his
theme, Adorno reflects: 'The task of a "societal biography" [*Gesellschaftsbiographie*], if I should adopt an expression I find a little unpleas-
ant, would have been to determine the social character of Offenbach's
music. Instead of which, it remains at the level of observing a pre-
established harmony between the monadological composer and the
given period' (AKB: 355).

The symbiotic relationship between Offenbach's music and the
Second Empire is not illuminated but presupposed. And so, Adorno
claims, Kracauer's monadological approach – detecting the general, the
totality, within the particular, the individual – fails in its avowed ambition to transcend the 'figure–background dualism' (AKB: 355) of banal
biographical writing. The music itself remains opaque and the backdrop appears 'just as abstract' (AKB: 356). Offenbach sits in 'an empty
societal framework ... filled with anecdotes, the telling or writing of
which probably provided more pleasure than the reading of them'
(ibid.).

The concept of the monad brings us to Benjamin, whose essay 'Paris
of the Second Empire in Baudelaire' was also to endure withering criticism from Adorno some eighteen months later on the same issue: how
artworks were conditioned by and conveyed their time and place.[22]
Conceived as the central section of a proposed Baudelaire book, Benjamin's text was to explore not only how the lyric poet's verses lent
voice to the 'capital of the nineteenth century' but also how Baudelaire
positioned himself and understood the duties and possibilities of the

artist alone and adrift in the modern and modernizing metropolis. Paris as envisaged in the writings of Baudelaire; Baudelaire glimpsed amid the jostling crowds of the city – Benjamin's study sought to fashion a similar double optic. And Adorno was unsurprisingly unimpressed. In his response of 10 November 1938, he complains: 'You show a prevailing tendency to relate the pragmatic contents of Baudelaire's work directly and immediately to adjacent features in the social history, and wherever possible the economic features, of the time' (ABC: 282). Adorno was unhappy with the positing of any *immediate* connection between a specific historical socio-economic circumstance and a contemporary literary figure, motif or text.[23] Such a straightforward equation constitutes an inexcusable oversimplification of the complex, indeed extremely elusive, relationship between artwork and material conditions. Cultural forms are not mere reflex responses to economic forces but involve manifold levels and moments of mediation.

Benjamin's riposte to this accusation of 'crude thinking' was clear and forthright. Firstly, his text itself should not be taken out of context and judged alone, since the 'theoretical armature' forming the first section of the Baudelaire book was yet to be written. Adorno's criticisms were premature. Secondly, a sense of mediation was not lacking, and for clues to its specific form one might turn directly to the *Arcades Project*. There, in his programmatic methodological reflections in Convolute N, Benjamin writes: 'Marx lays bare the causal connection between economy and culture. For us, what matters is the thread of expression. It is not the economic origins of culture that will be presented, but the expression of the economy in its culture' (ARC: 460). This is a key passage for Benjamin and for a reading of Kracauer. All forms of aesthetic production – whether major or minor works, whether popular or avant-garde, be they visual, literary or musical – may and must be read, not as direct reflections of current material circumstances, but rather as *expressions* of them. Paris in the Second Empire then finds *expression* in Baudelaire's verse and prose – this is Benjamin's claim, one that could be extended to Offenbach's operettas.

Indeed, Benjamin had already developed and demonstrated something akin to this approach some ten years earlier in his doctoral *Habilitationsschrift*, a work with which Adorno was very familiar.[24] Taking as his theme the obscure seventeenth-century German play of mourning, the *Trauerspiel*, Benjamin seeks to reveal the literary, theological and existential sensibility of the Baroque through a reading of some of its most neglected literary remains. For him, the allegorical poetics of these forgotten dramas give voice to, *express*, an epoch beset by war, disease and ruination, an era of creaturely despair at human futility and folly. Benjamin seeks to delineate the *Trauerspiel* as a particular historical and dramatic Idea in its own right, one distinct from the tragedy, a form with which it had all too often been confused. Drawing on Leibniz,

Benjamin conceived his work on the *Trauerspiel* as a monadological study, one in which each and every literary fragment contains within itself, patiently awaiting unfolding by the scrupulous critical theorist, the totality of which it is a part. The fragment is a miniature or abbreviated version of the whole.

And so it is with Baudelaire. In Convolute N once more, Benjamin explicitly states the exemplary character of the *Trauerspiel* study for the *Arcades Project*: 'The book on the Baroque exposed the seventeenth century to the light of the present day. Here, something analogous must be done for the nineteenth century but with greater distinctness' (ARC: 459). Where the allegory of the *Trauerspiel* was decisive for generating an image of the desolate, godforsaken world of the Baroque, Baudelaire's allegorical poetics would be unfolded as a monad to reveal and illuminate the ruinous tendencies, sufferings and melancholy sensibilities of the recent past, of modernity itself.[25]

While, for Kracauer, the carnival of the boulevards and comic claptrap of the salon find their *self-expression* in Offenbach's musical productions, what Baudelaire *expresses* in his poetry and prose is the desperate fate of the subject lost within the milling metropolitan masses and the inevitable destiny of the work of art en route for the marketplace. Crowds[26] and commodities – as forces of attraction and repulsion these are what moved Baudelaire and pervade his writings even if they are rarely made explicit.[27] To read and understand Baudelaire, then, one must uncover that which lies hidden, veiled, among his words; to appreciate Offenbach, one must look to the delights of the surface.[28] This holds not only for the poet and the composer; perhaps it is true of Benjamin and Kracauer, too.

3 Reception: Commodity and Popularity

The work of art as reflection, as expression, as self-expression, as monad – the exact status of aesthetic labour and object is an acute one given the changing perception and position of artist and artwork during the Second Empire itself. Discussion of how nineteenth-century Paris finds representation in lyric poetry and operetta leads necessarily to a consideration of how Baudelaire and Offenbach came to experience and articulate the commercialization and commodification of art and culture. Under such circumstances, how does the artist regard the exigencies of the marketplace and respond to the transient fashions and capricious whims of the public? In short, in the era of high capitalism, when art is increasingly recognized as just one more commodity in search of a buyer, how does the writer or composer come to view his/her own intimate connection with, and inescapable economic dependence upon, the anonymous crowd as customer? Does one pander to and appease popular tastes or, remaining imperiously aloof, revile such vulgarity? Should one appeal directly to the audiences, readerships and spectators of their time or, resigned to being misunderstood and maligned by myopic contemporaries, grandly lay claim instead to post-humous recognition and appreciation, the judgement of 'posterity'? As we will see, such issues are intimately bound up with the very notion of modernism (*modernité*) itself as a distinctive aesthetic sensibility and practice.

One of the reasons for Adorno's dismissive response to the Offen-bach book was the nagging suspicion that it was less a critical scholarly study and more an act of calculated opportunism, an unprincipled attempt to write a 'light' and 'popular' book so as to benefit from the current vogue for the biographical genre, a fashion which Kracauer himself had earlier identified and critiqued. It was a suspicion Ben-jamin certainly shared: as a fellow exile, he could understand though not condone Kracauer's aberation.[29] But, for Adorno, the case was clear: Kracauer had hoped to write, of all things, a *bestseller*. Of course, the Offenbach book proved to be nothing of the sort,[30] but this issue of popularity does take us to the heart of the study.

For the duration of the Second Empire, Offenbach's works enjoyed remarkable popular acclaim and commercial success, bringing him fame and a fortune. Indeed, his skill in setting the fashion for the fash-ionable was such that his music became an international phenome-non.[31] Why was this? For Kracauer the answer is clear: not only did he have an acute ear for his times and a pleasing tune, but there was also a correspondence or an *elective affinity* between the fanciful world of the operetta and the illusions and pretensions of the Second Empire. Both composer and music were fully in tune and in step with the daz-zling 'spectacle of wealth and brilliance' (JOF: 49) that stood at the heart of the city. With its grand projects of urban renewal, colonial expansion and public works sustained by financial speculation, with its World Exhibitions showcasing the marvels of technological progress and the spirit of international capital, with its imperial pageantry and pomp, the reign of Napoleon III was itself ostentatious, outlandish and, as Marx famously observed, farcical. As the reality of dictatorship, exploi-tation and class struggle was forgotten, sidelined or ameliorated by short-term prosperity, illusion, theatricality and pretence took centre stage. Parisian society itself entered into a fantastical, flamboyant 'oper-etta world'. Kracauer observes: 'The operetta would never have been born had the society of the time not itself been operetta-like; had it not been living in a dreamworld, obstinately refusing to wake up and face reality' (JOF: 215).

Indeed, the operetta both captured and contributed to the phantas-magorias of the time. It mimicked and mocked (gently) the society in which it rose to favour. Its home was Paris and it made itself at home in Paris.[32] Whether set among the foolish gods on Mount Olympus or among poor quarrelling lovers on a metropolitan streetcorner, its subject matter, its vernacular language, its wit and charm, its sentimentalism were always Parisian because: 'Only in Paris were there all the elements, material and verbal, that made the operetta possible' (JOF: 215–16).[33] The Second Empire was a period of dreaming,[34] and the ballads and arias of Offenbach's operettas were the lullabies with which Paris sang itself to sleep. And so long as the Second Empire slept and dreamed, Offenbach's name and finances were secure. The catastrophic end of the Second Empire in 1870–1 was the end for operetta, too – Offenbach's operetta at least. Offenbach turned to more sombre themes: he was to die in 1880 just before the first performance of *The Tales of Hoffmann*. And a new composer of operettas of a different style was already on the scene, an Austrian by the name of Johann Strauss.

Apropos Austrian connections: Offenbach's epithet, the 'Mozart of the Champs-Elysées', was rather perceptive. In his fragmentary sociological writings on Wolfgang Amadeus Mozart, Norbert Elias (1994) regards the great eighteenth-century composer as a key figure in the history of music not just for *what* he composed, but for *whom*. It is Mozart, ejected unceremoniously from the house of the archbishop of Salzburg, who moves beyond the feudal relations of patron and composer-as-servant and enters a new domain, the marketplace. Liberated from the prescriptions of the Church and the court, the composer takes on the mantle of creative genius and free spirit, garb both fine-sounding and wholly deceptive. The freelance composer was anything but free. Mozart traded servitude to the good opinions of rich and powerful masters for a new and precarious dependence upon public tastes and the monies that flow from subscription concerts, musical soirées and commissioned compositions. And if Elias's Mozart marks the birth of the impecunious musician selling himself and his products in the marketplace, then Offenbach represents a much later stage of development, one in which compositions were conceived from the outset and wholly fashioned as popular commodities.[35]

Indeed, Offenbach was to become as much a theatrical impresario as a composer, a cultural entrepreneur who invested his time, money and reputation in managing theatres and concert halls, forming orchestras and companies, entreating and cajoling reluctant divas. These various ventures and unpredictable individuals often let him down. The spectre of ruin was never far away. A precocious virtuoso and prolific composer, Offenbach proved a moderately adept businessman and a sometimes profligate theatre-owner. Nevertheless, he was astute enough to recognize the importance of pleasing and flattering his audiences, even if these entertainments were to be laced with a good deal of irony. He was writing in full cognizance of the exigencies of the rapidly changing musical marketplace wherein new demands and challenges were appearing: not just more lavish sets and daring set-pieces, testing the budgets and technical limits of the theatre, but also the growing importance of newspaper critics, editors and publishers; the proliferation of gossip columns; the imperatives of advertising and promotion; the capriciousness of celebrities and stars; the opportunities for lucrative international tours; the fickleness of public opinion.[36]

Nothing distinguishes Baudelaire and Offenbach more than their attitudes towards their publics. Kracauer chooses Offenbach as his focus because he set the rhythm for his times; he was in step and in tune with them. Scorned by the scandalized Parisian public, Baudelaire appears as an untimely figure in Benjamin's reading, as one who penetrates to the heart of the Second Empire precisely *because he is out of step with it*. Benjamin points out:

> Baudelaire envisaged readers to whom the reading of lyric poetry would present difficulties. ... Willpower and the ability to concentrate are not their strong points. What they prefer is sensual pleasure; they are familiar with the 'spleen' which kills interest and receptiveness. It is strange to come across a lyric poet who addresses himself to such readers, the least rewarding type of audience. ... Baudelaire wrote a book which from the very beginning had little prospect of becoming an immediate popular success. (SW4: 313)

Baudelaire's poems were written without any expectation of a contemporary readership. Yes, like Offenbach's theatrical productions, his verses gave voice to the quotidian life of the city of Paris: the shock encounter with the crowd, the life of the boulevard, bohemians and outsiders. And Baudelaire was equally indebted to the Parisian vernacular for his language and expression.[37] But his tone was not light and his subject matter not sentimentalized. The public craved wit, charm and frivolity, the romantic and comic misunderstandings and misadventures of impoverished young lovers who finally stumble upon each other and good fortune. The bitter, brooding poetry of Baudelaire – sarcastic, salacious, sardonic – invoked the abjectness of drunken ragpickers, whores, outsiders and malcontents. That Parisian society was 'operetta-like' ensured both Offenbach's success and Baudelaire's failure. Or, rather, Baudelaire's success in his own terms. For he did not write to please the public of his time, but to spite them.[38]

The whirl of the crowd on the boulevard was as necessary for Baudelaire's creativity as it was for Offenbach's. But the poet's relationship with the masses was very different. Instead of enjoying comfort and complicity, his was an experience based much more on contempt, conflict and combat: for Baudelaire, the artist was a skilled fencer,[39] duelling with lethal adversaries. Out on the streets, bruised and wearied, he heroically plunged into the turbulent masses and 'battled the crowd – with the impotent rage of someone fighting the rain or the wind' (SW4: 343). Baudelaire's poetry constitutes a privileged expression of nineteenth-century Parisian life because he himself was willing to undergo its dangers and deprivations, to bear its wounds and scars as indelible stigmata.

Few readers meant little money. Baudelaire knowingly condemned himself to penury.[40] Yet he was anything but naïve about the commodification of art during the Second Empire.[41] Indeed, the significance of Baudelaire's poetry lies precisely in the recognition of the transformed status of artwork and artist under the conditions of capitalist modernity. Poems were mere commodities to be bought and sold like any other. And so, in placing his/her very soul into the work of art, the artist sells him-/herself at the marketplace to the highest bidder.[42] The poet becomes a commodity him-/herself – nothing other than a whore.[43] But it was another urban outcast that provided him with an abiding image for the contemporary poet: the ragpicker (*Lumpensammler* or *chiffonnier*). The sources of poetry, of all art in these ruinous times, are to be found not in the inspiration and imagination of the artist-as-genius but, rather, buried amid the dirt and detritus of the metropolis itself.[44] And so she/he must venture out early to salvage the linguistic scraps and fragments of the cityscape and then patiently stitch them together into a useable text for sale. Such waste materials, such wasted lives, are the stuff from which modern poetry is to be fashioned.[45] The poet as whore, as ragpicker – without pathos, all without the need of sympathy and sentiment – these are unattractive images. So it is little wonder that the 'operetta-world', with its 'joy and glamour', should find such subjects distasteful. Such thoughts do not make for sweet dreams, and the sleepers do not wish to be disturbed.

The poet as embittered ragpicker; the composer as popular mocking bird: here one is confronted with contrasting visions of the modern metropolitan artist. And perhaps Kracauer's own fall from grace, from the good opinions of Benjamin and Adorno that is, is intelligible in terms of a subtle shift from one to the other. In the course of seven years, Kracauer, that early-morning revolutionary ragpicker of *Die Angestellten*, has seemingly sacrificed his wry critical edge to become a witty raconteur of diverting anecdotes in the hope of pecuniary advantage, of writing a bestseller. Better a *chiffonnier* than a caged canary.

4 Redemption: Modernism and Critique

Whether seemingly in time or out of step with the society in which they appeared, both the gentle mocking spirit of Offenbach's libretti and the splenetic scorn of the untimely poet were critical of and complicit with the phantasmagoria of the Second Empire. Both composer and poet are subject to, and exemplify, the illusions and delusions, the deceptions and intrigues of the era. They, and their works, both enchant and disenchant modernity. And this ambiguity is, in part at least, a consequence of their myopia – neither Offenbach nor Baudelaire possessed a particularly acute understanding of their own real situation and interest within the prevailing class structure and political struggles of the time. The provocative and satirical tendencies of the works themselves owe precious little to any political predilections or conspiratorial activities of the artist. This makes them *more*, not less, interesting for the critical theorist. Offenbach and Baudelaire are *symptomatic* of their time *because of, not despite*, their eccentricities and absurdities. Hence, their texts are never to be taken at face value. Artworks are not intelligible in terms of authorial intention. Kracauer and Benjamin are readers *against the grain*, studying texts not just for what they said *then* but for what they might disclose *now*. Indeed, it is only posthumously, during the afterlife of the works themselves, so to speak, that the significance of these operettas and those poems unfolds, comes into view for the critical historian of the recent past, and in turn for us.

This temporal interplay between past, present and future preoccupied Baudelaire, too. In his famous essay 'The Painter of Modern Life' (1863) and various reviews of the *Salon*, he sought to articulate the principles and preconditions of a new art of the 'now' – *modernité*. According to Baudelaire, the task of the modern artist is not to imitate the great masterpieces of the past, copying their antiquated themes and styles, but rather to depict and describe contemporary life in all its vitality. To accomplish this, the artist must abandon the calm seclusion of the studio and immerse him-/herself in the flux of the modern itself. The genuine artist of today must describe and depict the marvellous mobile spectacle afforded by the metropolitan street. Contemporary crowds, parades, fashions – these fleeting phenomena are all subjects worthy of art, a sentiment certainly shared by Offenbach. 'By *modernité*', Baudelaire proclaims, 'I mean the ephemeral, the fugitive, the contingent, the half of art whose other half is the eternal and immutable' (1986: 13). In focusing on the transient manifestations of the present moment, the artist captures them for future times. Oriented to veneration by subsequent generations, the true artist shuns the shallow adulation of uncomprehending contemporaries. The ephemeral is transformed into the enduring, the modern, the new, becomes the 'classic', those masterpieces cherished by those who come after.[46] This helps us understand Baudelaire's attitude to his own time. Art does not curry favour with the public tastes of the day. The true worth of his poetry will be appreciated only in the fullness of time by readers yet to be born, by posterity. It is for them that the true artist paints, composes and writes.[47] Such work is like a message in a bottle (*Flaschenpost*), cast upon the seas

of time, with an unsure destination and an unknown recipient on a
foreign shore.

Baudelaire did not write for the reader of his time and was not disappointed. Offenbach directed his productions precisely to the contemporary audiences and in later years suffered the inevitable fate of all
fashionable things: his works fell *out* of fashion. But simply because his
ear was tuned to his present does not mean that Offenbach did not
have an eye for the future. Indeed, for Kracauer, Offenbach's music
possessed a utopian moment or promise that was irreconcilable with
the frivolity, complacency and self-deception of imperial Paris. Offenbach's levity and wit, while seemingly in accord with a society which
invented and privileged the *bon mot*,[48] were born of a melancholy recognition of the hypocrisy, triviality and inhumanity of the Second
Empire. The operetta's 'satirical spirit' ridiculed the very milieus from
which it sprang. Offenbach's music was an enchantment that disenchanted his world – unfolding this paradox was central to Kracauer's
study, for it was the composer's ironic sensibility and critical distance
that lifted the operetta above the banality and mediocrity of its time
and transformed it into an art form itself worthy of critical appreciation
and contemporary redemption. Here Kracauer presents an abiding
theme in his own work: the affinity of the comedic and the utopian, of
laughter and liberty:

> As light and airy as the spirit of the Boulevards seemed, it contained a
> secret which Offenbach was destined to reveal. There was something
> Utopian about him, something that pointed toward the future. His music,
> his whole being, looked forward to a state of society in which all the
> powers of darkness had been abolished – a state of affairs to which the
> spirit of the Boulevards perhaps also pointed. If Offenbach was magician,
> it was white magic that he practised, casting out evil spirits and conjuring
> up a better human world. (JOF: 112–13)

This carnivalesque ambience of merry debunking, of the eradication
of fear, and the overcoming of the mythic is that of the fairy tale. It
was a spirit with which Benjamin was very familiar and for which he,
too, possessed the greatest enthusiasm.[49] To confront and outwit the
forces of domination and cruelty with 'cunning and high spirits' – this
is the fundamental, the 'wisest' lesson of the fairy tale (SW3: 157). For
Kracauer, it is a message of hope amid hopelessness that Offenbach's
music keeps alive and in our minds. There was, as Baudelaire duly
recognized, much seriousness in Offenbach's frivolity.

The afterlife of the work of art is fundamental for both Kracauer and
Benjamin. Their preoccupation with the Second Empire is not motivated by idle curiosity or by an arcane interest in the past for its own
sake, a kind of *l'histoire pour l'histoire*. Rather their concern is precisely

with the dialectics of past and present moments: with how the recent past speaks to and informs what comes after, and how the present traces itself in and interprets what has gone before. This recognition of the mutual construction and illumination of past and present is articulated by Benjamin in his concept of the 'dialectical image', the key historiographical concept for the *Arcades Project* sketched in the 1940 'Theses on the Concept of History'. And it is to the production and mobilization of such dialectical images of Offenbach, Baudelaire and the Paris of their time that Kracauer and Benjamin dedicate themselves from the vantage point of the Paris of *their* time.

Kracauer's 'societal biography' of Offenbach was intended as a history of the origins of the present, of modernity itself. Both he and Benjamin recognized Paris, 'capital of the nineteenth century', as the site of 'diverse motifs that persist today' and as 'the immediate precursor of modern society' (JOF: 23). Commodification, the accelerated tempi of urban existence, shock experience, distraction and amnesia, exile and melancholy – these incipient features of everyday metropolitan life captured by Baudelaire's poetry have become the hallmarks of modernity itself. And dictatorial regimes combining superficial 'joy and glamour' with brutality and repression, militarization and the mobilization of mass populations for 'public works' were all too familiar to those forced to flee Germany in the 1930s. Only the most casual and complacent reader of Kracauer's narration of the stupidities and cruelties of the Second Empire could miss the parallels with the Third Reich.[50]

The Offenbach and Baudelaire studies are less accounts of the 'then' than allegories of the 'now'. They are anything but innocent histories, naïve biographies. Indeed, they are attempts to identify and redeem the critical energies and bellicose spirit of Baudelaire and the utopian intimations of Offenbach for contemporary political interventions. The essential question for Kracauer and Benjamin is clear: How do these works, composed then, resonate with, and provoke those who come after, those living now? *Now* is the 1930s here, but it is also *now*. And this then remains the crucial question for us today: How might one turn these words from the past – not just Offenbach's and Baudelaire's, but also Kracauer's and Benjamin's – into critical interventions in the present?

6

Orpheus in Hollywood

1 Long Shot

Paris. 1864. A crowded boulevard on a late spring evening. Ludovic Halévy and Henri Meilhac, Jacques Offenbach's librettists, are strolling along to the composer's house, exchanging pleasantries and witticisms with acquaintances encountered en route. The imperial carriage rolls past pursued by the usual procession of vehicles occupied by a motley array of notables, fashionable figures, courtesans and other hangers-on. Among them is Hortense Schneider, Offenbach's capricious leading lady for the last decade. Her carriage pulls up. She 'waves the two men over and, with slightly vulgar aplomb, rails against Offenbach' (MPT: 2). The carriage moves off. Meilhac's response to this petulant outburst is telling. He turns to Halévy and declares that Hortense was 'born to play the part of Helen of Troy in an operetta' (ibid.).

This comic incident opens Kracauer's 'Jacques Offenbach: Motion Picture Treatment', a 22-page German text now held in the Deutsches Literaturarchiv. With this rather peculiar script, written around 1938, Kracauer hoped to interest Hollywood film companies, producers and directors[1] in acquiring the motion picture rights to his then recently published *Jacques Offenbach und die Paris seiner Zeit* (1937), a book already translated into English. Had the 'Motion Picture Treatment' plan succeeded, the ensuing rights sale would not only have generated much needed funds for the impoverished exile but also have initiated an important contact with, indeed a potential lifeline to, influential figures in America. It failed. Although Kracauer later notes in a letter to Max Horkheimer[2] that Metro-Goldwyn-Mayer did indeed take out an option on the American edition of the book, nothing came of it. The rights remained unsold, the film unrealized. Kracauer remained poor and in Paris.[3]

The prospect of Kracauer, then nearing his fiftieth birthday, becoming a Hollywood screenplay writer should not surprise us. The 'Motion Picture Treatment' was certainly not his only (unsuccessful) attempt to write for the cinematic medium which so fascinated him. Sometime between 1933 and 1936 he had penned a five-page 'Thematic sketch [*Ideen-Entwurf*] for a short film' to be entitled *Dimanche*;[4] and in the mid-1940s he was involved in writing the script of *The Accident*, later retitled *Below the Surface*, a so-called test film intended to elicit and examine audience reactions as part of the Frankfurt School's ongoing studies in prejudice and anti-Semitism.[5]

Moreover, Kracauer had reason to be quietly optimistic: in a letter of 22 August 1939, he points to the production of a Fox film biography of Offenbach starring Lily Pons.[6] Indeed, Offenbach's music was enjoying fresh acclaim on the East Coast: the 1937 New York Metropolitan Opera House performance of *The Tales of Hoffmann* remains today one of the great recordings for collectors. Furthermore, in 1938 MGM released Julien Duvivier's *The Great Waltz*, a musical film biography of Johann Strauss, Offenbach's great rival and eventual successor. If this production could be a box office hit then why not an Offenbach movie? Duvivier's film was to prove a mixed blessing for Kracauer, however. On the one hand, it was to provide, in Kracauer's terms, an exemplary instance of the cinematic realization of a musical film based on the life and work of a composer, demonstrating the reconciliation of apparently uncinematic subject matter with the inherent realistic tendency of the film medium.[7] On the other, Kracauer observes, its financial failure was decisive in MGM's decision not to take up the option on *Orpheus in Paris*.[8]

The Offenbach 'Motion Picture Treatment' is neither a brief overview (like *Dimanche*) nor a detailed, finalized shooting script (like *Below the Surface*) but rather a half-way house: a sketch of the main scenes of the film as a series of vignettes culled from the book; indications of the tenor and direction of the dialogue; and various specifications regarding the use of Offenbach's music, both as background accompaniment and as actual performance. From the very outset, Kracauer makes it clear that the text itself was not to stand alone but rather must be read in conjunction with the book. This elaborated the essential context and delineated the principal characters on which the 'Motion Picture Treatment' drew. In short, the book is the key to the 'Motion Picture Treatment': this is Kracauer's view. I want to reverse this formulation and suggest the following: to appreciate the book, one should read the 'Motion Picture Treatment'. My argument here is this: viewing the Offenbach book through the lens of this film sketch brings into sharp focus its intentions and inventiveness and facilitates a new appreciation of its critical power, complexity and playfulness. In short: the book appears in its true, vibrant colours only when understood as the literary product of a profoundly *cinematic* imagination.

As we have seen in the previous chapter, *Jacques Offenbach and the Paris of his Time* was intended to be something other than a conventional biography detailing Offenbach's life and musical achievements. Kracauer's study was explicitly intended as a *Gesellschaftsbiographie* – that is to say, as a critical attempt to discern, decipher and reconstruct a particular society and historical epoch – the Paris of the Second Empire – through the lens of one particular, exemplary individual and opus: Offenbach and the operetta. But while such a biography was for Kracauer both necessary and legitimate – and he was quick to extol its merits and virtues – the reception given by his closest colleagues at the Institut was both unanimous and unequivocal: the book was an utter embarrassment, the surest sign of Kracauer's destitution, both economic and intellectual. Without doubt, the prospect of a cinematic version as outlined in the 'Motion Picture Treatment' would simply have added insult to injury, confirming their worst suspicions. Whether Adorno and Benjamin had any inkling as to Kracauer's plans is unclear, but by 1938 there were other arguments to be had: between Adorno and Kracauer over the rewritten 'Mass and Propaganda' text for the *Zeitschrift*, and between Adorno and Benjamin over the Baudelaire. And so it is left to Martin Jay, writing many years later, to pick up the critical baton and beat Kracauer with it. Had it been made, Jay remarks (1986: 167), the Offenbach movie would have been precisely the kind of film Kracauer himself would later condemn in *Theory of Film* as utterly uncinematic: namely, a historical costume drama. As such, it would have been an act of self-betrayal – Jay's conclusion curiously echoes Adorno and Benjamin's verdict on the original book. But even if they were written with an eye to money-making, as so-called *Brotarbeit* – a charge Kracauer utterly refuted – the Offenbach study, taken together with the subsequent 'Motion Picture Treatment', demands more sustained consideration than this. Indeed, there is a clear precedent for the critical reassessment of minor media works undertaken by impecunious intellectuals: a series of scripts for radio broadcasts for children in the early 1930s written and presented by none other than Dr Walter Benjamin.

Jeffrey Mehlman (1993), among others, has persuasively argued that Benjamin's radio scripts – among them, children's radio dramas, tales of extraordinary figures and events, historical and contemporary stories of Berlin – be understood as 'theoretical toys' (1993: 4), as playful opportunities to test out the author's fundamental philosophical ideas and theological motifs. And if Benjamin's radio writings are really intellectual experiments, allegories for adults disguised as 'enlightenment for children', surely one should not exclude the possibility that Kracauer's 'Motion Picture Treatment' might be something other than schmaltzy, waltzy entertainment for those 'little shop girls' who go to the movies. *Brotarbeit* or not, the 'Motion Picture Treatment', read as a 'theoretical toy', as the articulation in miniature of the Offenbach book's critical themes and motifs, might provide for new insights and a fresh appreciation. To detect in the fragment or minor work the kernel of and key to the greater one, the totality – such a way of reading is not only reminiscent of Benjamin's monadological practice but also imitates a conventional scientific and cinematic technique for the exploration of physical reality: the long-shot – close-up – long-shot sequence.[9] If the book forms the panoramic long shot – the context, the background, the whole – then the film treatment constitutes the close-up scrutinizing and penetrating the detail. What might such a close-up reveal?

2 Close-up

Let us take Jay's dismissal of Kracauer's proposed Offenbach film as uncinematic, as shunning the fundamental qualities and possibilities of the medium. True, Kracauer argues that in its very artificiality and closure the historical drama compromises film's predisposition for capturing unstaged reality as an endless continuum: 'Whenever a film-maker turns the spotlight on a historical subject or ventures into the realm of fantasy', he warns, 'he runs the risk of defying the basic properties of his medium' (TOF: 77). But, given such dangers, Kracauer is also keen to explore how film-makers seek to 'mitigate the inherently uncinematic character of films that resuscitate the past' and alleviate their inevitable 'staginess and finiteness' (TOF: 79). Far from compromising Kracauer's cinematic imperatives, the 'Motion Picture Treatment' might better be understood as an exemplary cinematic compromise. Even a cursory consideration of the proposed film substantiates this thesis.

It is significant, for example, that the film's opening scene is the Parisian boulevard, since, as Kracauer repeatedly insists in *Theory of Film*, the metropolitan street with its crowds, distractions, contingencies and ephemera constitutes the most cinematic of subject matter.[10] Film not only has an 'elective affinity' for the city, it exhibits a special and 'unwavering susceptibility to the street' (TOF: 62). Moreover, in the dawdling duo of Halévy and Meilhac, we are immediately presented with the image of the flâneur, the great observer of the flow of modern urban life, whose predilection for the visual, for the fleeting and fortuitous, makes him an exemplary cinematic figure.[11] Indeed, let us follow them for a moment. The next scene finds Halévy and Meilhac entering Offenbach's house in the rue Laffitte. As they climb the stairs to his apartment, a growing din is audible. People are milling on the staircase. The hallway is crowded with journalists, theatre types, artists and dilettantes. Pushing through this throng into the salon, we notice Offenbach, surrounded by, yet seemingly oblivious of, the noisy hustle and bustle around him. Unperturbed, he sits at a table composing. In accordance with Kracauer's insistence on the primacy of the visual in film, these first images of Offenbach tell us much: he is at home here. From the boulevard to the salon, this is his social milieu, the creative atmosphere and essential raw material for his musical labours.[12] He is at the height of his powers and popularity amid the superficial 'joy and glamour' (JOF: 151) of the Second Empire. The operetta is inspired by this world – petty and pretentious, frivolous and fashionable, insincere and eccentric – and provides its signature. This is *'la vie parisienne'*.

These loud and lively opening scenes provide a compelling contrast with a sequence towards the end of the film (MPT: 20) which envisions the waning popularity of Offenbach's operettas amid the transformed social, cultural and political conditions of the 1870s. Images appear in 'rapid montage' (*Schnellmontage*) of the 1878 World Exhibition. A sandwich man appears, a figure who, according to Benjamin, is none other than the ruinous 'last incarnation' of the flâneur.[13] The camera follows him as he trudges along the boulevard past a stand publicizing a new invention: Edison's phonograph. We wonder what is to be the fate of the 'little work' of art, the operetta, in the age of mechanical reproduction. A carriage crosses the screen and, leaving the sandwich man behind, the camera follows the vehicle. It comes to a halt. In the background we see theatrical posters bearing the names of Johann Strauss and Charles Lecocq. There is no mention of Offenbach. The camera peers into the carriage – an ageing, failing Offenbach is its lone occupant. We recognize that Offenbach's world has been transformed, indeed, that it is no longer *his* world at all. He and his operettas are anachronisms. What is important here is that all this is conveyed not through captions or dialogue but through the use of simple street images. The film's narrative is advanced as the camera pursues moving figures and objects – crowds, flâneurs, sandwich men, passers-by, carriages, and so on. In other words, ideas are manifested as we follow the 'flow of life' on the boulevard. Such scenes suggest that, had it been filmed, Kracauer's Offenbach motion picture would have been far more cinematic than one might initially imagine. Indeed, I think Kracauer the film theorist would have rather approved of 'Offenbach: the Motion Picture'.

Let us rejoin Monsieur Offenbach in his salon. Above the hubbub of the assembled company we suddenly hear a snobbish young man recounting the latest rumours concerning the mutually destructive affair between Hortense Schneider and the ailing duc de Gramont-Caderousse. Halévy, and the camera, are alone in noticing that Offenbach has stopped writing. In the next scene, we encounter the unhappy lovers themselves. The camera pans through the rooms and corridors of the rowdy Café Anglais,[14] just as it previously made its way into

Offenbach's home. The camera struggles through crowds of dandies and demi-monde, *bon viveurs* and bohemians, snobs and society figures, know-it-alls and nonentities. Gramont-Caderousse is at the head of a group of boisterous revellers, making a drunken spectacle of himself.[15] He finally collapses. In the grey morning light, only Hortense Schneider has remained behind to tend to him.

What is the significance of such images? It seems to me that Kracauer's 'Motion Picture Treatment' presents imperial Paris as an empire of gossip. It appears as a cacophonous realm of chatter and conjecture, tittle-tattle and trivia, scandal and slander, speculation and rumour, a world of whispers delivered at full volume. Ironically, while the 'sole object was to kill time, not to give it a meaning' (JOF: 122), this craving for novelty, intrigue and distraction ensured precisely what it most feared: silence and boredom.[16] In the seamless movement between salon and street, café bar and boulevard, the opening scenes of the film suggest the blurring of public spaces and private lives, public lives and private spaces, the symbiosis of society figures and the popular press, artists and critics, celebrities and journalists, bourgeois and bohemian. These are all interlaced through the endless circulation of small talk. And in seating Offenbach so comfortably at the centre of this pantheon of prattle, this all too fragile house of visiting cards, Kracauer envisages him in a similar manner perhaps to Benjamin's 1929 image of Marcel Proust. For Benjamin, Proust's reflections offer incomparable insight into the aristocratic circles of *fin de siècle* Paris in which he moved as a 'satiated society' (SW2: 241). As Benjamin suggests: 'it was Proust's aim to construe the entire inner structure of high society as a physiology of chatter' (ibid.), and this is surely the best description of the initial scenes of Kracauer's proposed movie: a filmic 'physiology of chatter' by means of a panorama of chatterers.

If this is plausible, then it might lead us to reconsider two aspects of Kracauer's Offenbach book. Firstly, it might suggest a new way of interpreting the controversial notion of a *Gesellschaftsbiographie*. Rather than being understood as a 'biography of a society' in general terms, might this concept not better be seen as a depiction of the life and lives of 'society' in a narrower sense – that is, as particular social echelons and as intimate social circles, as 'polite society'? In German, of course, the word *Gesellschaft* can mean 'company' and 'social gatherings' as well as 'society' as a socio-economic and political totality. Admittedly, this would mean reading Kracauer against the grain of his own explicit intentions, as outlined in his 'preface' to the book, but this may be, as Benjamin claims, the most productive, indeed the only proper, way of reading anything anyway.

Secondly, the notion of a 'physiology of chatter' might lead us to revise our understanding of the style and structure of the Offenbach book and, in particular, Kracauer's continual reliance upon anecdotal material. Far from being mere 'old wives' tales', as Adorno was all too quick to complain, the anecdote serves as a device for the immanent unfolding of the innermost tendencies of a society nourished by hearsay and rumour. The use of anecdotes is, moreover, a critical technique for disclosing the distinctions and contradictions between surface appearances, perceptions and underlying realities, for unmasking the ideological pretensions and phantasmagorias of a particular era and class. This is absolutely decisive for Kracauer's 'Motion Picture Treatment': conceived as a series of anecdotal episodes highlighting the mismatch between what is and what seems to be, between words and deeds, the film fosters the possibilities of comic debunking to the full.[17]

In this sense, Halévy and Meilhac's initial encounter with Hortense sets the tone for everything that follows. After listening to the courtesan's histrionics, Meilhac is convinced that Schneider was born to play the role of *La Belle Hélène*, Helen of Troy, the epitome of female beauty. We laugh at the incongruity suggested by Meilhac's remark, and, as if to drive home the point, images of Hortense singing at the premiere of *La Belle Hélène* are intercut with the final moments of the dissolute Gramont-Caderousse dying alone in a squalid hotel room. But is Meilhac really joking? His conviction is actually sound, but only because the operetta itself is a satirical form in which nothing is as it seems and comic reversals and absurd contradictions are the order of the day. This is, after all, the topsy-turvy, operetta world of the Second Empire. Hortense *will indeed be* the perfect Helen of Troy for Offenbach's operetta.[18] Meilhac is telling us the truth, but we find it incredible. One is reminded here of one of Benjamin's radio scripts, a story concerned with bootlegging during the Prohibition era in the United States. An African-American boy walks along beside a train waiting in a station selling what he claims is 'iced tea' to the passengers. With a knowing smile and sly wink, they readily pay exorbitant prices in the belief, of course, that this 'iced tea' is actually alcohol. They are mortified to discover that this 'iced tea' is in fact iced tea. As Mehlman (1993: 7–12) points out in his discussion, notice is hereby given: things are exactly what they are and precisely what they are not. Everything is deception, trust nothing. This warning also applies to Kracauer's 'Motion Picture Treatment'.

The episode following the Café Anglais debauchery is the clearest example of this. The film presents, through the intercutting of two narratives, an anecdote concerning Offenbach's 'reception' at a little town on the Rhine while en route to the fashionable spa resort of Bad Ems.[19] The composer's stopover at the unnamed location unfortunately coincides with a visit by the lieutenant governor (*Regierungspraesident*) from Wiesbaden, who has failed to keep the engagement. Coincidentally in the company of the deputation sent to bring the indisposed dignitary, and with the local band playing music from *Orpheus in the Underworld*,

Offenbach steps off the Rhine steamer and greets the expectant crowds in the erroneous belief that *he* is being honoured. They in turn cheer the unwitting impostor and a festive procession ensues. Offenbach is duped and happy; the crowds are duped and happy. Everyone – save the embarrassed deputation – is duped and happy, temporarily at least. Offenbach finally realizes his mistake when asked by the local mayor to say a few words to commemorate the town's new gas lighting system. The now enlightened and humiliated composer makes a discreet exit from the proceedings.[20]

These German provincials are not the only ones fooled by appearances. Arriving in her cabriolet at the World Exhibition of 1867, Hortense is stopped by an attendant because she has inadvertently come to the entrance reserved for visiting royalty and nobility. Our quick-thinking heroine immediately announces that she is none other than la Grande Duchesse de Gerolstein – the eponymous character she was then playing – and the gate is opened with much servile bowing and scraping.[21]

While the film derives most of its comic force and critical edge from such ironic incidents, Kracauer is also not averse to inserting the occasional straightforward joke. It is 1871. On a Viennese street Offenbach chances upon and comes to the aid of the aged and impoverished Rudolf Zimmer, composer of the eight bars of waltz music that have haunted him since childhood. When Zimmer has suitably recovered, Offenbach asks him to play the waltz in its entirety. Seated at the piano in a hotel room, Zimmer immediately plays the first eight bars but then stops – he has forgotten the rest too. This whole sequence is intercut with images of the Paris Commune culminating in pictures of Paris ablaze and the Commune's bloody suppression.[22] In this intricate interlacing of narratives, a smile is brought to, and immediately wiped off, our faces.

The juxtaposing of reality and illusion, ridiculous discrepancies and reversals, farcical impersonations and misunderstandings, ironies, parodies, and jokes that fall flat – these were, of course, the very lifeblood of Offenbach's operettas. His stage works sought precisely the puncturing of pretension and the dispelling of phantasmagoria through comedy. And, as Kracauer observed, the Offenbach book was intended to partake of and correspond to this satirical spirit, this sense of the carnivalesque. So, too, was the Offenbach film. But one should be careful here. Although a comedy, and a musical one at that, Kracauer's 'Motion Picture Treatment' should not be thought of as an attempt to turn Offenbach's life into some kind of operetta and/or to reproduce the operetta on screen. The reason for this is clear: Kracauer's Offenbach film is, *contra* Jay, conceived as *cinematic*, not theatrical. In *Theory of Film*, Kracauer emphasizes the antithetical moments of the operatic and the cinematic: 'Opera on the screen is a collision of two worlds detrimental

to both' (TOF: 154). He then explicitly rejects two common film strategies for managing this clash: firstly, the 'canned opera' or 'photographed theater' (TOF: 155) approach, in which a stage performance is
simply recorded by the cameras. Not surprisingly, Kracauer condemns
this as wholly uncinematic. Worse still, though, is the attempt to fuse
film and opera, to create a spurious synthesis of realistic (that is, cinematic) and formative (artistic, theatrical) elements, to produce some
kind of *Gesamtkunstwerk*. Kracauer writes: 'As should be expected, this
allegedly superior whole invariably reveals itself as an eclectic compromise between irreconcilable entities – a sham whole distorting either
the opera or the film or both' (TOF: 154).[23]

Neither 'canned operetta' nor *Gesamtkunstwerk*, Kracauer's 'Motion
Picture Treatment' nevertheless sought to incorporate Offenbach's
music in multiple and complex ways, and this leads us to the very heart
of his proposed film. The Offenbach movie is conceived as a musical
film of a particular kind: not of the film musical variety, with characters
suddenly bursting into song and launching themselves into dance in
the midst of otherwise seemingly mundane activities – a genre which
Kracauer perhaps surprisingly endorses – but, rather, of the kind which
seeks 'to narrate the life of some virtuoso, composer or showman'
(TOF: 150), which integrates music as a 'component of the narrative'
and, with its images of the composer at work and rehearsal scenes,
presents music as a 'product of real life processes' (TOF: 151).[24] In the
'Motion Picture Treatment', music weaves in and out of the drama,
sometimes as background accompaniment linking together simultane-
ous or succeeding scenes, sometimes in the foreground as actual music
– as when a fragment of a performance is presented – and sometimes
as both: beginning with actual, synchronous music in the theatre, the
image of the stage then dissolves and, with the music still playing,
other images appear. The use of music from *La Belle Hélène* is typical.
We begin in Hortense Schneider's salon, where Offenbach is trying to
persuade the reluctant diva to play the operetta's eponymous heroine.[25]
With Offenbach at the piano playing an extract from the score to tempt
her, Schneider instinctively begins to sing ... cut to the premiere with
her on stage in the closing bars before the interval. The camera then
focuses on the intrigues of the celebrities and notables among the audience. The music begins playing again but, instead of the stage, we are
presented with a montage of shots of European capitals and theatrical
billboards suggesting the international success of the operetta[26] ... cut
to a Parisian hotel room and Gramont-Caderousse on his deathbed.
Now actual music, now commentative, now synchronous, now asynchronous, now in parallel,[27] now in counterpoint[28] – Offenbach's music
becomes the very glue which holds the anecdotes together, creating a
sense both of the ubiquity of this music and of how it was inextricably
interwoven with this society.

But there is more to it than this. Offenbach's music is no mere cinematic soundtrack. Kracauer's 'Motion Picture Treatment' makes continual use of one particular device: asynchronous, actual music. We hear music as it is being performed on stage but we do not see the performance itself. *La Belle Hélène* is a case in point, but there are also occasions when the camera seems wilfully to avoid focusing on the stage. At Bad Ems, for example, the singer Zulma Bouffar has scarcely opened her mouth before Offenbach leaves the theatre box – and we leave with him. Later, when Zulma sings a duet in the one-act *Lieschen und Fritzchen*, the camera is turned not on her, but on the audience watching her. In *Theory of Film* Kracauer argues that this deliberate *inattention* to actual musical performances has a paradoxical effect: it heightens the viewer's sensitivity to the music. In film one comes to an appreciation of music not so much through its direct representation as through a series of digressions and diversions, through interruption and disturbance, above all, through the alternation of concentration and distraction. Ironically, film does justice to music only when it stays true to its own cinematic imperatives and seemingly decentres it. Kracauer's example here is René Clair's 1931 film *Le Million*:

> loyalty to the medium might prove singularly rewarding. Precisely because it launches the spectator on visual pursuits, it might lead him to the kernel of the music he unavoidably neglects, so that he resembles the fairy-tale prince who, after a series of trials testing his devotion and steadfastness, ultimately finds his beloved at the most unexpected place. In the opera episode of LE MILLION the camera does not pay much attention to the fat singers and their love duet but literally turns its back on them, meandering through the painted stage world and focusing on the quarrelling lovers gone astray. We watch the reconciliation between the two, a pantomime to the sounds of the duet which ends with a fiery embrace; and we realize that the lovers are transported and driven into each other's arms by the enchanting voices and harmonies. And then something miraculous happens: absorbed in the sight of the lovers, we enter so completely into them that we are no longer aware of their presence but, as if we were they, yield to the impact of the duet. Having penetrated the images we find at their core, waiting for us, the very music we were forced to abandon. (TOF: 151–2)

Benjamin would surely have appreciated this passage. After all, for him, digression was the only genuine mode of illuminating the 'truth content' of the artwork, distraction the precondition for the technical mastery of the everyday object world. In his essay on Goethe's *Elective Affinities*, Benjamin emphasizes the necessity of circumspection and circumlocution in philosophical enquiry. We cannot approach philosophical ideas and truths directly but, rather, since these have their counterparts in the domain of art, only indirectly through the analysis of artworks. Benjamin presents us with an analogy here. Imagine encountering a shy, enigmatic, intriguing stranger: one wants to learn more, but direct questioning would be impolite and embarrassing. To avoid any such unpleasantness, one asks friends, relatives and neighbours, subtly, discreetly. From such sources we gain an impression of the stranger. This is how we approach philosophical truths – not through rude interrogation but rather through what others (artworks) have to say. Here, ironically, Kracauer's vision of a world of chatter and gossip becomes a metaphor for a method of critical analysis in which hearsay is transformed into a heuristic device. And perhaps this is how Offenbach's music is presented to us in both book and film versions. We are to develop an ever more intimate acquaintance with it but only by paying attention *elsewhere*: by exploring the social milieus from which it springs; by understanding the circumstances attending its rise to popularity; by gauging the responses it elicits from its admirers and detractors; by envisaging the conditions which will ensure its ultimate demise. In Kracauer's 'Motion Picture Treatment' we discover something of the truth of Offenbach's music through another medium: film. This is Kracauer's purpose. The camera turns its back on the music so that we may discover it anew. Adorno's bitterest complaint regarding Kracauer's book – that it ignores Offenbach's music – is characteristically perceptive and myopic. It does, but for good reason: what Kracauer presents in his Offenbach studies is the operetta 'recaptured' (TOF: 151). The 'Motion Picture Treatment' brings this sharply and unmistakably into focus. The panoramic quality and continual, anecdotal digressions of *Jacques Offenbach and the Paris of his Time* owe their origin not to the *dialectical imagination* prized by Adorno but, rather, to Kracauer's own *cinematic imagination*.

Dialectics have their place here too, though. Kracauer's enthusiasm for the film musical genre derives from his understanding of its inner dialectic. For him, the musical is to be valued not *despite* its theatricality but precisely *because* of it. By its very nature, the film musical is concerned with juxtaposing realistic episodes with staged flights of fancy and artifice. In so doing, the musical draws attention to and articulates the enduring tension at the heart of the film medium: 'Through its very structure', Kracauer writes, 'it illustrates the eternal struggle for supremacy between the realistic tendency, suggested by the threadbare intrigue, and the formative tendency, which finds its natural outlet in the songs' (TOF: 148). The musical alternates between the intellectual demand for narrative coherence and consistency (characteristic of the non-story film) and the emotional participation generated by fictional contrivances (typical of the story film). Kracauer writes:

> The conflict between these two antinomic moves, which are natural outlets for the realistic and formative tendencies respectively,

materializes in the very form of the musical. No sooner does the real-life intrigue of a musical achieve a certain degree of consistency than it is discontinued for the sake of a production number which often has been delineated at a prenatal stage, thereby corroding the intrigue from within. Musicals reflect the dialectic relation between the story film and the non-story film without ever trying to resolve it. This gives them an air of cinema. Penelope fashion, they eternally dissolve the plot they are weaving. The songs and dances they sport form part of the intrigue and at the same time enhance with their glitter its decomposition. (TOF: 213)

Kracauer's 'Motion Picture Treatment' is clearly more musical film than film musical. Nevertheless, his use of montage to counterpoise appearance and reality, anecdote and actuality, theatre stage and urban street,[29] operetta and operetta world, is clearly concerned with maintaining this same tension, with setting in motion this dialectical play of enchantment and disenchantment. And what emerges from and survives this process of dissolution – 'corroded intrigue' and 'glittering decomposition' – is the best possible description of the phantasmagoria of the Second Empire itself and of the remnants to be collected by a radical ragpicker. 'All that is solid melts into air'[30] – the 'air of cinema', that is. And in this evaporation lay Kracauer's aspiration that the Parisian 'dreamworld' of the nineteenth century might find its true expression in the Hollywood 'dream factory' of the twentieth.

3 Long Shot

In his writings on Baudelaire and the image of the metropolitan crowd, Benjamin draws a simple but important distinction: the representation of confusion is not the same as confused representation. Similarly, when reading Kracauer's writings on Offenbach one should remember that the examination of the superficial is not to be mistaken for superficial examination. Adorno's attitude indicates his own confusion on this point. His hostility is, in any case, understandable in other terms. In refraining from critical aesthetic judgements on Offenbach's music itself, and in illuminating the circumstances which brought it to fleeting prominence, Kracauer did what Adorno was so conspicuously incapable of: treat light music lightly. And it is Kracauer's deftness and wit that are so striking in the Offenbach writings: an irony and charm that correspond faithfully to his subject matter. In Kracauer, Offenbach's operetta finds not its abject apologist[31] but rather its most astute sociologist. It finds its would-be cinematographer, too. As the 'Motion Picture Treatment' suggests, Kracauer's work was informed by cinematic imperatives: he sought to set images in motion, in dance to the merry rhythms of Offenbach's melodies. Such music was the accompaniment to the 'flow of life' on the street, a score which found its perfect libretto in salon gossip. In envisaging the Parisian boulevard, in rendering the 'physiology of chatter', Kracauer understood the medium of film as a possible digression leading to the heart of the operetta. If it had been produced, his film would have constituted a popular entertainment portraying and penetrating the popular entertainment of the recent past. Perhaps it is as well that nothing came of it – just imagine Adorno's scornful letter addressed to Kracauer in Beverly Hills!

But, while Adorno failed to probe beneath the surface of Kracauer's work on Offenbach, we must come to appreciate its depths if it is to be anything other than a dead book and forgotten screenplay. I will spare the reader the obvious Orpheus analogies here. Suffice to say, if we are to appreciate Offenbach and the Paris of his time afresh, if we are to stumble upon Kracauer's writings anew, if they are to be 'recaptured', we too must make a detour – via Hollywood.

Part IV

FROM THE NEW WORLD: MONSTROUS STATES, MENTAL IMAGES

7

The Caligari Complex

Now nothing stands in the way of my long cherished ambition. At last I can put the Caligari theory to the test – I now shall soon know if this patient can be compelled to perform deeds he should shrink from in his normal waking state.

Can he be made to commit *murder*?

I must know. I will become Caligari.

(Notes found on the desk of the asylum director Dr Caligari)

1 A Backwards-Looking Prophet

First published in April 1947, *From Caligari to Hitler* arguably remains Siegfried Kracauer's most famous[1] and controversial book. It split the critics then,[2] and it continues to divide them now – to the extent that it is still discussed at all, that is.[3] But, whatever its intellectual merits and theoretical shortcomings, one thing, certainly the most important, is indisputable: it helped save the Kracauers' lives. In June 1939, following a correspondence[4] with John E. Abbott, then director of the Film Library at the New York Museum of Modern Art, Kracauer was offered the post of 'special research assistant' to undertake a project on the historical and sociological significance of German film. Working with the curator Iris Barry, Kracauer was occupied for the next six years in intensive archival research and repeated film screenings which ultimately resulted in the *Caligari* study. And it was precisely this guarantee of official – albeit temporary – employment and income[5] in America that was vital in finally securing the US entry visas enabling the Kracauers to escape from occupied France as late as February 1941, make their way across Spain, and finally depart on 15 April from Lisbon as third-class passengers on board the SS *Nyassa*. On 25 April 1941, they stepped ashore in New York to be greeted by Leo and Golde Löwenthal.[6] At the age of fifty-two, Kracauer's French exile was over; his American exile was just starting.

Both the *Offenbach* and the *Caligari* books are, albeit in different ways, characteristic of what one might term 'exile literature': the first, after all, deals with the life of a German-Jewish émigré in Paris of the Second Empire;[7] the second, published ten years later, is distinctively Janus-faced. In so many ways the very culmination of his various writings on Weimar culture and society, *Caligari* also constitutes his first major study of the cinematic medium which had so long fascinated him and which was to become the focus of his work in New York, eventually spanning three decades. Accordingly, Kracauer's *Caligari* is perhaps best understood in three main intellectual contexts.

Firstly, it elaborated his critical vision of metropolitan mass culture initially pioneered in journalistic form for the *Frankfurter Zeitung* during the 1920s and 1930s. Indeed, 'firmly rooted in a middle class mentality' (CAL: 8), popular German cinema provided a temporary refuge for all those 'spiritually shelterless' white-collar employees whose everyday lives and tastes were the subject of *Die Angestellten*. And the connection with these Weimar writings is methodological as well as thematic. It is in the 'Mass Ornament' essay that Kracauer first developed the notion that popular cultural phenomena, film among them, could be understood as the 'surface-level expressions' of more fundamental social, political and economic tendencies and processes – indeed, of the prevailing spirit or rather *spiritlessness* of modern times. This insight proves absolutely decisive for Kracauer's attempt to reconstruct a 'psychological history' of German cinema. Indeed, the book is premised on the assumption that film constitutes a privileged medium for the analysis of a historically specific and ever changing collective national unconscious. He gives two reasons for this: on the one hand, he observes, films are always collaborative ventures and products and, contrary to theories of the directorial *auteur*, never the vision of any one particular individual; on the other hand, for reasons of commercial necessity, films are intended to appeal to widely shared tastes and sentiments so as to 'satisfy existing mass desires' (CAL: 5). Given these premises, Kracauer argues, one may examine films for recurrent themes and motifs which, subject to critical interpretation, disclose common sensibilities and longings.[8] Accordingly, *From Caligari to Hitler* was and remains – however naïve and contentious – a pioneering attempt at some form of *collective psychoanalysis of Weimar cinema*. And so it is that, as we will see in chapter 10, while Kracauer's *Offenbach* studies certainly reward close comparison with Benjamin's *Arcades Project*, his *Caligari* study also bears a close affinity, certainly methodologically if not thematically.[9] For Kracauer, it is not so much the luxurious interiorized shopping streets of Second Empire Paris as the opulent picture palaces of Berlin, cinematic capital of the 1920s, wherein the collective dreams of an epoch take to the screen as haunting phantasmagoria, that constitute the *Traumhäuser* of modernity.[10]

Secondly, while it is important to note the 'substantial continuity' (CAL: xxi) with Kracauer's Weimar writings, a significant shift in perspective is also discernible. Many of the films discussed in the *Caligari* study were ones he had already reviewed for the *Frankfurter Zeitung* at the time of their release.[11] The extensive collections of German film held in MOMA's Film Library enabled Kracauer to watch them again, but this time in a different guise: no longer as a film *critic*, but now as a film *historian* or, rather, as a *film psychohistorian*. With rare exceptions, Kracauer refrained from quoting his own earlier reviews,[12] and several of his evaluations changed in retrospect.[13] Indeed, it would have been extraordinary had his understanding of such films, now filtered through the lens of the most traumatic events and experiences of the twentieth century, remained unaltered, even if such reappraisals seem inferior to his original impressions and insights.[14] As critics have pointed out in no uncertain terms, the problem here is that Kracauer's revisitations and revisions of Weimar films for the *Caligari* project were constrained by the demands of his overarching argument and the teleology that structured the entire study. In retrospect, the films were chosen and tailored to fit his central thesis, closing down any alternative lines of interpretation.[15]

In the light of such concerns, Quaresima claims Kracauer's approach, in which 'history is read backwards and made to follow in its own footsteps' (CAL: xxxviii), is nothing other than 'retroactive historicism' (CAL: xxxiv) – that is to say, telling the past supposedly 'as it really was' but with the considerable benefit of hindsight.[16] I would suggest a more generous reading: Kracauer's concern with a past that is already known or, to be more exact, with the catastrophic future of a past that is itself now also past, corresponds to the situation of Roland Barthes in *Camera Lucida* (1993). When looking at Alexander Gardner's photograph of the condemned Lewis Payne, or the 'Winter Garden' image of his own mother, Barthes becomes a 'backwards-looking prophet' pondering 'over a catastrophe that has already occurred. Whether or not the subject is already dead, every photograph is this catastrophe' (1993: 96). Such a position is not so much a *problem* for Barthes as *the only one available* for the observer of the photographic image; it is, indeed, this inescapable temporal vortex or vertigo of the picture that constitutes the 'ecstasy' of photography (1993: 119). To be clear: for Barthes, this is not a prohibition on reading the image of the past in the present but rather the very reason for doing so at all. Perhaps Kracauer likewise offers us something akin to an *ecstasy* of Weimar film.

Thirdly, the *Caligari* book developed in parallel with the exiled Institut's various studies in authoritarianism, propaganda and prejudice initiated in the 1930s and continued in the USA during the 1940s under the auspices of the American Jewish Committee. Kracauer was a not insignificant figure in this work. As corrections were being completed on the *Offenbach* book, he was commissioned by Horkheimer in January 1937[17] to write an essay on fascist propaganda for publication in the *Zeitschrift für Sozialforsching*.[18] Eventually entitled 'Totalitarian Propaganda' ('Die totalitäre Propaganda'), this substantial text was to be so radically edited and attenuated by Adorno during the course of 1938 that an incensed Kracauer could only denounce the final version as a betrayal of his original argument and refuse publication under his name. All this palaver exacerbated the damage already done to their relationship by the scathing reception given to the Offenbach *Gesellschaftsbiographie*. With the rift repaired and relations restored by the time of his arrival in New York, however, Kracauer was once again involved in collaboration with the Institut and charged with the scripting of a screenplay for a 'test film project' (*Below the Surface*), a social psychological experiment designed to uncover latent anti-Semitism among American student audiences. As we will see in the next chapter, in using film to probe for the deep-seated predispositions and prejudices of viewers, this project involved something of an inversion of the underlying principles and methods of the *Caligari* study. Indeed, it is no surprise that, although Kracauer's 'psychological history' ends with the accession to power of Hitler in 1933, the final edition of the book in 1947 included as a supplement a 1942 study entitled 'Propaganda and the Nazi War Film'. This suggests his own frame of reference: the hours of painstaking research and endless screenings of obscure films for *Caligari* were prompted neither by mere intellectual curiosity nor by financial expediency, but rather were envisaged as an ongoing contribution to the Allied war effort and the defeat of Nazi Germany and, thereafter, to ensuring no repetition of such genocidal totalitarianism.[19]

2 Daydream Believers

Back in 1927 Kracauer could little have imagined that, in penning his mini-series of sketches satirizing both the clichéd plots of contemporary mainstream popular cinema and the naïve appetites and aspirations of their audiences, he would be sowing the conceptual seeds for an analysis twenty years later of those authoritarian predilections and predispositions of an entire nation that would usher in National Socialist totalitarianism within just six years and culminate in the Holocaust the following decade. In retrospect, though, and mindful of Hannah

Arendt's famous thesis as to the 'banality of evil', the connection between all those little shopgirls and little office boys – holding hands in the cinema, dabbing away a tear or two, dreaming of Riviera weddings, breathing easily again only when all those conflicts and complications besetting on-screen lovers were at last overcome – and Hitler's 'willing executioners'[20] should come as less of a shock. Of course, neither Kracauer's feuilleton pieces nor his early film reviews identify proto-fascistic tendencies as such amid the powdered noses and morally pink complexions ensconced in the movie theatres of Frankfurt and Berlin. Nevertheless, the 'Little Shopgirls' episodes do contain two key ideas that were to prove decisive for his later re-reading of Weimar film and filmgoers.

The first of these concerns the ideological character of commercial film production in the context of the newly emergent culture industries. Kracauer recognizes that film as a commodity form is 'financed by corporations, which must pinpoint the tastes of the audience at all costs in order to make a profit' (MOR: 291). As a result, films are concocted in the image of the proclivities and preoccupations of their publics in so far as these are identified by the producers themselves. As a result: 'Films are the mirror of the prevailing society' (ibid.), or rather, and more specifically, in keeping with Kracauer's increasingly Marxist leanings in the late 1920s, they present a vision of society which is imbued with the values, and which enhances the interests, of the dominant classes within capitalism. 'Society', he notes, 'is much too powerful for it to tolerate any movies except those with which it is comfortable. Film must reflect society whether it wants to or not' (MOR: 292). Even when the settings, characters and plots seem most innocuous or outlandish – in fantasy movies, epic adventures or historical melodramas[21] where 'things are pretty unrealistic' – contemporary 'films do not ... cease to reflect society. On the contrary: the more incorrectly they present the surface of things, the more correct they become and the more clearly they mirror the secret mechanism of society' (ibid.).

Secondly, while individual films themselves may vary enormously as to characters, costumes, historical and geographical settings, and so forth, there may be a number of recurrent genres, plots, devices and narrative schemes. Kracauer sees these shared tendencies and trajectories as indicators of underlying wishes and desires among cinema audiences. In studying such unsuspected regularities and patterns, as with other 'surface-level expressions', the conscious *and unconscious* predispositions of spectators as a collective entity may be discerned and deciphered. In other words, films seek to appease, and in some way screen, the otherwise inaccessible contents of the minds of audiences. It is here that Kracauer's ideas start to take a more complex turn, away from the idea that film simply reflects some independent and pre-existing societal reality. His version of the relationship between film and society becomes more intricate and intriguing – less a case of mere *reflection* and more one of complex, prismatic *refraction*. Indeed, films *imagine* (that is to say, *turn into images*) the *daydreams* of their audiences.[22] Popular films depict a *collective dreamworld* which may be subject to the same kind of psychoanalytical investigation and interpretation as dreams themselves – this insight is decisive for the *Caligari* study in underpinning the very conception of a 'psychological history' of German cinema. Indeed, even in 1927 there is already an anticipation that the whole of Weimar society might be stretched out on the analyst's couch and subject to Freud's remarkable 'talking cure':

> In order to investigate today's society, one must listen to the confessions of the products of its film industries. They are all blabbing a rude secret, without really wanting to. In the endless sequence of films, a limited number of typical themes recur again and again; they reveal how society wants to see itself. The quintessence of these film themes is at the same time the sum of the society's ideologies, whose spell is broken by means of the interpretation of the themes. The series 'The Little Shopgirls Go to the Movies' is conceived as a small collection of samples whose textbook cases are subjected to moral casuistry. (MOR: 294)

In retrospect, as with Dr Caligari himself, German film and its audiences would prove to be a rather more complex and convoluted case than first thought.

The *Caligari* book makes three important additions to this embryonic analytical and interpretive scheme. Firstly, as is made clear in Kracauer's opening comments, it is not only the collective reception by the 'anonymous multitude' (CAL: 5) but also the *collaborative production* of films that is both distinct and definitive for cinema: 'films are never the product of an individual' (ibid.). Combining the work of screenwriters, actors, lighting and staging crews, set designers, camera operatives and make-up artists with that of editors, directors and producers, it is this collective technical-industrial character of film that 'tends to exclude arbitrary handling of screen material, suppressing individual peculiarities in favor of traits common to many people' (ibid.).

Additionally, in the *Caligari* book, Kracauer goes beyond the consideration of standardized film storylines and stock characters to a rather more sophisticated analysis of cinematic techniques, styles, images, figures and motifs. In discerning these as signs and symbols, his approach has been intriguingly aligned with the work of Erwin Panofsky,[23] pioneer of iconology as a method for reading the polyvalent imagery invested in medieval and Renaissance painting.[24] Kracauer approaches filmic motifs in terms of their 'symptomatic rather than aesthetic value' (CAL: 56) – that is to say, as "visible hieroglyphs" (cited in CAL: 7) whose decipherment reveals the 'deep psychological predispositions' (CAL: v) and unconscious motivations of the time. In his discussion of the *Caligari* film itself, for example, he points to the repeated appearance of the circle and of circularity (spirals, whirlpools, vortexes and carousels) as figures of chaos and confusion.[25] Similarly, the setting of the fairground as portrayed in both *Caligari* and *Waxworks* (*Das Wachsfigurenkabinett*) four year later also stands for labyrinthine incoherence and disorder, with its milling crowds, discordant sounds and sensory tumult.[26]

Finally, Kracauer comes to emphasize the distinctive *national* characteristics of film in *Caligari*: 'The films of a nation reflect its mentality in a more direct way than other artistic media' (CAL: 5). While in 1927 he points to the homogeneity of both films – whether American or German – and audiences, twenty years later his focus is unequivocally *German* cinema and its petit-bourgeois spectators. For the book's detractors, this exclusive concern with the products of the German film industry is a major weakness. It disregards the inconvenient fact that Weimar cinema audiences were enjoying American westerns, slapstick comedies, romantic dramas and historical romps, a circumstance to which so many of Kracauer's own film reviews during the 1920s attest. It is legitimate then to ask exactly how popular German films were with German audiences in the 1920s compared with American movies. Was there no cross-fertilization of themes and ideas? Moreover, from the other starting point, were these German films only ever intended for German audiences? Was there no concern with international markets and appeal to mass tastes in other German-speaking countries and beyond?

Kracauer was certainly mindful of such issues – the *Caligari* book opens with the startling impact of German films on American, British and French audiences following the lifting of wartime embargoes from 1920 onwards[27] – and they are clearly awkward for his central argument. His principal response, though, is to stress the uniqueness and specificity of the German historical situation. In his 'Notes on the Planned History of the German Film', sent to Panofsky with a letter dated 16 October 1942, Kracauer states:

> Many a German film succeeded in influencing the American and French cinema, and on the whole the German contribution to the general history of the film can scarcely be overestimated. But it is certainly not for this reason alone that the project devotes itself to the German effort. Decisive rather is that German films, more directly than the films of other nations, point to the background from which they emerge. That they express and mirror in so immediate a manner the world in which they grow up is chiefly the outcome of Germany's history since the last world war. It is as if the despair after the war and the violence of the interior struggles had removed some of the opaque layers which, in more normal times, separate the course of art from that of contemporary reality. German films are particularly transparent. (KPB: 16–17)

And, with respect to audiences, he is at pains to distinguish his approach from any notion of immutable transhistorical collective (Jungian) archetypes:

> To speak of the peculiar mentality of a nation by no means implies the concept of a fixed national character. The interest here lies exclusively in such collective dispositions or tendencies as prevail within a nation at a certain stage of its development. What fears and hopes swept Germany immediately after World War I? Questions of this kind are legitimate because of their limited range; incidentally, they are the only ones which can be answered by an appropriate analysis of the films of the time. In other words, this book is not concerned with establishing some national character pattern allegedly elevated above history but it is concerned with the psychological pattern of a people at a particular time. (CAL: 8)

For Kracauer, the 'secret history' (CAL: 11) disclosed by Weimar cinema is conceived as nothing less than the exposure of the 'German soul' (CAL: 3) between 1919 and 1933.

3   Screening the Soul

Kracauer states: 'CALIGARI shows the "Soul at Work"' (CAL: 72). The reference to the (German) 'soul' here and elsewhere in his text[28] is both striking and significant. It should remind us of Simmel's account of Rembrandtian portraiture and the artist's attempt to depict the inner light imbuing the souls of those seventeenth-century Amsterdamers. This in turn should alert the reader to an important point that has been largely overlooked by commentators and critics: the *Caligari* study is the continuation not only of Kracauer's Weimar writings on mass culture and film but also of his earlier preoccupation with the manifestation and representation of inner life in visual media. The 1947 book is another episode in Kracauer's engagement with the thematic complex addressed some thirty years earlier in his 'On Expressionism' essay. This is not just because the *Caligari* film itself, in order to portray the sense of disequilibrium, disorientation and distortion of a crazed mind, famously used Expressionist sets and designs as backdrops. It is because, while the language has now shifted from that of *Lebensphilosophie* (soul, spirit, the manifold of inner life) to the terminology of a rudimentary psychoanalysis (dream, double, the unconscious, regression), the *expressivity* of cultural phenomena in relation to individuals and collectivities remains the very heart of Kracauer's intellectual enterprise.

Mixing, then, the vocabularies of metaphysics and medicine, of *Geist* and *Gestalt*,[29] Kracauer's *Caligari* study presents a curious collective case-history, one marked by all manner of delusion, disturbance and derangement. The seventeenth-century Dutch soul of illumination and indomitable faith in God captured on canvas by Rembrandt finds its antithesis in the morose doubts and existential uncertainties of the gloomy German soul found on the Weimar cinema screen. Above all, the German mentality during the 1920s and 1930s is characterized by forms of irrationalism and psychological retrogression: immature fears of self-determination and responsibility; a paralysis of critical and reasoning faculties; and a search for solace in sentimentalism, romanticism and fate. In its flight from the spectre of genuine freedom, the German psyche, Kracauer argues, was only too willing to embrace the authoritarianism and totalitarianism to which it had long been predisposed and for which German film-makers had readied and reconciled it.[30]

In tracing this trajectory, Kracauer proffers a controversial cinematic chronology dividing German film production into four phases based primarily on the fluctuating socio-economic and political conditions of the time: the 'archaic period' (1895–1918); the immediate post-war era (1918–24); the 'stabilized period' (1924–9); and the pre-Hitler years (1930–3). Significantly, the history of German film is not to be recounted immanently – that is to say, in terms of changes and developments in cinematic technologies, techniques, practices, aesthetics or themes. Rather, Kracauer seeks where possible to map these aspects directly onto the prevailing societal and collective psychological circumstances they express.

Although 'It was only after the first World War that the German cinema really came into being' (CAL: 15), with the foundation of Ufa (Universum Film AG) as an incipient instrument of war propaganda in 1917, Kracauer's 'psychological history' opens with a consideration of the 'forebodings' of the 'archaic period' up to 1918. From the veritable 'junk heap of archaic films' (CAL: 28), distinguished only by the 'fascinating personality' (CAL: 26) of the Danish actress Asta Nielsen, he selects four movies of interest: two from 1913 featuring sinister doppelgänger (Paul Wegener's *Der Student von Prag*[31] and Max Mack's *Der Andere*); and two presenting the mayhem attending the creation and destruction of monstrous figures (*Der Golem*, another Wegener film, from 1915, and Otto Rippert's 1916 *Homunculus*). In the case of the 1913 films, Kracauer contends, the figure of the demonic double – for Otto Rank, the definitive figure of the psychoanalytic uncanny – is to be understood as the introjection of structural contradictions and societal conflicts into individual psychological tensions.[32] These figures of duality and bifurcation serve to dramatize on screen the irreconcilable imperatives tearing the bourgeois psyche asunder, ones which are echoed later in the Weimar years in the acute predicament of white-collar employees: middle-class antagonism towards the exclusionary imperial order, with its autocratic pomp and aristocratic privileges, compounded by fear of proletarian agitation and revolution. Kracauer writes:

> The opposition of the bourgeoisie to the imperial regime grew, at times, sufficiently acute to overshadow its hostility towards the workers, who shared the general indignation over the semi-absolutist institutions in Prussia, the encroachments of the military set and the foolish doings of the Kaiser. ... Yet notwithstanding this dualism the imperial government stood for economic and political principles which even the liberals were not unwilling to accept. Face to face with their conscience, they had to admit that they identified themselves with the very ruling class they opposed. (CAL: 30)

The German petite bourgeoisie was not merely 'spiritually shelterless' – it was schizophrenic to boot.

Monstrous creatures left to find their way in a world which treats them with contempt, the Golem and the Homunculus appear to Kracauer as embodiments of bourgeois fears and frustrations and the perennial failure of this class to recognize its interdependence and realize its independence:[33]

> The Germans resembled Homunculus: they themselves had an inferiority complex, due to an historic development which proved detrimental to the self-confidence of the middle class. ... The middle-class strata were in a state of political immaturity against which they dreaded to struggle lest they further endanger their already insecure social condition. This retrogressive conduct provoked a psychological stagnation. Their habit of nurturing the intimately associated sensations of inferiority and isolation was as juvenile as their inclination to revel in dreams of the future. (CAL: 33)

Interesting though these early films may be, it is those in the aftermath of defeat (1918–24), with the German 'soul wavering between tyranny and chaos' (CAL: 74), that constitute Kracauer's principal concern and point of departure. Foremost among these is, of course, the eponymous *Das Cabinet des Dr Caligari* (Robert Wiene, 1919).

4   The Casebook of Dr Caligari

Based on 'an outspoken revolutionary story' (CAL: 64) co-written by the Czech Hans Janowitz and the Austrian Carl Mayer as a pacifist, anti-authoritarian text in the wake of the Great War, *The Cabinet of Dr Caligari* opens with an inter-title telling of 'an 11th century myth' in which a mountebank known by the name of Caligari was able to exert a hypnotic control over a somnambulist, transforming him into a deadly instrument of his murderous bidding. The first scene of the film presents the viewer with the interior of a walled garden where a young man (a student, Francis, played by Hans Fehér) and a more elderly companion are seated on a bench. A strange young woman, dressed in a long white gown and seemingly in a trance, wanders past them, and Francis tells the old man she is his 'betrothed' (Jane, played by Lil Dagover). He then begins to speak of his 'remarkable' experiences in his hometown of Holstenwall, to which the viewer is now transported in the form of an Expressionistic backdrop. A travelling fair has arrived on the outskirts of the town, bringing with it the sinister figure of Dr Caligari (Werner Kraus), who, venturing into Holstenwall in search of an official permit from the authorities, is treated by the haughty town clerk with condescension and contempt. Another young student, Alan (Hans von Twardowsky), bored with his books and craving distraction, persuades his friend Francis to go along to sample the pleasures of the fair. They come upon Caligari's tent, where the showman is now inviting the passing crowds in to see the bizarre figure of 'Cesare the somnambulist' (Conrad Veidt), who, having purportedly slept for twenty-five years, is about to awaken. Back in the town, the corpse of the murdered town clerk is discovered. Meanwhile, at the fair, Alan and Francis are among the many who have thronged into Dr Caligari's tent. Standing in a coffin-like box, the 'cabinet', Cesare opens his eyes at his master's command. The astonished onlookers are encouraged by Caligari to ask questions about their future, since 'Cesare knows all secrets'. Alan jauntily steps forward but is aghast when, in reply to his foolish question 'How long shall I live?', he receives the terrible answer 'The time is short. You die at dawn.' Francis leads his shocked friend away and they return to town, where they are joined by Jane, the woman they both love. That night, Alan is murdered in his bed by a knife-wielding shadowy figure. Accompanied by Francis, Jane's father, Dr Olsen, leads the investigation, questioning Caligari and scrutinizing the sleepwalker in his cabinet, before events take another turn with suspicion thrown on a burglar, who, caught with dagger in hand prowling the nocturnal streets, nevertheless protests his innocence with respect to the killings. After Alan's funeral, Francis goes under cover of darkness to Caligari's tent to see what he can discover. Cesare creeps into Jane's house and abducts her, but her screams alert the household and they all give chase. Cesare drops the young woman and collapses. Francis is mystified: 'It can't have been Cesare. I've been watching him for hours, asleep in his box.' But with the somnambulist now safely incarcerated in a police cell, Francis and the authorities revisit Caligari and, discovering a dummy in the box, realize the deception. Francis follows the fleeing Caligari to a nearby psychiatric asylum. On enquiry, Francis discovers to his horror that, far from being an escaped patient from the institution, Caligari is none other than its respected director. Managing to convince the doctors of his tale, Francis gains access to Caligari's office and case-notes, which tell of the director's obsession with the medieval myth of Caligari and the opportunity when a somnambulist is admitted as a patient to test the hypothesis: that, in such a condition, the 'patient can be compelled to perform deeds he should shrink from in his normal waking state'. When the news comes in that the escapee Cesare has been found dead in a ravine, and the body is brought before him, Caligari collapses. The doctors seize him and lead him away into a cell, where orderlies secure him with a straitjacket. And, at this moment, we return to the opening scene once more as Francis concludes his tale: 'Today he is a raving madman chained to his cell.' Kracauer notes: 'The revolutionary meaning of the story reveals itself unmistakably at the end with the disclosure of the psychiatrist as Caligari: reason overpowers unreasonable power, insane authority is symbolically abolished' (CAL: 65).

Well and good – only this is not the end of the film. As the two men rise from the bench on which they were sitting, we realize that we are in the courtyard of the asylum, with the inmates wandering to and fro. To one side stands a Cesare-like figure with a doll; Jane sits transfixed. Francis points out: 'See, there is Cesare. If you let him prophesy for you, you will die.' He whispers to the young woman: 'Jane, I love you ... when will you marry me?' And all becomes clear: *Francis is one of the patients*. The man we have come to know as 'Dr Caligari', now shorn of much of the ghastly make-up, steps into the courtyard. He is indeed the director of the institution but an evil monster only in the troubled imagination of the unfortunate inmate. Francis screams: 'He is Caligari!' as he attacks the kindly director, before being overpowered by doctors and orderlies and led away to the very cell that Dr Caligari occupied at the close of Francis's tale. 'Caligari' calms the patient and is now optimistic: 'At last I recognize his mania. He believes me to be the mythical Caligari. Astonishing! But I think I know how to cure him now.' The film ends with a close-up of the face of 'Dr Caligari'.

So, what is the significance of this film for Kracauer? Why does it constitute a decisive moment in the history of Weimar cinema? The answer – and here Kracauer follows the account provided by Janowitz's memoirs – is that the framing of the story – the scenes of Francis in the asylum which book-end his narrative – were *the additions of the film-makers*. The original story by Janowitz and Mayer, now transformed into the delusional account of an asylum inmate, was intended as the radical critique of authority and control, of the ruthless tyrant who manipulates the unwary and vulnerable into committing horrific acts against their own will and better judgement, who dispatches unfortunate others to kill and be killed. Caligari stands for all the arrogant politicians and military leaders of Europe who, from the comfort of their ministerial offices and war rooms, sent so many thousands of young men, sleepwalking to patriotic anthems and jingoistic rhetoric, to their deaths across the battlefields of the Great War. According to Kracauer: 'The original story was an account of real horrors; Wiene's version transforms that account into a chimera concocted and narrated by the mentally deranged Francis' (CAL: 66).

What should have been a denunciation of the deadly abuses of power by a tyrannical figure is utterly reconfigured: the director of the asylum is no longer an obsessive, murderous arch-villain but rather a benign, paternal therapist who can now cure the unfortunate patient. Kracauer comments: 'Janowitz and Mayer knew why they raged against the framing story: it perverted, if not reversed, their intrinsic intentions. While the original story exposed the madness inherent in authority, Wiene's CALIGARI glorified authority and convicted its antagonist of madness. A revolutionary film was thus turned into a conformist one' (CAL: 66–7). Little wonder that the writers refused all association with the film. And little wonder, too, given the fate of his own 'Totalitarian Propaganda' essay at the hands of Adorno ten years earlier, that Kracauer was sensitive to the consequences of having one's work rewritten by others who self-righteously claimed to know better, and was accordingly sympathetic to the stance adopted by the co-authors.

However, as Quaresima points out (CAL: xliii), the veracity of Janowitz's own account has been called into question since the rediscovery of the original screenplay. This itself contains a framing device: ensconced on the terrace of a country house, and for the amusement of gathered friends, Francis relates the familiar tale at Jane's instigation. While the final pages remain lost, it seems highly likely that the film's conclusion would return once again to Francis, Jane and others on the terrace. This inconsistency prompts Quaresima to ask some pertinent questions: Were there really any unauthorized changes to the script? How radical was the story in the first place? Does the film really end as an outright celebration of authority? Perhaps, as he suggests, the concluding shot of Caligari's face is more ambiguous, since 'we can no longer tell whether he is a curing psychiatrist or a triumphant killer' (CAL: xliv). While these questions are certainly legitimate, their significance for the validity and credibility of Kracauer's argument is less clear. There is an enormous gulf between the two alternative framing devices: Francis as member of the amiable landed gentry regaling friends with his earlier experiences is a very different narrator from Francis as psychiatric patient pacing the asylum courtyard, attacking its benevolent director. If anything, far from undercutting the tale, the country house scenes might add credence to the testimony – these are now the memories of an established and reputable mature gentleman, not the fancies of a young and impressionable student. Whatever role Janowitz did or did not play in the proceedings, the crux of Kracauer's argument surely holds.

5 In Caligari's Footsteps

Kracauer's interest in *Caligari* extends beyond the issue of the framing device to the fiendish figure of the evil doctor himself: 'Caligari is a very specific premonition in the sense that he uses hypnotic power to force his will upon his tool[34] – a technique foreshadowing, in content and purpose, that manipulation of the soul which Hitler was the first to practice on a gigantic scale' (CAL: 72–3). As such, Caligari constitutes one of a whole 'procession' of screen 'tyrants' in the ensuing years, most notably F. W. Murnau's vampyric *Nosferatu* (1922), the notorious criminal mastermind *Dr Mabuse* (1922) and the character of Jack the Ripper, who stalks the fairgrounds in *Waxworks* (1924). But these were not the only films of the time suggesting that, when confronted with the alternatives of despotic domination or anarchy and chaos, the German mind would turn in upon itself and seek solace in authority and order. There were other premonitions of totalitarianism. In a genre Kracauer designates as 'films of fate', audiences were treated to the consequences of human passions and instinctual life. His example here is Fritz Lang's *Die Nibelungen* (1924), with its doom-laden Germanic legends reworked in Wagnerian fashion to form a bombastic mytho-logical spectacle. Kracauer unmistakably echoes his earlier critique of the mass ornament, with its elimination of the individual as auton-omous subject, as the precursor of the National Socialist 'aestheticizing of politics'.[35] In Lang's epic narrative and monumental compositions, with actors reduced to mere 'accessories of primeval landscapes or vast buildings' (CAL: 94), one witnesses

> the complete triumph of the ornamental over the human ... Absolute authority asserts itself by arranging people under its domination in pleasing designs. This can also be seen in the Nazi regime, which mani-fested strong ornamental inclinations in organizing masses. Whenever Hitler harangued the people, he surveyed not so much hundreds of thousands of listeners as an enormous ornament consisting of hundreds of thousands of particles. TRIUMPH OF THE WILL, the official Nazi film of the Nuremberg Party Convention in 1934, proves that in shaping their mass-ornaments the Nazi decorators drew inspiration from NIBELUNGEN. SIEGFRIED's theatrical trumpeters, showy steps, and authoritarian human patterns reappear, extremely magnified, in the modern Nuremberg pageant. (CAL: 94–5)[36]

Even in apparently 'escapist' films, mythological powers and ominous portents are not lacking. Kracauer focuses on the 'mountain films', a popular genre throughout the 1920s and early 1930s initiated by Dr Arnold Fanck. Pioneering the use of outdoor filming, these started life as sporting films profiling and celebrating the brave feats of mountaineers, skiers and other alpinists but, not content with documenting such achievements, increasingly developed fictional plots and storylines: tales of survival against the odds, avalanches, courageous rescues and narrow escapes. In mixing the 'idolatry of glaciers and rocks' (CAL: 112) with the daring exploits of heroic adventurers, such films became 'half-monumental, half sentimental concoctions' (CAL: 257) vaunting 'an antirationalism on which the Nazis could capitalize' (CAL: 112).[37]

Kracauer's account of films of the immediate post-war years (1918–24) sets the fundamental terms and tenor of his central thesis. As he proceeds chronologically with his analysis of movies produced during the years of relative economic stability in the mid-1920s, and then on through the catastrophic economic crises of 1929 and into the immediate pre-Hitler period, this argument is subject to ever more exemplification and some further elaboration. The films of the mid-1920s, Kracauer contends, demonstrate an all-pervasive sense of intellectual inertia and paralysis, as exemplified in the uncritical and apolitical *Neue Sachlichkeit*[38] of Ruttmann's experiment in 'rhythmic montage' *Berlin – Die sinfonie der Großstadt* (1927);[39] in the 'pompous ornamentation' (CAL: 149) of Lang's *Metropolis* (1926);[40] and in the half-hearted rebelliousness and sentimentality of the cliché-ridden 'street film' genre, melodramas in which middle-class adolescent sons, frustrated by bourgeois niceties, run off to live fleetingly like bohemians among the lumpenproletariat and demi-monde before, recognizing harsh realities, realizing their own responsibilities, they return older and wiser to the fold of their relieved families.[41] These tame and tedious films pandered to the need for escapism, distraction and the alleviation of boredom that was central to the demands of the white-collar employees, whose significance is reiterated once more:

> Compared to the workers with their firm beliefs and hopes, these three and a half million employees were mentally shelterless; all the more so as the middle class itself had begun to falter. They filled the cities and belonged nowhere. Considering their crucial position within the social structure, much depended upon their reactions. The films would have to take notice of them. (CAL: 132)

In so doing, the films of the 'stabilized period' evinced a 'morally pink complexion' (TSM: 38).

The economic collapse of 1929 brought an end to this cinematic stagnation. True, the early 1930s did witness some politically progressive films: pacifist films such as G. W. Pabst's *Westfront 1918* (1930), 'timid heresies' (CAL: 223) critiquing authority such as Leontine Sagan's *Mädchen in Uniform* (1931), and more radical visions such as Slatan Dudow's famous *Kuhle Wampe* (1930). But as protests and provocations these were muted, flawed and compromised. Kracauer contrasts their frailty and incoherence with a much more formidable series of films, the 'national epics', in which the spirit of youthful rebelliousness is transformed into heroic patriotism and martial duty: the war films of Luis Trenker, the glut of Napoleonic costume dramas, and a series of 'Fridericus' films[42] eulogizing self-sacrifice, national liberation and charismatic dictatorship. These ultimately reprised the fundamental tension besetting the German bourgeoisie:

> The moral of the Fridericus films was to submit unconditionally to absolute authority. Here a contradiction arises. On the one hand, a majority of Germans – in particular middle-class Germans – tried to fend off socialist notions by insisting upon the idealistic concept of the autonomous individual. On the other hand, the same people were keen on giving up individual autonomy in favour of total dependence upon an autocratic ruler, provided, of course, that he prevent any encroachments on private property. ... There remained only one way to preserve a semblance of self-determination while actually relinquishing it: one could participate in the ruler's glory and thus drown the consciousness of one's submission to him. The halo of glamour surrounding the screen Frederick lured the audience into acts of identification with this supergenius. (CAL: 118)

Such 'national epics' played their part in ensuring that the vacillating German psyche finally threw in its lot with the figure of the Führer.[43] And so, over a period of some twenty years, Kracauer concludes, in its depiction of murderous tyrants and sleepwalking assassins, fainthearted rebels and all-conquering kings, awe-inspiring mountain scenes and ornamental mass spectacles, Weimar cinema screened, as uncanny premonitions, those fantasies and phantasmagorias of the German mind that were soon to be realized in the actual political realm during the 1930s. In a memorable concluding paragraph, Kracauer writes:

> Irretrievably sunk into retrogression, the bulk of the German people could not help submitting to Hitler. Since Germany thus carried out what had been anticipated by her cinema from its very beginning, conspicuous screen characters now came true in life itself. ... Homunculus walked about in the flesh. Self-appointed Caligaris hypnotized innumerable Cesares into murder. Raving Mabuses committed fantastic crimes with impunity, and mad Ivans devised unheard-of tortures. ... In Nuremberg, the ornamental pattern of NIBELUNGEN appeared on a gigantic scale: an ocean of flags and people artistically arranged. ... The blare of military bugles sounded unremittingly, and the philistines from the plush

parlors felt very elated. Battles roared and victory followed victory. It all was as it had been on the screen. The dark premonitions of a final doom were also fulfilled. (CAL: 272)

It had all been foreseen on screen. By 1932, the audiences were primed and prepared: 'the bulk of the Germans adjusted themselves to totalitarian rule with a readiness that could not be merely the outcome of propaganda and terror' (CAL: 204). The groundwork for Goebbels had been done; it had begun in the picture palaces of Germany even before the declaration of the democratic republic – this is the unsettling lesson of Kracauer's book.

6   The Cesare Complex

Even if the detail does not always withstand closer critical scrutiny,[44] Kracauer's *Caligari* nevertheless constitutes a ground-breaking 'psychological history' of Weimar cinema. Its provocative central thesis is one which all serious subsequent histories and interpretations of the time and medium must confront and one to which many are deeply indebted. And there is more: the book is *theoretically* significant as well. It contains numerous intimations and anticipations of the concepts, techniques and examples that were to be explored later in *Theory of Film*, a study that was actually sketched before the *Caligari* study while Kracauer was stranded in Marseilles in 1940–1. And so the attentive reader will find in *Caligari*, mentioned in passing or as asides, references to the camera's special ability 'to scan the whole visible world' (CAL: 6) and its predilection for capturing the flow of metropolitan street life. Forms of cinematic montage and editing, the use of sound and music as forms of accentuation – these *technical* insights would also later be elaborated in Kracauer's ambitious attempt to articulate the imperatives and redemptive promise of the cinematic medium. Indeed, on at least one occasion in the *Caligari* book, he identifies the conflict between the sentimental narratives and pioneering camerawork of the Weimar period: commenting on two of G. W. Pabst's 'street' films – *The Joyless Street* (*Die freudlose Gasse*) (1925) and *The Love of Jeanne Ney* (*Die Liebe der Jeanne Ney*) (1927) – Kracauer laments how the gritty realism and potentially radical social comment of both are fatally compromised by the banality of the scripts. Indeed, what Pabst thereby exemplifies is precisely what Kracauer would later see as *the* fundamental tension in film-making: that between the claims of 'camera reality' and the constructions (including narrative) of the 'formative tendency'. He writes: 'Pabst is sufficiently courageous to detail the ghastliness of social misery, but he does not mind cutting short the conclusions that might be drawn from his report. His weakness for melodrama counterbalances those implications of his realism which a generation not yet accustomed to the free display of camera reality too readily took for granted' (CAL: 170).

Read in tandem, *Caligari* and *Theory of Film* constitute a complex vision of cinema: on the one hand, as the fundamental expression of inner life, the representation of individual and collective dreams and neuroses, what one might term 'psychological reality'; and, on the other, as faithfully recording the 'surface-level expressions' of the external object world, redeeming 'physical reality'. And Weimar cinema is exemplary here because of its unique combination of the most atavistic and the most advanced, of the depiction on screen of forms of psychological regression and at the same time the utilization of the most advanced and sophisticated filmic techniques and technologies. And this was no mere coincidence: the archaic and the most modern are born of the same German soul.[45] Kracauer's 'Notes on the Planned History of the German Film' contains the following fascinating passage:

> From the very beginning the German film contained dynamite. It inherited another dowry, too, thanks to the fact that it was nursed in a period of revolutionary crises and social insecurity. ... Under such conditions, the unhappy homeless soul not only drove straightway toward the fantastic region of horrors, but also moved like a stranger through the world of normal reality, embracing its conventional forms with a look that had the force to change them into weird abnormal structures. Here was an incomparable chance for a young cinema which had not yet conquered all its spheres. That free-wandering soul imagined the madmen, somnambulists, vampires and murderers who were haunting the expressionistic settings of the CALIGARI-film and its like, and, on the other hand, inspired such directors as Karl Grune, Lupu Pick, and G. W. Pabst to portray in their early pictures apparently familiar objects and make them seem new. These pictures feature the city street as the place where the 'Man of the Crowd' perceives the kaleidoscopic configurations of everyday life; they are full of house façades, window-dressings, strangely lit rooms and physiognomic particulars. Thus the Germans widened the dominion of the cinema in two directions: they incorporated in it the terrific visions of a mind put out of joint, and at the same time introduced a truly cinematic realism. This was done with a perfect insight into the language of lights and shadows, and by means of a camera that became as movable as the unfettered mind directing it. It is understood that from such technical devices important conclusions can be drawn with regard to the psychic organization in which they originate. (KPB: 17)

How is one to understand this curious correspondence of phantom and film? A final peek inside Dr Caligari's cabinet might help here. What is one to make of his unwilling accomplice, that innocent murderer: Cesare? The sleeper awakes! He has been dormant for a quarter of a century and now he, Cesare, opens his eyes. And we are there to see it – as onlookers inside the mountebank's tent, as filmgoers in the cinema. What must it be like to see the world again after so many dormant years, to see the world as it now is for the very first time? But, as all eyes are turned on him, Cesare stares straight ahead, like the ethereal figure of Jane in the asylum garden.[46] Yes, his eyes are open, as are hers, but neither of them seems to see. Entranced, with eyes wide open, they are sightless sleepwalkers. They remain caught in the world of dreams and nightmares. There is more to this than just an image of the spiritually shelterless Weimar audiences. This is an envisioning of the unfulfilled possibilities of the film medium. The promise of awakening as a restoration of vision; the betrayal of this promise by a new unblinking, unseeing – is this not precisely the hope that film itself has offered us and been found wanting? Is not Cesare another of our companions in misfortune?

Alternatively, is Cesare our guide or instrument in re-vision? Perhaps it is precisely in the macabre guise of the unseeing somnambulist that the world is also somehow made strange to us once more. And in this very estrangement from mundane things, this distortion of the quotidian encapsulated in the Expressionist decor, there lies the possibility that we may come, paradoxically, to see them anew. Cesare as phantasmagoria, as a wandering ghost in the labyrinths of fairground and nocturnal city, awakens us with a fright from our own long dream-sleep so that we may become physiognomists of everyday objects we use and habitual spaces we frequent. Perhaps the world has taken on the peculiarities not just of a 'photographic face' but of a 'cinematic countenance'. And one last thing: in foregrounding this uncanny moment of recognition, in which the familiar and unfamiliar, the 'real' and the dream-like, are collapsed and confused, Kracauer himself adopts the mantle of, as Adorno astutely observed, the most 'curious' (*wunderlich*) of 'realists'.

8

Re-Surfacing Work[1]

1 Introduction

The *Caligari* study may be, as Quaresima claims, 'the work most closely associated with Kracauer's name over the years' (CAL: xvii). This chapter deals with two other works written in America which do not figure at all: the first is *Below the Surface*, a screenplay of some twenty-four typewritten pages dating from 1944–5 for a so-called test film of approximately 20 minutes' duration forming the centre-piece of a social psychological experiment investigating the character, prevalence and intensity of anti-Semitism among particular American audiences;[2] the second, the co-written report *Satellite Mentality: Political Attitudes and Propaganda Susceptibilities of Non-Communists in Hungary, Poland and Czechoslovakia* (1956), constitutes – at nearly two hundred pages – by far the most substantial piece of work Kracauer was to publish between *Caligari* and *Theory of Film*. Two contrasting texts – a film script and a government report – which, for different reasons, have come to share a common fate: oblivion. In re-reading them here, my goal is to 'recapture' them not only as demonstrations of the varied scope of Kracauer's American writings but also for their originality and, importantly, their critical bite.

Kracauer's 'test film' project was conceived in the context of the ongoing Studies in Prejudice programme, an extensive and productive collaboration beginning in the late 1930s between the Scientific Research Department of the American Jewish Committee and the Institut, examining both social and individual features of anti-Semitism in America and involving empirical sociological and experimental psychological techniques. Horkheimer, then director of both organizations, played the key facilitating role in the realization of these studies and, with Samuel H. Flowerman, became general editor of a five-volume series of publications (1949–50), most notably *The Authoritarian Personality* by Adorno et al. (1950).[3] The other volumes in the series, along with a host of related studies in film propaganda techniques and other fragments on anti-Semitism, now receive scant scholarly attention.[4] Such neglect is in part attributable to a widespread and enduring perception of these writings as the least successful part of the Institut's work. Indeed, in many respects they appear to be characterized and compromised by precisely the kind of naïve methodology, empirical simplifications and pseudo-scientific experimental style that Horkheimer and Adorno so despised in prevailing American sociology. For me, however, even if they may lack some of the philosophical sophistication which makes the writings of the Frankfurt School so demanding and provocative, this does not necessarily diminish their value and significance, either as historical documents or as sources of theoretical and critical insight.[5]

The various studies in propaganda and prejudice from the mid-1940s should neither be dismissed as mere financially expedient *Brotarbeit* reluctantly undertaken by impoverished exiles nor discreetly passed over as embarrassing flirtations with an American positivistic social science that proved anathema to the true exponents of Critical Theory. Rather, for some Frankfurt School figures – Kracauer and Löwenthal in particular – these studies constituted nothing less than essential and urgent intellectual contributions to the Allied war effort and the desperate struggle of liberal democratic regimes against fascism and National Socialism. These studies were part of a pioneering examination of the social-psychological dimension of modern warfare and, in particular, of the manipulative use of media (principally film) and cultural forms in the mobilization of mass populations for the conduct of total war. Indeed, the studies in propaganda and prejudice were developments of, rather than departures from, longstanding intellectual trajectories: for Kracauer, a preoccupation with cinema and theories of film production and reception; for Löwenthal, an abiding concern with anti-Semitism, literature and the limits of European Enlightenment.[6] And even for Adorno and Horkheimer these projects were far from insignificant in that they brought central issues in Critical Theory sharply into focus: the ideological character and totalitarian tendencies of mass culture; the fundamental failure of the Enlightenment and the descent into modern barbarism; and the persistence and pervasiveness of deep-rooted forms of prejudice, irrationalism and anti-Semitism. For them, totalitarian propaganda stripped away the spurious pretensions of culture industry products and the modern mythologies of consumer choice, pluralism and individual taste to reveal the inherent logic of new forms of mass media and communication: domination, manipulation, stultification of human intellectual faculties and the ultimate eradication of the autonomous individual subject.

The projects on prejudice, propaganda and authoritarianism demonstrate a clear continuity with, and may serve to illuminate, those very cultural and aesthetic studies that have long since eclipsed them. For example, the 'test film' project itself suggests that Horkheimer and Adorno's perception of film was more differentiated than is customarily understood under the rubric of their culture industry critique. True, film is an ideological instrument and propaganda weapon involving mythic spectacle and the deception of the masses. But at the same time, in the right hands, it can disenchant those masses and lay bare their hidden predispositions and susceptibilities. Film has both critical and pedagogic potential. Most significantly for our understanding of Kracauer, *Below the Surface* can readily be understood in terms of his then emerging theory of the complex relationship between the medium of film, the collective unconscious and latent political tendencies. In this sense, the notion of a 'test film' is of special interest: the film not only tests audience reactions and discloses underlying prejudices but also serves as a litmus test for Kracauer's developing film theory itself. Accordingly, I would suggest that, in the studies on propaganda and prejudice, one may see the principal exponents of Critical Theory engaged in the search for an appropriate and adequate *critical method* for the investigation of mass culture and communications, for an approach 'combining European ideas and American methods' (Wiggershaus [1995] 2010: 410) in a sophisticated, powerful and empirically grounded historical materialist critique of modernity. And, significantly, this was to be a collaborative undertaking. For just about all of those connected with the Institut, both then and now, these studies constituted one of the main instances of the Frankfurt School genuinely working together *as a school* in accordance with its own founding interdisciplinary spirit. Such projects should not be dismissed prematurely as second-rate works but, rather, recognized as initial moves in an essential and enduring collective critical task.

2   The 'Test Film' Project: Towards a Reconstruction

The various versions of the screenplay and related archive documents permit a reasonably clear reconstruction of the general outlines of Kracauer's project, though the precise sequence of various drafts and memoranda is less easily specified. The intention was to devise and produce a short, narrative film which would be shown to selected audiences composed principally of college students. The audience members would then be asked to complete specially designed questionnaires[7] and participate in follow-up discussions in small focus groups each led by a researcher. The questionnaires and group sessions were intended to bring to light any latent anti-Semitic sentiments or other prejudices held by respondents so that these could, in turn, be analysed in terms of form, content, degree and demographic distribution.

The idea of developing some kind of film experiment was first mooted by Horkheimer as early as 1941 in the *Studies in Philosophy and Social Sciences*. In February and March 1943, the film project was, as Wiggershaus notes, 'provisionally cancelled for financial reasons',[8] only to be revived in 1945 under the title *Below the Surface*. It is clear that a number of the Institut's members and associates were preoccupied with the project during the course of 1945 and early 1946. The 'test film' appeared on the agenda for numerous meetings between Horkheimer and Adorno (based in Los Angeles) and Löwenthal and others (in New York). Of these others, Kracauer was almost certainly the most important figure, particularly during the early stages of the project from around March to July 1945. In his notes 'Project of a Test Film', he sketched the principal features of the film and made the decisive suggestion that it be made in three different variants to be shown to different audiences. Whether he alone wrote the first version of the screenplay remains unclear: Kracauer himself simply refers to 'my cooperation in the writing of the script as well as the production of the picture',[9] though later he claims rather more emphatically: 'I developed the first script of this "test film".'[10] Whether penned solely by Kracauer or not, the full first draft of the screenplay was seemingly completed by late 1944 and bore the provisional title 'The Accident: First Draft Screen Play' (a text of some twenty-six pages).[11]

In his letter to Horkheimer of 30 March 1945, Kracauer notes his continuing role in the development of the test film: 'I am confirming our agreement that I am to serve as your consultant with reference to the motion picture you are about to produce.'[12] However, his work as consultant was rather more marginal than this suggests. His three-page report dated 4 April 1945, 'Suggestions for the Dialogue',[13] arrived too late it seems. Decisions had already been taken and plans were seemingly proceeding apace. In a letter from John Slawson, executive vice-president of the American Jewish Committee, dated 22 March 1945, there is a contract (stipulating a $1,500 fee and deadline of 20 April 1945) for Gilbert Gabriel and Major Bernard Vorhaus 'to write the screenplay of a motion picture tentatively called *The Accident* that the American Jewish Committee is about to make for scientific purposes'.[14] Whether this was a deliberate attempt to sideline Kracauer or merely a case of wires getting crossed is unclear. In any event, the next version of the screenplay bears another title, *Below the Surface*,[15] and Kracauer is almost certainly its author. Thereafter, in June 1945, a so-called round table discussion, attended by Pollock, Adorno and others, produced a document entitled 'Notes and Suggestions re Experimental Motion Picture'.[16] It is probable that Adorno also wrote a subsequent

'Memorandum re: Below the Surface' (dated LA July 1945),[17] in which there are a number of suggested changes to the text and other comments. In the Horkheimer Archive there is a fourth version of the script (comprising some twenty-six pages), in which some of the characters in the film are, for the first time, given actual names: in this version we are introduced, for example, to 'Private Henry Brown and his girl' and the African American 'Walter Johnson'.

At the same time as these various memoranda were making their way from Los Angeles to New York and back, Horkheimer was on the lookout for a director and a producer for the 'test film'. In a letter of 19 June 1945, Alexander Hackenschmied informs Horkheimer of one particular meeting: 'This morning I had a talk with Mr Elia Kazan about the practical problems of your film project. He recommended very strongly to make the film in Hollywood and also to look there for a writer.'[18] Horkheimer and Adorno were also actively trying to interest Jack Warner (Warner Brothers Corporation) and the Hollywood film producer Eddie Golden in the project, but without success. *Below the Surface* was still a subject of discussion in the spring of 1946 – there is a 'Memorandum on Experimental Movie Project' dated 18 April 1946 and some 'Notes' dated a week later[19] – but thereafter, in the absence of the necessary finance and with interest probably waning, it was abandoned. The film, of course, was never made. All that is left behind is a confusing paper trail of archive documents. And few have shown any subsequent interest in these. Although the idea of an 'experimental motion picture' is mentioned at various points in Wiggershaus's ([1995] 2010: 378) exhaustive history of the Frankfurt School and a 'test film' is noted by Koch (2000: 92), it is never named, let alone considered in any detail. *Below the Surface*, Kracauer's unfilmed 'test film', has become an unread text.

3 *Below the Surface*

Although there are a number of different draft versions of the screenplay, the setting and key events portrayed in *The Accident* and then subsequently in *Below the Surface* remain largely the same: it takes place in a crowded New York subway carriage during the evening rush hour. As the camera lingers on the faces of a number of typical passengers, a series of voice-overs disclose their everyday thoughts and preoccupations. The carriage jolts suddenly and a woman standing encumbered by a large unwieldy vacuum cleaner is catapulted through the rear exit door. The train screeches to a halt. Saved by the rear guard-chain, the woman is dazed but unharmed – her vacuum cleaner, though, has fallen onto the live rail and caused it to short-circuit. With the train at a standstill and in the half-light provided by the emergency lights, a scandalous accusation is made: the woman did not fall, she was pushed, and the culprit was the man standing right next to her, a man who is (and here there are three variants in *Below the Surface*) Jewish or African American or (in the control variant) an ordinary white American white-collar worker. The man protests his innocence, an argument ensues and the various passengers now start to take sides. It begins to turn nasty. There is a standoff. Then, suddenly, the main lights flare on again and the train moves off. The woman, now recovered from her fall, gives the lie to the claims of the accusers – she insists that she simply tripped over her vacuum cleaner. They grudgingly back down. Calm is restored and the passengers continue their homeward journey.

Had it ever been made, the showing of this film in conjunction with questionnaires and focus group discussions[20] was intended to stimulate reactions and disclose deep-rooted unconscious dispositions. Subsequent analysis would lead to the construction of some kind of social scientific scale or index used to check and measure the degree of prejudice in prevailing American society. In his fragment 'Hypotheses: March 1945', Kracauer outlines the following rudimentary proposition:

> A person determined by an anti-Semitic outlook will introduce a relation of cause and effect between two unrelated parts of a situation. ... The crucial question is whether the person introduces the causal relation where it does not exist. If he does, this can only be on the basis of an anti-Semitic orientation. ... If this hypothesis is correct, then the reaction to the film indicates the presence or absence of an anti-Semitic orientation in the given situation. The validity of this inference can eventually be checked against the correspondence between the reactions to the film and other data, such as interviews and attitude scales.[21]

In this context, it is clear that the chosen title, *Below the Surface*, has at least three levels of meaning. Firstly, it is to be understood literally – the drama unfolds in a New York subway car below the surface of the metropolis. Secondly, we see in the events of the test film how the contradictory emotions and hidden prejudices of the various characters manifest themselves in a moment of conflict and crisis.[22] Thirdly, and this is clearly the principal goal of the 'test film' project, '[the] latent prejudice'[23] of audience members is to be brought to the surface: 'true feelings may come to the surface when he [the viewer] sees members of minorities in action.'[24] Kracauer here sees the need for the film to mask its own intentions in order to gain access to what lies below the surface,[25] to the human unconscious as the fundamental wellspring of our emotions and reactions. Below the surface, then, deep in the unconscious of the modern enlightened subject, lurk the powerful forces of irrationalism and primitive instinctual drives.

Such a view is in keeping with Kracauer's understanding of the relationship between surface and depth that we have already seen in his earlier work on mass culture in Weimar Germany. Popular dance troupes, variety acts, café pianists, trashy detective stories, hotel lobbies, shopping arcades, seedy bars, umbrellas – ultimately these are all so many 'surface-level expressions' of the 'spiritual shelterlessness'[26] of the metropolitan subject. And it is above all the new medium of film that has, for Kracauer, a special connection with, and privileged access to, this hidden domain of modern mental life. *Below the Surface* was conceived against the background of his ongoing research for the *Caligari* book, a study predicated on the view that film gives expression to and satisfies the fundamental desires, fantasies and aspirations of mass audiences and, in the particular case of German audiences in the Weimar period, their secret craving for authority and order.[27] Film articulates, envisions and appeals to the inner psychic life of a particular people at a particular historical moment. Films present '"visible hieroglyphs"' (CAL: 7) of the collective unconscious. In the 'test film' project, Kracauer utilizes this insight and *reverses* the direction of flow. Film is no longer just an *expression* of the unconscious but, rather, becomes an instrument with which to engage and elicit its elusive contents.

But there is more. If one accepts that the 'test film' project was conceptualized according to the theoretical principles Kracauer was developing in his *Caligari* study, then an intriguing possibility presents itself. Film not only addresses itself to the unconscious urges and wishes of the audience, it is also a medium which bears witness to the collective unconscious of those engaged in its *production*. As we have seen in the previous chapter, film is a distinctive cultural product in that it always involves the creativity and expertise of a number of differently skilled collaborators. Film is never the work of a solitary individual artist but instead always the output of cooperative labour, and hence serves as the expression of a collective, social mentality. For Kracauer, then, films disclose the sensibility not only of audiences *but also of the film-makers themselves*. And so, following Kracauer's argument, would it be legitimate to see *Below the Surface* as some manifestation of the collective unconscious of those who brought it into being – that is, of the members of the Frankfurt School themselves? Does the proposed film manifest that which lay below the surface of the 'dialectical imagination'? *Below the Surface* is precisely a fantasia of Critical Theory in that here we see a series of motifs, concepts and figures found in other writings of the Frankfurt School brought together in an imaginative configuration and translated into the cinematic medium.

4   Critical Theory Screened

On closer inspection, *Below the Surface* clearly depicts or envisions key figures and motifs drawn from Critical Theory. The scenes and events portrayed in the 'test film' are supposedly culled from the everyday life of the modern metropolis. The various anonymous figures (notwithstanding one version of the screenplay) are conceived as simple types, who conduct themselves in a manner reminiscent of Simmel's disinterested, *blasé* personality. The passengers in the carriage observe, Kracauer notes, 'that curt constrained politeness of the subway code'.[28] As the film opens, we find each of them immersed in their own private thoughts and interests, indifferent to one another, avoiding contact, concerned only to escape the company of strangers and longing to be home. They are quintessentially modern figures for Kracauer: crowded together and yet alone, marking time in transit, occupying a space that is neither here nor there, silently waiting in an indefinite in-between. Typical big-city dwellers, they are 'those who wait', figures of alienation and ennui.[29]

Intended as ciphers for the presentation of particular social and political viewpoints, these supposedly ordinary and representative characters would surely appear as crude stereotypes and caricatures to a reader today. Only writers of the Frankfurt School could provide descriptions such as the following:

TOUGH GUY: 'He is a huge, surly brute, Prussian type.' (MHA 1a: 3)

CLUBFOOT PEDDLAR: 'his face a mix of piety, truculence and dormant fanaticism' (MHA 1a: 7)

WOMAN WITH A VACUUM CLEANER: 'She is a mousey, puritanical little woman, middle-aged, middle-class, clutching her too-big burden with an air of frustration.' (MHA 1a: 1)

One cannot help but pity the unfortunate prospective actors who would have had to embody such figures and features. How is it possible that the members of the Institut, among the most provocative and insightful of twentieth-century intellectuals, could combine not only to produce such a banal storyline but also then to people it with a rogues' gallery of this kind? If a camel is a horse designed by a committee, then *Below the Surface*, a product of numerous meetings and memoranda, could indeed be said to be the veritable camel of Critical Theory. But such a verdict may be a little unjust. Clarity of the narrative structure and the legibility of action, not originality and aesthetic complexity, were the key priorities if the 'test film' were to succeed, and the figures presented should be predictable and familiar ones so as to put the viewers at their ease. The film as experiment should not be confused with the experimental film.

As bearers of ideas and representatives of particular political and ideological standpoints, the *dramatis personae* of the 'test film' exemplify many of the concepts and motifs of Critical Theory in what amounts to a kind of self-parody. It is noticeable that the figure of the white-collar worker serves as an exemplary urbanite, a vision which wholly accords with Kracauer's *Die Angestellten*. The opening shots of the film appropriately comprise images of office workers leaving their place of work and streaming towards the subway. So it is no coincidence that the control variant of the screenplay substitutes a white-collar worker for the accused Jew or African American. The office worker, the commuter, is a figure of mundane respectability against whom one can display minimal or no prejudice. He is the neutral background figure, the modern metropolitan man without qualities, 'the average American', 'Joe Public', the typical New Yorker as much as the typical Berliner.

Nor is it a coincidence that the OLD WOMAN, who scarcely figures at all in *The Accident*, comes to play a more central role in *Below the Surface*. As the avid reader of horoscopes – 'Something's gonna happen. The stars said so for today. Folks can make fun of it, but astrology explains a lot of things'[30] – she serves as the representative of superstition and fatalism. 'The stars don't lie!'[31] is her continual, nonsensical refrain. It is significant, of course, that, as a figure of irrationalism, the OLD WOMAN is among the first and the most forceful of the accusers. Mythic thinking and extreme prejudice are inextricably interwoven in her. She is no innocent bystander. Her elevation in the screenplay for *Below the Surface* from mere extra to key supporting role is perhaps indebted to Adorno's association of occultism with anti-Semitism and anticipates, even suggests, his later study 'The Stars Down to Earth' (1952–3), exploring the *Los Angeles Times* astrology column.[32]

The principal representative of prejudice in the film is the most virulent accuser – the bitter CLUB-FOOT PEDDLER. It is he who first tries to 'introduce a relation of cause and effect between two unrelated parts of a situation' – 'Well, *somebody* did it!'[33] he exclaims. He, too, is a figure of primitive and irrational thinking – 'We don't have to see what we know.'[34] He is, first and foremost, a pedlar of lies,[35] deploying a number of rhetorical devices typical of the petty propagandist: He seeks to de-individualize and characterize the Jew as an enemy – 'always pushing in first, always grabbing the profits!';[36] 'Him and his kind, they glory in it – they're always pushing.'[37] He seeks to promulgate a conspiracy theory – 'It's time people woke up to a lot of things going on in this country!'[38] – according to which he is a victim of a malevolent and omnipotent other. He calls for action, seeks restitution, demands justice: 'There's times when us plain, decent God-lovin' Christians – us white Americans – has got to take the law into our own hands and clean things up. Come on!'[39]

The PEDDLER is clearly recognizable as a prototype of Löwenthal and Guterman's fascist agitator. He is a 'prophet of deceit', a

'cheer-leader in reverse', as they put it. Indeed, one finds an echo of
Below the Surface in their book four years later:

> In a crowded New York bus a woman complained loudly that she was
> choking, that she was pushed and squeezed by other passengers and
> added that 'something should be done about it'. (A typical inarticulate
> complaint.) A second passenger observed: 'Yes, it's terrible. The bus
> company should assign more buses to this route. If we did something
> about it, we might get results.' (The solution of a reformer or revolution-
> ary. The inarticulate expression of the complainant is translated into an
> objective issue – in this case 'the faulty organization of the transportation
> services that can be remedied by appropriate collective action'.) But then
> a third passenger angrily declared: 'This has nothing to do with the bus
> company. It's all those foreigners who don't even speak good English.
> They should be sent back where they came from.' (The solution of the
> agitator who translates the original complaint not into an issue for action
> against an established authority, but into the theme of the vicious for-
> eigner.) (1970: 8–9)[40]

Of the other occupants of the subway car, the figure of the INTEL-
LECTUAL is also of special interest. With his facile preoccupation with
'objectivity' and his concomitant disparaging of 'intellectual theory' in
favour of 'solid virtues',[41] this character is nothing other than a wicked
parody of the American empirical social scientist. This intellectual is,
in fact, nothing of the sort – indeed, he is the very antithesis of the
thinker; he is the anti-intellectual par excellence. 'There are problems',
he pontificates, 'too important to be understood by the mind alone.'[42]
It is no wonder that he feels himself at home only among '"Doers"! –
businessmen and other red-blooded men of action'.[43] He is a representative of pseudo-intellectual servility, an advocate of the 'authoritarian
personality' – 'Face it, gentlemen, we need strong leaders – doers, like
Henry Ford'[44] – and an abject apologist for anti-Semitism.[45] Ironically
his 'objectivity' serves as his all-too-transparent excuse for inaction
when called upon to intervene in the escalating dispute.

The dramatic action culminates in the confrontation between two
heroes of the proletariat, the two burly SHIPYARD WORKERS, and the
irrational and superstitious forces embodied by the lumpenproletarian
figure of the PEDDLER and his cronies. At this moment of tension, the
main lights in the subway car are suddenly restored: 'Long shot of the
mob frozen into an ugly, sustained tableau. The antagonists still stand
immobile, hate-bound.'[46] One cannot read this without being reminded
of Benjamin's writings on Bertolt Brecht's dramatic innovations. In the
first version of *What is Epic Theatre?*, Benjamin writes: 'The thing that
is revealed as though by lightning in the "condition" represented on
the stage – as a copy of human gestures, actions and words – is an
immanently dialectical attitude. The condition which epic theatre

reveals is the dialectic at a standstill' (Benjamin 1973: 12). Brecht uses interruption to halt the flow of dramatic events and thereby reveal particular prevailing conditions and circumstances, above all, contemporary political situations. This moment of interruption is understood by Benjamin as one of illumination, discovery and recognition, in which the collective consciousness of the audience is transformed and their sensitivity to class distinctions and oppression is heightened. *Below the Surface* contains precisely such a moment in which action is frozen as part of a political pedagogy. The confrontation between the workers and the sinister pedlar is nothing less than a cinematic envisioning of the struggle between the powers of modern reason and liberation and those of enduring prejudice and hate. In this sense, it is nothing less than the 'dialectic of enlightenment' that finds representation in this moment of the 'dialectic at a standstill'. The restoration of light in the subway car is a moment of literal and metaphorical enlightenment. The riddle is solved, truth is revealed and prejudice is exposed. In this way, *Below the Surface* is not just an experiment but, rather, a piece of didactic film-making, an urgent political intervention. The Frankfurt School's Critical Theory of modern mass culture here begins to transform itself into a critical cultural *practice* which seeks to interrogate rather than merely investigate its audience. Film in the image of Critical Theory, film in the service of profane illumination and ideology critique – this is how Kracauer saw his 'test film' project. And, if this is the case, then something quite remarkable is happening below the surface.

5 The 'Lesser Evil'

Sometime between June 1951 and March 1952, somewhere on the border between East and West in a transit camp in Austria or Germany constructed to house the many refugees from one of the neighbouring Eastern countries all now under Soviet control, a young lad, one of some three hundred temporary residents eventually interviewed by representatives of an American organization,[47] provides answers that will later be singled out for special mention. We do not know his name, only his nationality; we do not know exactly what he said, but his sense of ambivalence and equivocation is evident to the two scholars back in New York, Siegfried Kracauer and the social psychologist Paul L. Berkman, who would be involved years later in the collation and 'qualitative analysis' of these transcripts. Just over half-way through their report they observe: 'This Czech, a bright boy, belongs among the intellectuals who find themselves in an ideological dilemma: he is stuck with the anti-capitalist socialist or Communist teachings, but at the same time craves individual freedom, the result being that he has come to consider the West the lesser evil after all' (SAT: 99).

Undertaken on behalf of the Bureau of Applied Research at Columbia University and eventually published in the autumn of 1956,[48] *Satellite Mentality: Political Attitudes and Propaganda Susceptibilities of Non-Communists in Hungary, Poland and Czechoslovakia*, like Kracauer's numerous less substantial projects around this period for the Bureau and others,[49] has elicited little in the way of subsequent scholarly or critical interest, notwithstanding a couple of reviews at the time of publication. This is unfortunate but not altogether surprising, especially since Kracauer himself was keen to make little of them.[50] When mentioned at all in his correspondence of the time, such writings are typically disparagingly dismissed as time-consuming irritations and impediments to his *real* work, his *own* work – that is to say, to progress on his ongoing book of film aesthetics, an undertaking intermittently speeded by grants from various foundations[51] but also further interrupted by recurrent ill health.

In a letter to Adorno of 1 October 1950, for example, one finds the following rather resigned reference to a report on Voice of America broadcasts, a text which had taken up the best part of his summer vacation: 'Perhaps I must do more of such things. I don't like to shoulder two tasks at once, but for practical reasons it may be necessary' (AKB: 449). Needs must: and, however reluctant a bearer of such burdens, Kracauer actively sought them out through the good offices of his relatively well-placed friend and colleague Leo Löwenthal.[52] Indeed, Kracauer successfully persuaded Löwenthal to regularize the 'nervous nightmare' (*Angsttraum*) of disparate, ad hoc commissions into one of the Bureau's 'inside jobs',[53] a proper position first as staff member and then as research director during the course of 1952.[54] Such relative security came at a cost, however: ten hours a day of report writing left precious little time, let alone energy, for progress with his own manuscripts. True, a one-year fellowship from the Boston-based Chapelbrook Foundation commencing in May 1954 promised him some temporary respite, but, even so, it is not always easy just to pick up where one has left off on longstanding research work. Indeed, with some four months of funding already gone, Kracauer was yet to refocus his attention when, in a letter to Adorno of 28 August 1954, he writes rather optimistically:

> As for me, I am now going to resume work on my film book that I have had to set aside for the last two years. I hope I will be able to finish it in one go. ... Small interruptions are of course unavoidable, above all due to my ongoing work in the Bureau. Among other things I have written a long essay culminating in the analysis of the relationship between empirical research and basic theory. A major project may develop from this. I have also directed another project. (AKB: 470)

Given Adorno's disdain for such things, it is perhaps to be expected that all these financially necessary but intellectually unfulfilling projects and report-writing duties for the Bureau scarcely figure in their subsequent correspondence. But it is surprising that the publication two years later of a substantial piece of research such as *Satellite Mentality* does not seem to merit a mention even in Kracauer's exchanges with Löwenthal, especially given the latter's key role in originally commissioning the project and facilitating his participation.

As a contribution to the critical recovery and reassessment of these writings, I want to suggest here that *Satellite Mentality*, even if a rather perfunctory study penned primarily for pecuniary reasons, might still reward more careful attention. Indeed, reading between the lines and/or against the grain of conventional interpretation might actually disclose a much more ambiguous and ambivalent text and even a surreptitious *textual strategy of critique*. Instead of a one-dimensional lambasting of the dehumanizing conditions of the Soviet system in Russia and elsewhere written to appease State Department bureaucrats and functionaries, *Satellite Mentality* offers a rather finely nuanced critique of everyday suffering under the Stalinist 'yoke' (SAT: 10), of the terrors of totalitarianism more generally and, also, of the failures of American capitalism. In their exploration of 'what people behind the Iron Curtain think of their regime, how they visualize America, and how they react to western radio communication' (SAT: 5), Kracauer and Berkman provide a complex commentary on Cold War perceptions and propaganda, a polarizing world in which, as our shrewd young Czech respondent concluded, damning here with faint praise, the West appears as no more than 'the lesser evil after all'.

6   Towards a Re-reading

Both thematically and methodologically, Kracauer's work for the *Satellite Mentality* report is more in keeping with his other writings, his *real* work, than he himself admits. In its concern with the displaced and dislocated of Europe, *Satellite Mentality* is congruent with, rather than a departure from, his longstanding preoccupation with the 'extra-territorial'[55] and interstitial,[56] with the conditions of life 'elsewhere' (*anderswo*), and with the 'spiritually shelterless' modern predicament itself. Indeed, the plight of those forced to flee from totalitarian regimes and the disorientating experience of exile were acute personal as well as political issues for him. Themselves refugees only a decade before, Kracauer and his wife Lili were to become active in supporting the work of organizations helping recent immigrants in New York.[57] Even by the mid-1950s, they were still ambivalent about being 'at home' in America.[58]

There is methodological continuity with earlier works, too. Kracauer and Berkman state their intention to bridge 'the gap between, on the one hand, studies of the systems in place in Eastern Europe (in which individual actors are absent) and, on the other, stories of particular individuals and experiences (in which some more objective picture of life in the system is missing)' (SAT: 1). Through the presentation and examination of personal testimonies and anecdotes, the authors seek to articulate 'the interplay between the given conditions of Satellite life and the very manifestations of this life' (SAT: 2) – that is to say, to capture how the social, political and economic structural conditions prevailing in the Eastern bloc at this specific historical moment pervade, frame and find expression in the everyday experiences and accounts of various individuals. This chimes with Kracauer's abiding concern with the exploration of how societal features and processes of a particular epoch are instantiated and/or embodied in the lives of exemplary or representative[59] figures. Now, there is no reason in principle why Kracauer's monadological method, his dialectic of self and society, should not apply to *any* individual, to lives more ordinary: the painstaking unfolding of *any* single human life (their experiences, attitudes, aspirations, perceptions of self and others, fears and foibles) should always provide insight into the society in which they have become what they are. The three hundred or so transcripts examined by Kracauer and Berkman constitute fragments of potential 'societal biographies' which, composed into mosaic, a composite[60] termed the 'satellite mentality', should prove decisive in understanding Soviet societies, the 'spirit of the times' not in the Berlin and Paris of the recent past, but in the Warsaw, Budapest and Prague of the Cold War, of the here and now. Late in the day, Kracauer resumes his guise of ragpicker.

7 The Dissident Imagination

There are, I suggest, three levels or moments of critique in the *Satellite Mentality* study:

a) firstly, in what one may designate the conventional reading, the text articulates and analyses a number of testimonies which combine to offer a withering critique of the Soviet Union and its dominion over Eastern Europe;

b) secondly, while recognizing the historical and political specificity of the experiences and accounts presented, one might argue that the text gestures towards a more wide-ranging critique of totalitarianism per se, rather than just Soviet communism, with several aspects (hatred of committed and zealous Party members, corruption of interpersonal relations, fear of informers, distrust of all

official 'information') clearly recognizable as features of fascist dictatorships as well;

c) thirdly, and this is certainly the most contentious claim, the text
   might plausibly be seen as a sustained though necessarily veiled
   critique of 1950s America: in terms of the glaring disparity between
   American rhetoric and reality; in its failure to support dissent in
   Eastern Europe while pursuing a ruthless neo-imperialist foreign
   policy elsewhere; and in the crudity and crassness of Western
   propaganda which, treated with the same scorn as its Soviet counterpart, plays its own role in shaping the thoroughgoing scepticism
   and suspicion that characterize the 'satellite mentality'.

That *Satellite Mentality* presents voices hostile to the Soviet Union
and the communist regimes it imposed across Eastern Europe is certainly not in question, and this is hardly surprising given that the
interviewees, at great cost and risk to themselves, have chosen to flee
these lands. As they make abundantly clear, the rule of the Party has
profound consequences for all aspects of mundane life in satellite societies. In relation to the economic sphere, the respondents complain bit-
terly of ever higher and more absurd production targets for the sake of
wholly inadequate piece-rate wages; of shortages of food and other
basic necessities; of expensive yet poor-quality consumer goods;[61] and
of the ideological indoctrination to which they are routinely subjected
at the compulsory works meetings, where the required singing of Party
songs and parroting of slogans is supposed to raise spirits and promote
solidarity. But, as Kracauer and Berkman highlight, any genuine sense
of collectiveness or togetherness is precisely what is lacking in such
societies because of the endemic and intense distrust of others that is
the logical consequence of the totalitarian system of surveillance, based
as it is on clandestine networks of spies, informers and infiltrators run
by the secret police. What emerges most powerfully from the testimonies is the impression that these are societies where mutual trust is
absent from all interpersonal relations, even the most intimate, where
one confides in no one. These are regimes which foster and feed upon
fear and the 'total insecurity' (SAT: 17) of their populations. Marked by
a justifiable sense of acute paranoia, 'Life in the Satellites, then, is
determined by fear and threatened with alienation. It is a life those
forced to lead it call "abnormal"' (SAT: 23). Indeed, these are systems
of control and manipulation geared to the total eradication of the individual subject:

> In the last analysis passive resistance represents the final barrier against
> the atomizing forces of Communist totalitarianism. For it prevents them
> from transforming the individual into a mere automaton. To attain
> this goal, the Communists must try to remove all obstacles to state

domination at their source – that is, they must destroy the individual's spontaneity and inner continuity, which are essential elements of the 'self'. As long as a man with 'self' exists – something essentially private and uncontrollable – he constitutes a threat to the Communist regime even if he were a committed Communist. Hence the remorseless attempts of Communist regimes to isolate individuals from all self-sustaining information and from all associations eluding their grip and to embed him in a situation where all meaning is established by the Party leadership.[62] Hence their eternal distrust of idealists, intellectuals and all those same groups whose actions may spring from internal sources. (SAT: 142)[63]

The 'satellite mentality' is what can be salvaged from this ruthless and relentless state violence directed against the foundations of the self as the regime operates to transform individuals into an undifferentiated, compliant mass.[64]

Only the most myopic of government officials in the State Department could read *Satellite Mentality* with unalloyed pleasure, however. Even within the parameters of a scathing critique of the Soviet system, Kracauer and Berkman draw attention to the interviewees' highly differentiated understanding of, and responses to, various communist 'types'. For the non-communist refugees, their communist compatriots were anything but a monolithic or homogeneous group of adversaries and enemies. For example, the respondents distinguish between indigenous veteran communists, many of whom were resistance fighters during the war, and the puppet governments and their lackeys installed by the Russians following 'liberation'. Indeed, for some respondents it is not the communists that are the real problem but, rather, the annexation and domination of Moscow. Liberation from the Russian yoke, not necessarily an end to communism, is the fundamental aspiration in some cases. Moreover, Communist Party members themselves are understood by the respondents to compose a motley assortment of characters with varying motives and levels of commitment.[65] So, for example, they carefully distinguish between those who join and participate only because they must, having little choice if they are to survive at all (the 'forced'); those who do so to retain their jobs and secure their positions (the 'jobkeepers'); those who were once keen members and organizers but who have become disenchanted, now harbouring resentment at the gross betrayal of ideals and principles (the 'disillusioned'); those who are simply ambitious and instrumental, seeing active Party membership as a way of advancing their careers and accessing certain privileges (the 'opportunists'); and, finally, the new zealots, reverentially repeating the Party line, the dogmatic true believers (the 'convinced'). While the first two of these groups, the 'forced' and the 'jobkeepers', are tolerated and excused, the third group, embittered and disaffected former communists, are actually highly regarded by the interviewees for their integrity and honesty. Only those who fall into the last two categories, the unscrupulous and devious 'careerists' and the present-day Party proselytizers, the 'convinced', are unequivocally detested.[66] Indeed, it is perhaps surprising how much the escapees are prepared to condone rather than condemn the actions, attitudes and adaptive strategies of those they have left behind.

The non-communists themselves are not a homogeneous group either. While the attempt to specify a distinctive 'satellite mentality' may be understandable, this is a doomed task and a rather misleading title: there is rather a plethora of contrasting *satellite mentalities* rooted in nationality, class, gender, age, level of education, and so forth. At various times, Kracauer and Berkman distinguish between the responses of the vast majority of interviewees (former workers and peasants) and those few provided by individuals designated as 'intellectuals' (SAT: 48), our 'bright boy' from Czechoslovakia among them. Tellingly, the complaints and criticisms of the former group are exclusively economic and material: the poor working conditions and long hours experienced by industrial workers; the absurdities of inefficient management systems and practices; low wages and the scarcity of goods and products; corruption and the 'black market'. It becomes increasingly clear from the report that, while motivations are always complex and various self-justifications abound, many if not most of the respondents have fled their homelands because of the enticing prospect of a higher standard of living with greater financial rewards based on individual enterprise. Those other freedoms typically imputed to dissidents by Western critics – of thought and expression, of religious faith and affiliation – concern, and indeed come to define, only a minority, the 'intellectuals'. The suffering of 'captive minds' features little. In other words, for most of the respondents, perceived monetary opportunities and material advantages rather than any ideological commitments or political/religious convictions have proved decisive. With all due respect for their hardships, in today's ruthless perception and parlance, many of these interviewees would simply be deemed 'economic migrants' and sent back.

Tempering their critique, Kracauer and Berkman devote a whole chapter of their study (chapter VII) to the perceived strengths and achievements of the satellite regimes. Certain transformations brought about by the communists are actually endorsed by the respondents: post-war reconstruction and (re)industrialization (SAT: 82); land reforms and collectivization of farming as a break with the peasant past (SAT: 85); social security and 'full employment' (SAT: 85–6); and extended and improved educational provision (SAT: 87). The responses of interviewees to these accomplishments are mixed: 'admiration goes hand in hand with disapproval of the methods used in achieving such imposing results' (SAT: 83). While the changes and reforms themselves are grudgingly acknowledged as beneficial, the rapidity of their implementation and their human costs are criticized. True, the sacrifices made by the satellite populations greatly outweigh the perceived advances, but that such progressive and positive features are appreciated at all allows a rather more nuanced picture of these societies to take shape.

Notwithstanding the caveats outlined above, *Satellite Mentality* might still seem an exemplary instance and clear proof of Kracauer's abandonment of Marxism and Critical Theory and his adoption and endorsement of the American model of liberal democratic politics. But this view, shared by his radical detractors, Adorno among them, would be misguided for two main reasons. Firstly, one should remember that the critical interrogation and indeed rejection of Soviet-style Marxism is one of the hallmarks of 'Frankfurt School' Critical Theory. It is no mere coincidence that, at the same time Kracauer was working on *Satellite Mentality*, Marcuse was also busily engaged with Columbia's recently formed Institute for Russian Studies, writing his *Soviet Marxism: A Critical Analysis* (1958). I would suggest that these two texts, Marcuse's 'immanent critique' of Soviet philosophy and Kracauer and Berkman's 'qualitative analysis' of the lived reality of Soviet satellite systems, constitute complementary projects which lend themselves to potentially fruitful comparison.

Secondly, it would be to overlook its double-edged critique. While not wishing in any way to efface the important and specific differences between various forms of totalitarianism and the programmes of persecution they unleash upon their unfortunate populations, only the most casual reader of *Satellite Mentality* would fail to recognize that many of the inhumanities and injustices identified by the report might also be understood as everyday experiences under dictatorships more generally. The notions of 'total insecurity' and 'captive minds' might be useful concepts for characterizing the daily suffering endured under National Socialist and fascist regimes and occupations. Paralysing fear and paranoia; the perennial prospect of denunciation by informers; the threat of torture and murder; the corruption and impunity of authority; all those various types of spineless accommodation to the rule of the Party and ingratiation with members and elites; the destruction of all interpersonal relations based on trust; endless subjection to censorship and propaganda: none of these is unique to the Soviet satellites but, rather, only too typical of all manner of totalitarian systems. The testimonies of these interviewees would doubtless correspond in many ways with those of escapees from countries on Europe's south-western margins at this time – from Franco's Spain and the para-fascist Portugal of Salazar's *Estado Novo*. And then there are the refugees from the tyrannies sponsored by the USA across Latin America. In short, in the Cold War such conditions and sufferings are shared in the 1950s between the Soviet *and* capitalist satellites. For an attentive reader, this accusation lies beneath the surface of Kracauer and Berkman's text.

And this brings us to America itself. For, while *Satellite Mentality* is undeniably and manifestly an indictment of the USSR, there is, I suggest, a veiled or subterranean critique of the contemporary USA as well. This is because the 'satellite mentality' is informed and shaped by the ongoing propaganda war between America and Russia (and, note here, Kracauer and Berkman specifically identify US communications as *propaganda*).[67] This has two main consequences: on the one hand, it provides the authors with plenty of critical perspectives on and portrayals of the West as claimed by the Soviet media. Noting that 'the subject of American imperialism is one of the Communists' most successful propaganda themes', the authors write:

> Non-Communists in Czechoslovakia speak quite often about the fact that American foreign policy is determined mostly by commercial interests; that is, Americans intervene only where their economic and political interests seem endangered; in short, that Americans are not led by ideals but by pure commercial reasons. (The otherwise well-informed and persistently anti-Communist Slovak lawyer.) (SAT: 101)

What is decisive here, of course, is the phrase 'otherwise well-informed', a remark which serves to impugn the validity of what has gone before. The next page finds another anti-American barb: Czechs, in particular, are of the opinion that rich 'American capitalists control or strongly influence the US government' (SAT: 102), only for this to be immediately undermined by the authors' comment: 'It would thus appear that a not insignificant segment of the Czechoslovak population lends a willing ear to the Communists' incessant vilification of the American capitalists' (SAT: 103). On the same page one reads: 'the inference is that these people have been conditioned to believe in the existence of serious working class disadvantages wherever capitalism flourishes' (SAT: 103). These three examples share a particular rhetorical technique in which an assertion is made, attributed to others, and then subjected to qualification, questioning or denial of its force and legitimacy. I think this constitutes a repeated tactical and textual game which succeeds in both offering up astute critical insights into American politics and society and at the same time avoiding any responsibility for their utterance so as to appease the bureaucrats.

There is a second, equally cunning tactic: presenting the often utopian visions of life in the USA that some of the respondents have developed as a result of American propaganda itself. America has become a fantasy for many: 'To them freedom is tantamount to freedom from all restrictions. This comes out clearly in their image of America. They imagine the American worker to possess all the freedoms of which they themselves have been stripped by the regime' (SAT: 38).

Some are convinced that, with higher wages, shorter working hours and choice of an array of modern consumer goods, one can understand 'America as the land of "real socialism"' (SAT: 46). Indeed, even the otherwise well-informed 'intellectuals' enthusiastically describe the USA as a 'workers' paradise' (SAT: 52). Others have bought into the American dream of entrepreneurial self-interest and competitive accumulation – 'the America of these people somehow resembles a jungle' (SAT: 41). This second critical tactic then is not to relay Soviet propaganda messages (with deflating commentary) but rather to confront 1950s America with some of its own claims and pretensions. It is the very mismatch between the naïve image of an ideal America envisaged by the 'satellite mentality' – a New World blessed with liberty, equality and fraternity, with democracy and justice for all – and the grim realities of Cold War America still haunted by McCarthyism (1950–4), and still segregated in the South (Rosa Park refuses to surrender her seat on the bus in 1955), that is so damning here. As Kracauer and Berkman helpfully point out, propaganda is discredited where and when it is found to be in direct conflict with experienced reality (SAT: 117–19). The real America, the America that Kracauer has come to know, may indeed be a 'jungle' perhaps, but it is certainly no workers' Eden. And as such it is not lacking in its own sources of insecurity, both material uncertainty and the fear of the powers-that-be, encouraging, ensuring intellectual self-censorship. And so it is that he is limited to this subtle smuggling in of critique, this writing which demands to be read between the lines. One cannot be certain of this, but such tactics are precisely those in which, according to Kracauer and Berkman, satellite populations themselves engage whenever they deal with officialdom: every word chosen with care, every opinion cautiously qualified and nullified, attributed to some unnamed other; every utterance duplicitous, deceptive and double-edged; the whole suffused with irony, inversions and evasions of meaning, in-jokes told poker-faced (see SAT: 131–2); and, at the same time, every government proclamation subject to scrutiny and suspicion, read as the surest sign of its very opposite (see SAT: 111–14). Saying one thing, communicating another, is the very skill that has been perfected by the 'satellite mentality'. And it is, I suggest, a lesson and a practice put to good use in Kracauer and Berkman's report.

Given the time and expected readership of the report, it is remarkable that it contains any subversive mention of the virtues of the USSR and any unpatriotic acknowledgement of the vices of the American way of life at all. Then again, *Satellite Mentality* is written by a critical theorist, not a bureaucrat. For Kracauer, it may have been disarmingly downplayed as mere *Brotarbeit*, but, when viewed as a complex and cunning critical text, it is also to be appreciated as a sophisticated and finely judged balancing act.

Part V

FROM THE SCREEN: REDEEMING IMAGES, REMEMBERED THINGS

9

Film, Improvisation and 'the Flow of Life'

1 'The Spirit of Film'

If, during the 1940s, Kracauer's work on the 'Caligari complex' required him to swap the role of journalistic film reviewer for that of psychoanalytical film historian and experimental social psychologist, then the actual publication of *From Caligari to Hitler* in 1947 allowed the resumption of a third guise: that of scholarly film *theorist*. Kracauer returned to the project that had already been sketched out in the three volumes of notebooks penned in Marseilles before his escape from occupied France and that would eventually be published as *Theory of Film* (1960). Indeed, there are even earlier indications of his theoretical/aesthetic preoccupations traceable beyond his film criticism for the *Frankfurter Zeitung* during the 1920s, back to his own formative pre-Weimar writings. Central to his critical interpretation of Expressionism, for example, is the distinction between the two competing imperatives Kracauer sees as shaping all forms of visual representation: the mimetic impulse to render the external world and the artistic will to vent their own inner life. And it is but a short step from this 1918 conceptualization of the work of art to the key tension he identifies some thirty-two years later between the 'realist' and 'formative' tendencies, competing or countervailing currents with which the film-maker must inevitably contend. Kracauer's repeated insistence upon a number of inherent cinematic qualities and themes finds expression in two main forms: most strikingly in some (if not most) of his numerous film reviews and journalism, but also, a little less obviously but nevertheless unmistakably, in his own drafts for film ideas, scripts and screenplays.[1]

In working chronologically through Kracauer's film reviews and reflections from the 1920s and 1930s, now collected together and published in volume 6 of his *Werke*, it soon becomes evident, firstly, how

prolific he was as a critic, penning two or three reviews for the newspaper week in, week out,[2] and, secondly, how he seldom missed an
opportunity to insert some comment as to the distinctive and determining features of the film medium. Indeed, these often *explicitly* serve as
the very interpretive principles and evaluative measures of the film in
question. Hence, Kracauer's vision of film develops and appears in
piecemeal fashion over the course of a decade. In a particularly telling
review of *The Merchant of Venice* (*Der Kaufmann von Venedig*) (Peter Paul
Felner, Germany, 1923) published on 24 November 1923, we learn, for
example, not only that motion pictures should on no account be mere
filmed theatre, the confines and conventions of the stage having no
place on the cinema screen, but also of the importance of two abiding
principles: film as a kind of physiognomy and as foregrounding the
unforeseen. Kracauer writes of Felner's production:

> The whole is lacking in terms of content [and is] strictly contrary to the
> spirit of film [*Geist des Films*]; [instead of] lively visual movement there
> are ponderous transitions and superfluous connections; instead of comic
> surfaces, phoney depths of the soul [*Seelentiefe*]; instead of surprising
> improvisation, carefully prepared scenes. In short: this is no genuine
> piece of cinema but rather bad theatre and sparkling revue. (WK 6.1: 38)[3]

And other historical costume dramas, again partly as a result of
their static and stagey feel, fare little better. In a review published a
week earlier,[4] Kracauer states his preference for two otherwise banal
German films involving swindlers, fortunes and romantic intrigue (*Die
Männer der Sybill*, Friedrich Zelnik, 1922; and *Der Frauenkönig*, Jaap
Speyer, 1923):

> Compared with historical epics, which have recently become modern,
> they do at least have the advantage that they show no carefully prepared
> scenes, no polished action which can just as well be seen in the theatre,
> but instead improvise exciting events from everyday life; and, what is
> more, that they forgo the presentation of the contents of the soul in favour
> of the filmic rendition of the appearances of superficial life. (WK 6.1: 37)[5]

A month later (28 December 1923), in his review of the epic drama
Peter der Grosse (Dimitri Buchowetzki, Germany, 1922), he expresses
his forlorn wish that the film-makers had rendered the spectacular
mass scenes and impressive battlefield choreography in such a way
that is

> truly in keeping with the spirit of film. Historical material is not really,
> because it leaves human beings and things in their natural contexts and
> affords too little opportunity for the embodiment of the improbable and
> fantastic. Their representation is still reminiscent of theatre, and only

when film has wiped out every trace of the stage is it completely cinematic [*ganz Leinwand*]. (WK 6.1: 46)

The preference for the 'improbable' and 'fantastic' may itself seem
rather curious, but only if one were to equate Kracauer's advocacy of
the 'realist tendency' with a simple-minded demand for mere cinematic
realism. In a review dated 4 November 1923, Kracauer praises both the
main feature – a circus film entitled *Zwischen Flammen und Bestien* (Fred
Stranz, Germany, 1923) – and the short animation film (one of a series
of *Münchener Bilderbogen*) which opens the programme. In the former:

> The shots deserve every praise; no technical possibility which film affords
> is left unused. Conflagration at the festival. Panic. Nocturnal strolls on
> the tightrope in the middle of the fireworks. The lion escapes with the
> child: all these fairy-tale happenings slip past so quickly that the unreal-
> ity which attends the circus world experiences one last intensification
> and completely removes any remnants of reality. (WK 6.1: 35–6)

In his appreciation of the latter, Kracauer observes how such animation is 'born straight out of the spirit of film' (WK 6.1: 35) and is
enchanted by how 'its improbability, running counter to any kind of
Naturalism, corresponds entirely with the essence of film [*Wesen des
Films*], which, if it is to be true to itself, must completely shatter the
natural contexts of our life' (WK 6.1: 36). Kracauer takes aim at both
Naturalism and the 'natural' here. Naturalism, with its emphasis upon
primordial human drives and instincts as the compelling force of
actions, presents violence and death as the inescapable *telos* of inner
life under the sway of myth and fate. Nothing could be less cinematic
for Kracauer: the film camera should attend to the light surfaces of the
everyday external world and not seek to penetrate where it simply
cannot venture – the murky depths of the human psyche. Film has a
penchant not for the morbid inevitability of fateful dramas but, rather,
for the serendipity and good fortune of comedy and the fairy tale. As
for the 'natural', Kracauer's point is this: by means of de-familiarization
and estrangement, the film camera should disturb habitual conditions
and circumstances, familiar things which appear as 'natural' and unal-
terably given, so as to discover them as contestable social constructions.
In capturing and re-presenting the mundane world from unexpected
and indeed hitherto unimaginable perspectives, the audience sees
anew the world to which indifference and amnesia have largely blinded
us.[6] Film enables the *de-naturalization* of what surrounds us understood
as a critical act of de-reification or disenchantment. And so, film is more
conducive to the depiction of the contemporary and quotidian than the
heroic and mythic, whose own proper medium is not cinematic images
but rather the words of poets and orations of the stage.[7] In 'Der Mythos

im Grossfilm', a review of *Helena* (Manfred Noa, Germany, 1923/4),[8] Kracauer admonishes film-makers who forget

> that the object of film is solely the apparent, silent outside of the world, that film finds fulfilment in the rendition of actions which are pieced together like the film shots themselves. A series of momentary images, an aggregation of (pointillist? splendid?) events: that really is its world. … One thing though is certain: that it would be better to plough the wide field of American silent comedy and detective hits than to bring kitschy versions of heroic sagas and great battles to the screen for everyone. (WK 6.1: 80)

At least three points of interest arise from this passage. Firstly, the notion of film as an 'aggregate', a bringing together and composing of a plethora of filmic fragments into a coherent whole for the purpose of depiction, anticipates Kracauer's notion, in both the 'Mass Ornament' essay and *Die Angestellten*, of the mosaic as the model of and for the critical representation of reality. The minutiae of everyday life in themselves tell us little; it is only when these atomistic particles are collected, collated and composed into a pattern that their individual and collective meanings come to the fore. The mosaic is a spatial construction and configuration of tesserae; the film is constituted through the physical contiguity and temporal continuity of frames. The role of the film editor becomes crucial here in the concatenation of the movie,[9] though this alone is insufficient to guarantee political insight.[10]

Secondly, Kracauer's reference to detective fiction and slapstick comedy (*Grotesk*) as exemplary filmic forms directs us to those quintessentially Anglo-American genres which were, according to an early aside in the *Caligari* book, largely alien to German cinema even if popular with audiences. Silent comedy is lauded by Kracauer not because it somehow captures the prevailing reality of American society and the Fordist system, but rather because it runs directly counter to them, upending their principles and subverting their logics. Slapstick is an anarchic, destructive character, the disorderly and disordering doppelgänger haunting and taunting the *Ratio* of modernity. He writes with tongue firmly in cheek: 'You have to hand it to the Americans: in their silent film comedies they have created themselves a form which counterbalances their reality: if in reality they discipline the world in an often unbearable way, so, as is only right and proper, they dismantle this self-made order in film' (WK 6.1: 199).

Finally, the film industry should stick to what it does best. Neither the Americans nor the Germans should dabble in screen versions of the mythological or epic. Kracauer is scornful not only of *Helena*, with its Greek myths, but also, of course, of Lang's Teutonic monstrosities and monumentalism in *Die Nibelungen* (1924). Both would be dwarfed a year later by the American sword and sandals epic *Ben Hur* (Fred Niblo), a film whose gargantuan scale and cost constitute its only points of interest. So many involved and so much invested, and all for so very little. Kracauer rejects the cinematic colossus: 'The shortcomings of the content open a gulf between BEN HUR and the POTEMKIN film. The latter is about a reality which is captured in the aesthetic medium of the film; in the former, a small private affair is painted large against the background of world historical events' (WK 6.1: 265–6).[11]

In the right hands, those of the Soviet film-maker Sergei Eisenstein, for example, the historical epic was not to be ruled out entirely as inherently incompatible with the true 'spirit of film'. Kracauer's advocacy of Eisenstein's *Battleship Potemkin* (USSR, 1925) here is perhaps not surprising given its cinematic significance and status, but it is less obvious in the light of his avowed aversion to intrusive montage techniques, indeed to the indulgence of the technical trickery characteristic of Formalist film-making. Kracauer praises Eisenstein's film on two counts: firstly, notwithstanding its grand scale and scope, it lays bare the revolutionary struggle of oppressed against oppressor bereft of any sentimentality and in the absence of any happy ending, genuinely capturing the brutality and actuality of contemporary political struggle. There are no heroic stars, no romantic distractions, no reconciliatory gestures: the film presents, in exploratory but never obfuscating visual terms, the simple and powerful story of suffering, mutiny and violent repression. Kracauer writes:

> Eisenstein uses the medium of film to represent perhaps for the first time a reality. He remains at the surface which is turned to the camera: he illustrates no text, he limits himself more to the sequencing of optical impressions. But *who* is doing the work of associating here? A fantasy full of outrage, terror and hope circles around a goal and possesses certainty. It catches sight of the automatic movements of the legs of the Cossacks and pans over the faces of the crowd to stop at a child's pram. The people of Odessa and the great harbour steps fuse into an indissoluble unity, the procession of people on the mole appears endless. This same fantasy, stirred by each thing, tosses the bodies of the sailors hither and thither, sees human shadows through iron railings, stretches the shining gun barrels across the sea. ... fragments of things are as important as the mutinous crowd to this fantasy, because mutiny is also to be found in them. (WK 6.1: 235–6)

This recording of the material world, and in particular the interaction of human bodies and things, is the other principal virtue of Eisenstein's film. Through the intricate camerawork and felicitous composition, modern technology and our complex relationship with it find faithful representation. Soulful inner life and mechanical external existence are not antithetical moments but set in genuine dialectical interplay. Just as in the fairy tale, the benign forces of Nature come to the aid of the weak and powerless in their confrontation with the seemingly omnipotent evildoers, so here it is as if 'second nature' were conspiring in the revolt against servitude and subordination. Eisenstein's great accomplishment is to have made a film which, 'unlike western films, does not rely for excitement on sensations behind which boredom stretches out. The thing is exciting because it is true' (WK 6.1: 235). This moment of truth has a name: '*Revolution*' (WK 6.1: 234).

2 *Terra Incognita* on Screen

From these extracts and examples, one can identify a number of emergent principles underpinning Kracauer's theoretical reflections on the film medium[12] and his designation of its genuine subject matter.

a) For the unfolding of film narrative, he privileges the imagistic and pictorial over other forms of representation and communication (sound, music, dialogue, titles); film stories[13] are to be *envisioned*, not told, by means of the selection and sequencing of *pictures*.

b) These visual elements composing the film must always perform some necessary *work* – advance the drama, disclose circumstances or reveal character – and must never constitute redundant decoration or excess ornamentation.

c) In imagining confrontations between, and collaborations of, the human and the technological, film must on no account exhibit technological/technical virtuosity for its own sake.

Further, there should be

d) a focus on the exteriority of everyday experiences, events and encounters as forms of action in the world (and not as inner states or forms of cognition/consciousness);

e) a preoccupation with recording and re-presenting the unpredictable world of objects and manifold manifestations of the natural environment at the level of surface for the purpose of de-reification; and

f) a predisposition for the *unstaged*, understood here not only in the limited sense of an aversion to the theatrical but, more generally, as the enthusiastic embrace of the unpredictable, the unintended and the improvisional.

While never formulated and specified in quite this way during the 1920s, nevertheless these tenets become paradigmatic, indeed almost programmatic, for Kracauer's own suggestions and scripts for short films in the early 1930s as his reviewing for the *FZ* came to an abrupt end. Each of the three film projects reproduced in volume 6.3 adheres to one or more of these principles.

His 1932 *Exposé (zu einer Kurztonfilm-Serie)* proposes various scenarios which, in presenting those usually unnoticed 'little everyday things', would assume 'an instructive character in addition to any aesthetic appeal' (WK 6.3: 515), the amusing incidentals attending foreign travel, for example. Or, reversing the logic of conventional travelogues, Kracauer suggests films foregrounding 'the exotic of our everyday' (WK 6.3: 516), explorations of the *terra incognita* of contemporary Germany: images documenting the Berlin skyline and its 'quite wonderful formations of roofs' (ibid.); the various trials and tribulations of moving house; and an alternative overview of current events featured in the newsreels and, more interestingly, of those censored out of them.

The other two projects are both comic creations. Based on the 1885 novel *Tartarin sur les Alpes* by Alphonse Daudet (1840–97),[14] Kracauer's film sketch of October 1933 tells of the misadventures of the eponymous president of the local alpine club, who, seeking re-election, forsakes his Provençal hometown of Tarascon and sets off for Switzerland, where a whole host of eccentric characters (exasperating tourists, refugee Russian anarchists, mischievous guides) lead him into all kinds of escapades. Foremost among these figures is Bompard, Tartarin's fellow townsman and now a local guide, who decides to play a little trick on the gullible, Ginster-like newcomer. Conspiratorially, Bompard lets Tartarin in on a fabulous and closely guarded 'secret': 'Switzerland doesn't exist at all. What we generally call Switzerland is nothing other than a gigantic health resort run by a large corporation for the amusement of travellers from all four corners of the world' (WK 6.3: 519). Switzerland is a simulation: its spectacular natural scenery is in reality, so Bompard reveals, only the most convincing artificial constructions built at enormous cost by the company's designers and engineers. The 'Swiss' themselves are all employees, sworn to secrecy so as not to spoil the illusion for unsuspecting holiday-makers: 'for example, they are not allowed to give the game away, telling tourists that the apparently so perilous alpine scenery is in reality a harmless artifice. The fact is nevertheless that if, say, an alpinist inadvertently falls into a crevasse, a porter will be waiting for him at the bottom' (ibid.).

Bompard's deception allows for two highly cinematic sequences. The first, shown as he relates his duplicitous tale to the credulous Tartarin, is the imaginative depiction of the Swiss landscape as it is in the process of 'construction' by teams of company workers. In foregrounding this work of simulation, the film mirrors the customary work of the film industry which, as Kracauer's visit to the Ufa studios at Neu-Babelsberg documented in his 'Calico-World' essay (1926) confirmed,[15] involves the creation of sets, settings and backdrops which are intended to appear 'real'. Bompard's story, in calling into question the distinction between the real and the fabricated, reminds the filmgoer of the fakery of all film-making. In Switzerland, as in the studios' scenery department, one finds 'everything guaranteed nature' (MOR: 288).

Secondly, Bompard's 'confession' emboldens Tartarin to attempt the most foolhardy of mountaineering exploits, safe and secure in the 'knowledge' that no harm can befall him. Slapstick comedy comes to the fore here in what may be intended as a parody of the high-altitude heroics found in Fanck's 'mountain' epics. To the amazement of veteran alpinists, Tartarin climbs the Jungfrau with aplomb:

> Why should he worry? Cheerful and carefree he crosses the most difficult snow bridges and crevasses, and when the mountain guides make him aware of the imminent dangers he winks at them with a knowing smile to let them know he is in on the secret and that they don't need to be so anxious about him. Eventually the guides are convinced that Tartarin is indeed a mountaineer of the highest calibre. (WK 6.3: 520)

As with Harold Lloyd on the girders of the construction site in New York, it is as if Tartarin could not have fallen even if he had tried.

This 'happy conquest of the Jungfrau' (WK 6.3: 521) leads to, and is then contrasted with, an attempt on Mont Blanc. By this time Bompard has disabused Tartarin of his deception, but, having committed themselves to the expedition, the two now see no way of backing out. After a perilous ascent and seemingly calamitous descent, in which each thinks himself responsible for the death of the other, Tartarin and Bompard are joyously reunited back at camp and our 'hero' is unanimously re-elected club president. Instead of a death-defying triumph over natural forces and fate, we witness a credulous coward and conniving conspirator not only surviving through selfishness and sheer chance but also winning the plaudits of all concerned. In true slapstick style, the last laugh belongs to Tartarin and Bompard: Fanck would indeed have been appalled at such a 'happy ending'.

Under the title *Sunday* (*Dimanche*), Kracauer's '1000-m children's film' (WK 6.3: 526) from early May 1933 opens with a conventional and convivial domestic scene of a bourgeois family relaxing after lunch. But, as parents and young child prepare for their afternoon walk, a change in perspective occurs: through enlargement and the shift of the camera to a low angle, it is as if the world had suddenly grown in scale and the viewer were now inhabiting a land of giants. He notes: 'thereafter everything is filmed from the *perspective of the child*' so that, in what follows as the principal part of the film, 'the Sunday afternoon outing is shown as the child experiences it' (WK 6.3: 523). Leaving the calm of the home, a series of dramatic outdoor adventures now begins:

an encounter with a Father Christmas (*Weihnachtsmann*); a terrifying chase by a ferocious hound; an expedition into the wilderness; a ride on a wild stallion; a monsoon; a quarrel with a violent stranger. Safely at home once more, the camera returns to its conventional position and the events we have just witnessed on screen are now replayed from the vantage point of the adults:

> The humour comes from correcting the child's imaginings. What seemed to him to be an adventure turns out to be mundane events: what he experienced with laughter or tears is not even noticed or is downplayed by the adults.

> Principle: *The repetition of the excursion must have the effect of solving the picture puzzle of the main part.* (WK 6.3: 526)

And so: the Father Christmas is merely the bus conductor in his uniform; the vicious dog is a playful puppy running hither and thither; the dark forest a few bushes; the mustang ride a turn on a carousel; the monsoon rain on the way home; and a bit of back-slapping between old friends completes the retelling. The film closes with the child sleeping soundly in his room, cuddly toy dog in his arms. The shifting perspectives of adult–child–adult corresponding to the dialectical structure of *Dimanche* de-familiarize the everyday world. Estrangement here serves a doubly didactic purpose: the spectator is reminded, firstly, that the film camera is never neutral with respect to the events it records; and, secondly, that the world is never simply given: it can be, and is, seen differently through other eyes. In encapsulating these experiences of contingency and alterity, the quotidian becomes a perpetual *terra incognita*. Whether chatting on a Berlin train or going for a walk in the park, Kracauer makes good use of his Sunday afternoon excursions.

3   Into the 'Thicket'

The culmination of Kracauer's longstanding fascination with the cinematic medium, *Theory of Film: The Redemption of Physical Reality* constitutes his most sustained and systematic attempt to explore its essential properties and possibilities and remains today 'a canonical work of classical film theory' (TOF: viii).[16] Like the earlier *Caligari* study, and as the preceding discussion has shown, the book had a 'long and complex gestation period' (CAL: xxii)[17] even before Kracauer's American exile; like *Caligari*, too, it was born in the context of a double catastrophe – the 'spiritual shelterlessness' of the subject in a disenchanted modern world, and the National Socialist terror and the Holocaust – or, contentiously, of their 'double repression' or 'near-elision';[18] and, like its predecessor, *Theory of Film* was subject to caustic criticism for its supposed naivety and presumptuous normativity.[19] By the time of its belated appearance,[20] and ironically given the title of its epilogue ('Film in our Time'), the book's emphasis upon 'reality', its penchant for films of the pre-war years and neo-realism, and its disdain for experimental film all seemed anachronistic in the newly formed film schools of the 1960s abuzz with Althusserian Marxism, semiotic decoding and Lacanian psychoanalysis. Kracauer certainly did himself no favours: his approach is straightforward and his writing style all too lucid for aesthetes and intellectuals; his appreciation of popular film genres is both eclectic and unpretentious, with a preference for slapstick comedies and Hollywood musicals over avant-garde art-house 'masterpieces'; and his work runs counter to the pretensions of the film-maker as artistic *auteur*. In its exploration of the use of dialogue and sound, its examination of the varied roles and possibilities of film music, and its conceptualization of the experiences of actors and spectators, *Theory of Film* quickly proves to be a far more complex and sophisticated text than its high-handed and high-brow critics would have us believe. And yet it remains much misunderstood and maligned to this day, despite the best redemptive endeavours of rare enthusiasts such as the late Miriam Bratu Hansen.

My hope here is to make a small contribution to the work she has so brilliantly inaugurated. My purpose in this chapter and the next is neither to trace further the genealogy nor to conduct an exhaustive, exegetical tour of *Theory of Film*, but rather, after briefly sketching the book's fundamental principles, to take two exploratory paths in the company not only of Kracauer but also, because the comparisons seem so fruitful, of Benjamin. The first excursion considers the significance for Kracauer of (American) slapstick comedy, a genre which, as Hansen points out, was paradigmatic for the 'Marseilles notebooks' and the early development of the book even if it takes on a more subterranean existence in the final version.[21] The second expedition, in chapter 10, ventures into the oft-posited elective affinity between the film medium and the modern cityscape, or, more precisely, the experience of the metropolitan street. While, in his 'Work of Art' essay, Benjamin curiously invokes architecture as the very model of a medium experienced in a state of collective distraction, Kracauer, erstwhile architect, contrasts the static and enduring forms of the urban built environment with the tantalizing and transient encounters and experiences of the urban crowd. The correspondence between the cinematic and 'the street' leads us back to the 'street films' of the 1920s and 1930s, a genre much discussed in the *Caligari* study. And this is indeed our intended destination: for, in returning to the uncanny figure of the sleepwalker in need of awakening, and, concomitantly, of the city as a dreamscape, we will stumble once again upon, or into, Benjamin's *Arcades Project*. And so these outings are digressions leading us, like the film medium itself, on 'paths that wind through the thicket of things' (TOF: 309).

The first few pages of *Theory of Film* leave the reader in no doubt as to the fundamental premise and 'basic concepts' of Kracauer's *'material aesthetics'* (TOF: xlix): the 'moving' images of film are 'essentially an extension' (ibid.) of the 'still' images of photography, since their 'basic properties' are 'identical' (TOF: 28). Accordingly, film and photography come to share the same essential imperative and 'unspoken affinity' (TOF: 18) for revealing, recording and representing the visible world – what Kracauer terms variously 'physical', 'material' or 'camera' reality. In conforming with this inherent 'realistic tendency' (TOF: 30), the film medium 'gravitates towards' (TOF: 28) this external realm and is most forcefully attracted by particular phenomena and moments:[22] the 'unstaged' (TOF: 60) and unceasing 'flow of life' (TOF: 71) as manifested at the level of surface; the 'indeterminate' (TOF: 68), incidental and accidental; and myriad trajectories of movement, instants of change and intimations of evanescence.[23] Film as glimpse, as trace or vestige of the vanishing, has, Kracauer argues, a particular predilection for portraying certain kinds of subjects: for example, the street life of the contemporary city, with its circulating traffic, milling crowds and urban detritus[24] all encountered and experienced *en passant*; and the realm of nature understood here similarly as an endless restlessness, as a manifold in motion to be caught only and ever 'on the wing' (TOF: xlix).[25] Be it first nature, be it second nature, film must seek out the very 'reality' that would elude it. Indeed, one might say that, for Kracauer, the true subject matter of film is the modern itself, understood here as Baudelaire's famous conception of *modernité*: 'the ephemeral, the fugitive, the contingent' (Baudelaire 1986: 13). The film-maker has inherited the mantle of the 'painter of modern life'.

Kracauer contrasts this 'realistic tendency' or 'cinematic approach' (TOF: 38) with another, competing gravitational pull: the so-called formative tendency (TOF: 30). This refers to the actions and interventions of the film-maker to give coherence, structure and narrative to films so as to render them as stories and as works of art. All films necessarily involve this 'formative tendency' for their very existence as material objects. The camera always has to be pointed at something by someone, and this involves decisions and choices as to what, and what not, to film.[26] Such artistic concerns start to become a problem for Kracauer when they intrude upon or displace the primacy of the 'realistic tendency', as happens in, for example, infelicitous attempts to film inappropriate subjects – theatrical plays, operas, novels, tragedy. But this privileging of the 'cinematic approach' of the film medium should be read neither as a dogmatic insistence upon 'realism' in film nor as some blanket endorsement of (Italian) neo-realist cinema. As his surprising enthusiasm for film musicals and their exemplification of the very 'air of cinema' (TOF: 213) indicates,[27] Kracauer does not simply dismiss the artifice of the 'formative tendency' but rather recognizes that it is always and only in the intricate interplay of these competing tendencies that film develops.[28] In the 'cinematic approach' the 'realistic' and 'formative tendencies' are symbiotic. He writes: 'All these creative efforts are in keeping with the cinematic approach as long as they benefit, in some way or other, the medium's substantive concern with our visible world' (TOF: 39).

Indeed, while Kracauer is scathing of the *uncinematic* qualities of much avant-garde, experimental 'film art' for its narcissistic absorption in technique for its own sake, technological possibilities and 'creative' touches may serve to extend the scope of 'camera reality' itself. Two examples of this should suffice. In his reflections upon the twin 'recording' and 'revealing functions' (TOF: 41) of the camera, Kracauer pays special attention to its capacity for capturing 'things normally unseen' by the human eye (TOF: 46), an elaboration of what Benjamin suggestively termed the 'optical unconscious' in his 'Work of Art' essay. Through the speeding up or slowing down of images, through the use of close-up or wide-angle lenses, the 'blindspots of the mind' (TOF: 53), unsuspected worlds within worlds, are disclosed. In regard to close-up, for instance, Kracauer writes: 'Such images blow up our environment in a double sense: they enlarge it literally; and in so doing, they blast the prison of conventional reality, opening up expanses which we have explored at best in dreams before' (TOF: 48).

Moreover, the use of obtuse camera angles may also disturb our complacent, conventional perspective on the world. The defamiliarization of the quotidian is wholly in keeping with the 'cinematic approach': films, Kracauer notes, 'alienate our environment in exposing' (TOF: 55) it to our eyes from new and disorientating vantage points and as part of unexpected and challenging configurations. We see the hitherto unseen, the *unforeseen*. As a visual prosthetic, 'The cinema, then, aims at transforming the agitated witness into a conscious observer. Nothing could be more legitimate than its lack of inhibitions in picturing spectacles which upset the mind. Thus it keeps us from shutting our eyes to the "blind drive of things"' (TOF: 58).

Kracauer's implicit appeal to the 'optical unconscious' is one of numerous thematic and conceptual echoes of Benjamin's understanding of film. The stress upon the physical extends, for example, to his understanding of the staccato bodily performance of the actor in the film-making process. In slapstick comedy, above all, the actor becomes, Kracauer notes, just another 'object among objects' (TOF: 97) and must wrestle with the disorderly and disobedient world of things. Indeed, since films are seldom shot in the actual sequence of scenes screened, the filming process itself inevitably involves a fragmentation of the actor's performance and physical presence. The bodily movements, gestures and expressions of the actor are broken down and then reconstructed along with the narrative in the editing room: 'This decomposition of the actor's wholeness corresponds to the piecemeal manner in which he supplies the elements from which eventually his role is built' (ibid.). For both Kracauer and Benjamin, the consequence and significance of this 'testing' attitude of the camera cannot be overestimated.[29] In his 1950 'Stage vs. Screen Acting', one of a number of essays published in the early 1950s in which specific themes of *Theory of Film* are first aired,[30] Kracauer notes how close-ups can *'challenge* the spectator to find errors in an actor's depiction of character' and *'force* the actor to relinquish ... gestures and inflections' (KAW: 202). Since 'the camera catches, and can magnify, the most ephemeral glance, the slightest shrug of the shoulder', to be convincing, to avoid the impression of 'overacting' and theatricality, the film actor 'must act as if he were not acting at all, as if he were the person in real life who happens to be photographed. He must seem *to be* the character' (ibid.). The actor must assume not just a 'photographic face' but a whole *photographic physis*. This returns us once more to the issue that has troubled Kracauer from the start: the relationship between visual representation and inner life. He writes:

> Contrary to what is usually assumed, photographic portraits are not explicit definitions of character. They are momentary records of mood, fragmentary, casual, even fortuitous. For this reason, the film actor must make his gestures, poses and expressions hint of the moments in the life of the character that are not photographed. His performance is photographic only when it impresses us as one incident out of many possible incidents in the life of the character being portrayed. Only then does the film actor render life in a truly photographic way. ...
>
> This explains why the film actor is bound to his physical appearance more than the stage actor, whose face never fills the whole field of an audience's vision. The camera catches all things, all the outer movements that reveal inner psychological changes. The nuances are impossible on the stage. (Ibid.)

Film acting is an exercise in minimalism: movements and manipulations, ephemeral and 'indefinite intimations' (ibid.) extricated from, and expressive of, a continuum of life lived invisibly elsewhere.[31]

And there is another dimension of corporeal experience which is transformed by film: the sense of shock and sensuous stimulation experienced by the distracted spectator in the cinema. In its eradication of aura and its emphasis upon tactile proximity, Benjamin enthusiastically emphasizes the 'physical shock' and the 'percussive effect' (SW3: 119) of film as the hallmark of cinematic experience, the corollary indeed of the very metropolitan existence to which film 'gravitates'. In his extraordinary epilogue to *Theory of Film*, Kracauer's advocacy of distraction as a new and positive mode of reception, as *an attention directed elsewhere*, leads to a different understanding of film's potential. Rationalization, abstraction and quantification – in the modern age, these processes have led to a diminution of the human senses and an indifference to the unique qualities of things. In its very ability to disclose and penetrate reality – whether through revealing what was previously invisible, through transforming perception by means of innovative camerawork (estrangement), or through techniques of comic debunking and playful digression – popular film is, Kracauer argues, capable of enhancing our faculties, heightening our sensitivity and receptivity, and restoring our aesthetic appreciation of the world around us. In a quasi-theological twist, Kracauer sees film as promising a threefold 'redemption': of the physical reality it (re)discovers; of the music that is 'recaptured';[32] and, above all, of humankind, of all those spectators who, through its sounds and images, come to bear witness to the world anew.

4   Critical Clowning I: Mimesis

The publication of Hansen's seminal work (2012) has served to emphasize how seldom the writings of Kracauer and Benjamin on film are brought together for mutual illumination and critical comparison.[33] The remainder of this chapter is concerned with exploring their shared interest in, and appreciation of, some of the critical promise of American silent film comedy, in particular the pioneering slapstick shorts of such celebrated figures as Charlie Chaplin and Harold Lloyd. Neither Benjamin nor Kracauer elaborated a sustained theory of these miniature film comedies. Kracauer's 'Silent Film Comedy' essay[34] is perhaps the closest to such an undertaking and brings together ideas and examples otherwise scattered across his many film reviews from the 1920s and 1930s. As for Benjamin, there are a couple of very brief overlapping essays from 1928–9 reflecting on Chaplin.[35] Together these rather disparate writings foreground two intriguing concepts: for Benjamin, the notion of mimesis; and, for Kracauer, the concept of improvisation. These are not mutually exclusive terms, and both imitation and improvisation are intricately and intimately connected to a wider set of thematic concerns: the medium of film and its affinity for the modern cityscape; wit, childhood and the fairy tale; and autonomy and utopia.

Mimesis, understood as the copying of reality, as the identification and fabrication of resemblances, and particularly as the re-presentation/representation of the natural world by means of an image, is, of course, a central concept in the theory and history of art. It is also an intriguingly polysemic term. Etymologically the word originates with the Greek *mimos* ('imitator'), giving rise to *mimus* (Latin: 'actor') and thence, in one derivation, to our contemporary usage of the word 'mime' as a special form of wordless, often comic, performance using bodily and facial gestures to communicate, and of 'mimic', as one who imitates or impersonates another. Mimesis involves the act of acting, of pretending to be someone or something else. 'Mimesis' as imitation shares the same Latin root (*imitari*) as the word 'image' (*imago*). Mimesis involves the work of imagination understood here specifically as the forming into and rendering of images.

In two fragments from the early 1930s, 'Doctrine of the Similar' and 'On the Mimetic Faculty', Benjamin understands mimesis to refer specifically to two aspects: the human ability to imitate the natural world so as to create resemblances, and our capacity to perceive correspondences between things that may or may not have any actual relation with each other. Humankind possesses the 'highest capacity for producing similarities' and the most acute 'gift for seeing similarity ... a rudiment of the once powerful compulsion to become similar and to behave mimetically' (SW2: 720). Early forms of cultic and ritualistic dance in which participants dressed and moved about as – temporarily 'became' – a venerated or magical animal would be an example of the former; the reading of the entrails of a sacrificed animal to divine the future would be an example of the second. That modern humankind possesses only a residue of these mimetic practices is central to Benjamin's argument. Eschewing mimesis as an aesthetic category and debate in art history, his concern is with the phylogenetic (historical) and ontogenetic (developmental) transformation of mimesis as a human capacity and activity. He contends that, far from witnessing the diminution and disappearance of mimetic practices, these are reconfigured and recast via the notion of onomatopoeia into language and then, through pictorial representations such as hieroglyphs, into script. Modern-day writing is, he claims, an (unrecognized) archive of 'non-sensuous correspondences' (SW2: 722). At the same time, Benjamin discerns the remnants of sensuous correspondences in one domain that is of particular significance for him, and for us in the context of clowning: the play of children.[36]

This notion of mimesis as child-like playfulness in the mimicking of others and of nature is the key to understanding Benjamin's subterranean interest in slapstick. True, Benjamin does not make any specific connection with the silent comedian here, but, as his reflections on Chaplin from 1929 and then 1934 make clear, imitation is more than just an essential aspect of the comic actor's repertoire and stock in trade; it is the very hallmark of Chaplin's comic character and the wellspring of the figures which people his films. Chaplin has become, Benjamin notes, his own 'walking trademark' (SW2: 200), his appearance and manner distinctive, unmistakable, and endlessly imitated by other actors. Dressed in an ill-fitting suit – tight jacket, baggy trousers, bowler hat askew – and armed with his twirling, whirling walking stick, Chaplin takes on forms of attire and accoutrements which at once portray and parody the respectable petit bourgeois employee, the ordinary office clerk, the insignificant pen-pusher, the little shop assistant. Chaplin's whole comic persona is a copying of the down-at-heel anonymous nobody of the big city. Benjamin approvingly cites the work of Philippe Soupault on the metropolitan roots of Chaplin and his comic creations:

> In his endless walks through the London streets, with their black-and-red houses, Chaplin trained himself to observe. He himself has told us that the idea of creating his stock character ... first occurred to him on seeing office workers walking along the Strand. What he saw in their bearing and dress was the attitude of a person who takes some pride in himself. But the same can be said of the other characters that surround him in his films. They, too, originate in London: the shy, young, winsome girl; the burly lout who is always ready to use his fists and then takes to his heels when he sees that people aren't afraid of him; the arrogant gentleman who can be recognized by his top hat. (SW2: 223)

Let us linger in the metropolitan setting. It is not just the typical inhabitants of the city that inspire and inhabit slapstick comedy: the buildings, objects and encounters of the cityscape also provide manifold settings and opportunities for imitative activity. For example, in *From Hand to Mouth* (1919), a film reviewed by Kracauer in 1924, an innocent Harold Lloyd is suspected of stealing a woman's purse in the street; a policeman arrives and gives chase as Lloyd makes a run for it; the fugitive hides behind a car which, the moment his pursuers arrive, pulls off, leaving Lloyd cowering in full view; the pursuit resumes until Lloyd finds another refuge, this time a barrel; discovered once more, he makes off, darting now into a second-hand clothes store, where he swipes a walking stick, a hat and a long coat. Disguised as an old man, Lloyd toddles off down the street until unmasked by the police and chased yet again before escaping on the back of a car occupied by a gang of real crooks. Multiple forms of copying are at work in this series of scenes: the chase, perhaps the most common and characteristic element of slapstick comedy, is itself mimetic. To follow someone, to shadow them, is nothing other than a kind of imitation, the copying of the movement, speed and direction of a pursuant by the pursuer. And hiding is an imitative act, and one so characteristic of children's play: to conceal oneself behind or inside objects means to take on (or accommodate oneself to) their shape. Lloyd's chase sequence is an adult game of hide-and-seek in the city. Indeed, the oldest trick (and, in nature, the origin of mimicry itself) is to avoid detection by imitating one's surroundings, by standing still and becoming a part of the scenery, so to

speak, quietly watching one's adversaries rush by. Lloyd finally impersonates the old man by taking on particular clothes and a doddery gait,
becoming another character altogether, an innocent passer-by. Lloyd
exits the shop like a child emerging from the dressing-up cupboard.
Indeed, here we see another very common trope of slapstick films: the
portrayal of the act of acting itself, with Harold Lloyd the actor playing
the part of a fugitive who is pretending to be someone else. Here the
mimetic faculty itself is acted out, *screened*.

Interestingly, and this is why I have chosen this particular comic
chase, it is staged again later in the film, when Lloyd actually wants to
be followed by the police so as to lead them to the gangsters' hideaway
where a kidnapped young heiress is being held for ransom. Lloyd
deliberately incites the police: kicking them, throwing stones at them,
smashing the windows of the precinct headquarters, so that, by the end
of such provocations, he is eventually pursued by a great posse of officers who finally pile into the criminals' lair. Lloyd escapes, hand in hand
with his beloved. Lloyd's antics ensure that the police are compelled
to chase him, to copy his every move as he twists and turns his way
through the city streets.

5   Critical Clowning II: Improvisation

Kracauer's understanding of improvisation is also bound up with film
and the cityscape. Once again, a little etymological work is valuable:
the term is derived from the Latin *provisus* – *pro* (beforehand) and
videre (to see). The 'provisional' – in its origins, then, this refers specifically to that which is seen beforehand, discerned in advance, to that
which is somehow anticipated, expected, to that which can be provided
for. The 'improvisional' or 'improvisation', then, is the very antithesis
of this 'seen beforehand': the 'unforeseen'. And slapstick film comedy
is a storehouse of images of improvisation as well as imitation.

a) *Improvisation as quotidian practice* It is an aspect of quotidian met-
    ropolitan experience, the incessant 'flow of life' to which we pay
    perhaps little heed but to which the film camera is uniquely devoted
    as a redeemer of the inconspicuous, disregarded and unnoticed.
b) *Improvisation as bodily practice* It involves a seemingly seamless,
    spontaneous physical performance; and I use the qualification
    'seemingly' because, of course – and here there is another
    paradox – that which appears as improvisation is invariably
    painstakingly practised, repeatedly rehearsed and scrupulously
    staged. The musician, the dancer, the acrobat – their level of
    accomplishment, their expertise and effort, is so often propor-
    tional to and manifest as the apparent ease and effortlessness

of the performance itself. On screen we witness the image, or, better, the *illusion* of improvisation, of the extempore.[37]

c) *Improvisation as material practice* There is a special relationship with the object world in which things are not reduced to specific functions and ends but, rather, are used and reused in playful and unexpected ways, as material for *bricolage*. When things are not provided, one must make do with whatever is to hand. Improvisation in this sense involves quick-wittedness and an optimism of the spirit that whatever is coincidentally present will suffice, that provisioning is not necessary. Providence will provide. What is simply there will be enough, what is there will do the trick – for Kracauer, this is one of the fundamental principles of slapstick comedy.[38]

Improvisation and mimesis are both essential ingredients of clowning. In the *Strassen in Berlin* collection, one finds a 1932 review of a theatrical performance by the three Andreu–Rivel clowns, 'Akrobat – Schöön'. Kracauer initially wonders whether such clowning can really survive transplantation from the circus to the Scala theatre: Can, indeed should, such tomfoolery ever aspire beyond random pranks and absurd antics? Kracauer is astonished: he witnesses a performance in which an identifiable and coherent narrative structure emerges from accidents and contingencies, a miraculous unity composed of the most disparate circumstances and actions. He comments: 'By uniting to carry out a joint task the clowns pursue practical dialectics; that is, they do not improvise obviously and from the outset but feign a willingness to work which they then constantly disavow. Thus the creation of opportunities, which, after all is their profession, is doubly and boldly underlined' (SBA: 101).

The performance of the clowns involves the continual formation and dissolution of orderliness, intention and attention, a fluctuation between purposive actions and apparent distractions of all kinds. Together, Kracauer tells us, the clowns determine to construct some kind of bridge somehow, a human bridge – a bridge to where and what end remains unclear. Nevertheless, this project provides the narrative thread through the performance. But, of course, the clowns repeatedly stray or are led astray from their labours, their task of constructing themselves as construction elements: they squabble, fight, and tickle each other. The bridge building is begun, interrupted, resumed, forgotten, remembered once more, ignored, renewed, and finally even completed, but this is achieved despite the clowns' best efforts, not because of them. The bridge, the mimetic imperative, is only an impetus, an alibi for everything else. Indeed, the inability to concentrate on the matter at hand is the clowns' greatest achievement. For both Benjamin and Kracauer, to be thus distracted is not failure of attention, rather an attending to something or someone somewhere else.[39] And this is characteristic, above all, of children and their play. In their susceptibility to distraction, the clowns are true to the wondrous capacity of children to find delights in the most unlikely things at the most inopportune times. Kracauer notes how the Andreu–Rivel performers 'reproduce in an exemplary fashion the entire course of the child's imagination. In fact, not content with presenting one comical childlike turn or another, they show how in the child each turn develops from the one before' (SBA: 103).

As in the case of the 'drunken pianist',[40] what seems incomprehensibly idiosyncratic might actually involve the coherent workings and consequences of another, unrecognized, unsuspected logic, one that does not conform to the conventions of the (sober) adult world:

> The adult generally considers children to be absentminded and distracted. They are forever changing the subject, do things in fits and starts, and appear to live entirely in and for the moment. Is it not genuinely the case, however, that these capricious associations made by the child develop coherently and not at all capriciously? That they are in fact based upon a legitimacy which only remains unfathomed because it is not determined by the wide-awake consciousness and highly important purposes of adults? The Andreu–Rivel clowns underline quite emphatically the strict logic governing the sequence of child-like notions. (SBA: 103)

The adult errs in thinking the child lives in a perpetual present. Rather, children's distraction is better understood as a living out of time, as living *extempore*. It is a sensibility antithetical to the adult temporal economy with its quantification and calculation of time and task, its emphasis on time-keeping and clock-watching. What appear as diversions, digressions and dawdlings are part of a denial of the scarcity of time. Time can never be wasted or frittered away, lost or gained. Time is not there to be made use of, like some instrument or tool. And time is certainly not money. Time is an opportunity for and the occasion of play. There is enough time, there will be time – such a *chrono-logic* runs counter to the modern metropolitan sensibility where the exigencies of busyness and business set the daily tempo and punctuality, predictability and synchronicity are essential.

Clowning, play, distraction and childhood: this complex is critical to both Benjamin and Kracauer and links with one particular narrative form: the fairy tale. Kracauer writes:

> the logic we see here isn't any normal logic but closest to that of the fairy tale. By adopting this logic the Rivel clowns not only unhinge their serious, all too serious, bridge building, the senselessness of which would in itself fulfil the clowns' very being, they also moreover point to a sense in the senselessness. Their comical antics are more than mere fun and games intended to shatter malign reserve and fake earnestness. While

this is a function of all clowning, the tomfoolery of the Rivels has another which lends it greater significance: thanks to the special logic supporting it, it evokes the idea of a reality not identical with our own; a reality as at odds with the quotidian as that of fairy tales and many dreams. (SBA: 104)

The fairy tale has a special significance for Kracauer and Benjamin (and Ernst Bloch). In his 1936 essay 'The Storyteller: Observations on the Work of Nikolai Leskov', Benjamin identifies the fairy tale as 'the first tutor of mankind', providing insight into 'the earliest arrangements that mankind made to shake off the nightmare which myth had placed upon its chest' (SW3: 157). In the 'happy ever after' of the fairy tale we see a reversal of the everyday world, in which the small and weak bravely confront and surprisingly triumph over the seemingly overwhelming powers of the demonic and despotic. With the help of kind animals and enchanting figures, children outwit those who mean them harm, undo their spells, and turn the powers of evildoers back upon their source. Benjamin observes: 'The wisest thing – so the fairy tale taught mankind in olden times, and teaches children to this day – is to meet the forces of the mythical world with cunning and with high spirits' (SW3: 157). The fairy-tale world for Benjamin is one of liberation, happiness and convivial complicity with the benevolent powers of nature.

Such intimations of an alternative reality, of a utopian realm, are key themes in understanding comedy in general and slapstick in particular. Slapstick is not simply about a contrary chronology, a dreamtime of distraction; it envisions radically new and harmonious relationships between human beings and the material and natural world, forms of recognition and appreciation that are both felicitous and fraternal. Here imitation and improvisation involve particular forms of material practice which share the clear-sightedness and cunning to recognize that things are not just what they seem.

6   The Reinvention of Things

Early in the first volume of *Capital*, Marx astutely and presciently recognized the commodity as 'a very queer thing abounding in metaphysical subtleties and theological niceties' (1977: 435). The object of misperception and misconception, it is an artefact whose origins in human labour are forgotten while being imbued with independent powers and potentialities. And in the world of slapstick comedy – for good and for ill – the material world of things certainly seems to possess a life of its own, though this enchantment is far from the fetishism identified by Marx.[41] Objects become obstinate, refuse to co-operate, conspire as obstructions; objects are unexpectedly obliging and useful in ways that were never foreseen; or *both*, changing suddenly from one moment to the next. Yes, things are unreliable, not to be trusted; things will trip you up, things are ticklish, tricky and treacherous. But this duplicity of things has a positive aspect, too. If things are unpredictable it is because they are more than inert objects with their uses inscribed and predetermined. Things are versatile and adaptable. In the slapstick world one can be sure that things will turn up, that, even without the proper tools for the job, what needs to be done will be done. Whatever is at hand is turned to the matter at hand, to this, ad hoc. Improvisation involves *the inventory* and *the inventive*: taking heed of what is to hand, and then an ingenious refunctioning of things, a crafty[42] extension of their use-value, so to speak. Improvisation looks to the re-use-value of objects. And such talents are both improvisional (one lacks the right implements, they are not provided) and provisional (one sees in other objects new and unintended possibilities). Such an attitude to the material world is precisely that of the fairy tale in its combination of 'high spirits' and 'cunning'. Fairy tales have not only their own chronologic but also their own technologic.[43] And we might term it *bricolage*.

In a 1924 review of a programme including Lloyd's *From Hand to Mouth* (1919) and Chaplin's *Dough and Dynamite* (1914), Kracauer captures the hallmarks of the slapstick world:

> The recipe is always the same:[44] one makes one's way through the world in the most improbable way, suffering every conceivable trickery of objects with an air of innocence; one behaves foolishly, stirs up melancholy but finally emerges as the noble soul one is. The essential thing is also this: that one is always smarter or at least nimbler than the stupid many-headed monster of the police which lies in one's way with great earnestness after the most ridiculous pranks. One swings over them and away, hounds them until they are out of breath, and gets up to the same madness with them as with the inanimate objects which are everywhere in the way. Boxes are there to be toppled over, manholes to be crept into. The entire mechanized world is placed in a comic light by Chaplin and his contemporaries, its stress is transcended, its gravity turned into fun, its way of moving derided and banished through exaggeration. (WK 6.1: 64–5)

The benevolence of nature is emphasized in Kracauer's review of Chaplin's *The Gold Rush* (1925):

> Because the human is presented in this way here, it is therefore fitting that he proceeds as if in a fairy tale. In the face of this little mite, Chaplin, creeping helpless and alone through the snowstorm and the gold-digger town, elemental forces stand back. In the nick of time something always happens to pluck him from the dangers he has failed to reckon with.

> Even the bear feels friendly towards him like a bear from a fairy tale. His
> very impotence is dynamite; his comedy conquers those who laugh and
> more than stirs the emotions, for it touches the very condition of the
> world. (WK 6.1: 270)

Chaplin has nothing to fear from the bear. But characteristic of the
slapstick comedian is oftentimes a particular kind of reluctant heroism,
as exemplified by Tartarin in his alpine adventures. Timid and timor-
ous, such comic figures nevertheless find within themselves – but
only when time and circumstance absolutely demand it – a sense of
resolution and resilience, a readiness to risk everything for the sake of
winning through. They thereby demonstrate what Benjamin refers to
as 'character':

> While fate brings to light the immense complexity of the guilty person,
> the complications and bonds of his guilt, character gives this mystical
> enslavement of the person to the guilt context the answer of genius.
> Complication becomes simplicity, fate freedom. For the character of the
> comic figure is not the scarecrow of the determinist; it is the beacon in
> whose beams the freedom of his actions becomes visible. (SW1: 205–6)

But such courageous characters are sometimes just more lucky than
anything else, or rather perhaps they are lucky because they are courageous. They are lucky and plucky. They have to be, given the circumstances in which they sometimes find themselves. Kracauer notes how
silent comedy

> did not highlight the performer's proficiency in braving death and sur-
> mounting impossible difficulties; rather it minimized his accomplish-
> ments in a constant effort to present successful rescues as the outcome
> of sheer chance. Accidents superseded destiny; unpredictable circum-
> stances now foreshadowed doom, now jelled into propitious constella-
> tions for no visible reason. Take Harold Lloyd on the skyscraper: what
> protected him from falling to his death was not his prowess but a random
> combination of external and completely incoherent events which, without
> being intended to come to his help, dovetailed so perfectly that he could
> not have fallen even if he had wanted to. Accidents were the very soul
> of slapstick. (TOF: 62)[45]

It should be remembered here that Lloyd's miraculous survival high
up on the girders follows his reluctant resolve to commit suicide: he is
still alive only because a series of the most absurd incidents have con-
spired to sabotage his half-hearted attempts to take his own life: by
poisoning himself – thwarted by an irritating fly settling on his nose
– by stabbing himself, by throwing himself from a high window, and
finally by shooting himself. When really confronted with death, Lloyd

clings to dear life. And, as is often the case with such comedies, the film's optimistic or ironic maxim forms the title: *Never Weaken* (1921).

For Benjamin and Kracauer, slapstick comedy, in its invocation and imagination of mimetic play and improvisation, in its congruence with childhood distraction and the fairy tale, envisions a ludic world of liberty and laughter. These are utopian premonitions, intimations and anticipations:

a) of the medium of film itself and its promise of a critical redemption of the world around us and a restoration of human faculties and sensibilities;

b) of a body that is unconstrained, unrestricted, unfettered, a body of airy lightness and youthful suppleness, a body of both grace and strength, of playfulness and joyfulness;

c) of a special *chronology*: a temporal freedom, an abundance of time to devote to playful distractions and digressions not only because there is no particular hurry but because such diversions are themselves the destination. One is at liberty to pursue whatever time and chance may bring along;

d) of a distinctive *technology*: slapstick comedy imagines freedom from material necessity, a benign relationship between the human body and the natural and human-built environment, and a sense of the world as serendipity. Dangers are avoided, death is defied, enemies are outwitted. And all these follow from the good fortune that accompanies those in full possession of their wit (in both senses);

e) of laughter itself, as a critical and subversive response to the condition of the world. 'In his films', Benjamin observes, 'Chaplin appeals both to the most international and the most revolutionary emotion of the masses – their laughter' (SW2: 224).

In his 1964 radio broadcast on Kracauer, Adorno concludes with:

In Kracauer, the fixation on childhood, as a fixation on play, takes the form of a fixation on the benignness of things; presumably the primacy of the optical in him is not something inborn but rather the result of this relationship to the world of objects. One looks in vain in the storehouse of Kracauer's intellectual motifs for indignation about reification. To a consciousness that suspects it has been abandoned by human beings, objects are superior. In them thought makes reparations for what human beings have done to the living. The state of innocence would be the condition of needy objects, shabby, despised objects alienated from their purpose. For Kracauer they alone embody something that would be other than the universal functional complex, and his idea of philosophy would be to lure their indiscernible life from them. The Latin word for thing is *res*. Realism is derived from it. (1991: 177)

Here, Kracauer's 'curious realism', his 'redemption of physical reality', is attributed by Adorno etymologically and explicitly to his (comedic) vision of 'the benignness of things'. And a little more etymological work may prove rewarding here. I suggest that liberty is at the very heart of Kracauer's 'fixation on play' and playfulness. To improvise is to ad-lib, to act freely, from the Latin *ad libitum* ('according to pleasure'). To live according to pleasure: to live in a benign world in a state of 'high spirits': what could be more enchanting than this utopian promise?

10

Film, Phantasmagoria and the Street

1   The Cinematic City

Benjamin and Kracauer were certainly not the first to identify an elective affinity or 'structural homology'[1] between film as the most modern mass medium and the metropolis as the most modern human habitat and pre-eminent locus of mass experience. Indeed, by the late 1920s and early 1930s such correspondences and connections were rather commonplace for both pioneering film-makers and early film critics and theorists. Nor do Benjamin and Kracauer really provide any systematic mapping or definitive theory of any such relationship, confining their observations to asides and digressions within texts concerned principally with other matters. Benjamin's typically elusive reflections pepper his various writings on the cityscapes of Europe, his recollections of childhood Berlin, and his unfinished study of the Parisian arcades. But even in the famous 1936 essay 'The Work of Art in the Age of its Technological Reproducibility', Benjamin's most sustained and substantial engagement with the film medium and one where its complex relationship with urban architecture is foregrounded, the precise character of any affinity remains ambiguous. Kracauer's thoughts on the interplay of cinema and city are similarly disparate, spanning his journalistic cultural and film criticism during the Weimar Republic before finding fuller elaboration in his *Caligari* and *Theory of Film* studies. But in these books, notwithstanding the careful, detailed analyses of specific films depicting the urban environment and the frequent references to the camera's penchant for the metropolitan 'flow of life', such connections between cinema and cityscape appear only in the context of other concerns – namely, his attempt to decipher motifs of authoritarian dispositions in interwar German cinema and to delineate the proclivities and potentialities of the film medium itself.

If the affinity between film and the city is made less explicit in Benjamin's and Kracauer's writings than one might expect, it is significant nonetheless. Indeed, the filmic qualities, experiences and moments of the metropolitan environment, and the urban sensibility of cinema-goers and the character of film reception per se, lie at the very heart of their writings. The cinematic medium contains a radical and popular political promise. For both, the film camera is uniquely able to penetrate and capture in myriad and novel ways our environment, in particular, the built environment composing the cityscape. Film not only represents and reveals what it has recorded with unprecedented felicity and fidelity but also allows for the critical reconfiguration of visual material. For Benjamin in particular,[2] techniques of editing, montage, slow motion and superimposition enable the construction of provocative juxtapositions, sequences and patterns. In various ways, for both Kracauer and Benjamin, these complex and illuminating moving images will irrevocably transform our weary everyday perception of the quotidian lifeworld. Film stimulates our sensibilities, sharpens our sensitivities, such that the great cities we inhabit will be recognized anew and radically transfigured.

Predictably, this revolutionary, transformative vision of the film medium incurs Adorno's censure. Responding to Benjamin's 'Work of Art' essay in a letter of 18 March 1936, he recalls a visit to Ufa's studios outside Berlin: 'When I spent a day in the studios of Neubabelsberg a couple of years ago, what immediately impressed me most of all was how *little* montage and all the advanced techniques you emphasize were actually used; rather, it seems as though reality is always constructed with an infantile attachment to the mimetic and then "photographed"' (ABC: 131).[3] According to Adorno, then, film fails to disclose and disturb reality; rather, the film industry manufactures the semblance of reality by way of studio sets, models and technical trickery. Film-makers erect infantile illusions, fabrications and fictions which are then merely 'photographed' (*abphotographiert*). Film fails to lay bare the capitalist city as the site of modern phantasmagoria (commodification, reification, the myth of progress) and human suffering (alienation, exploitation, domination). Instead, the simulation of the city in the film studio is deceptive and duplicitous. Due to the very production process itself, film cannot but be phantasmagoric.

Adorno's remarks are both astute and misplaced. The phantasmagorias of Neubabelsberg would surely not have been news to Benjamin. Indeed, Adorno could have spared himself the trip to the Ufa studios altogether and instead consulted Kracauer's account of a visit to Neubabelsberg published in the *Frankfurter Zeitung* on 28 January 1926. Kracauer's essay 'Calico-World' not only predates Adorno's remarks by a decade but also, in its emphasis on a realm of simulations and simulacra, anticipates Jean Baudrillard's explorations of hyperreality some sixty years later. For Kracauer, the Ufa complex is a 'world made of papiermaché' (MOR: 281), where nothing has substance, nothing endures.[4] He observes: 'The things that rendezvous here do not belong to reality. They are copies and distortions that have been ripped out of time and jumbled together. They stand motionless, full of meaning from the front, while from the rear they are just empty nothingness. A bad dream about objects that has been forced into the corporeal realm' (ibid.).

Here, amid the warehouses and studio sets, the most extraordinary and absurd juxtapositions are to be found: the exotic, the fantastic and the most mundane nestled incongruously next to each other. Props from a western saloon are stored amid the flourishing tropical vegetation of colonial dramas. The towers of medieval fortifications stand alongside futuristic skyscrapers, mere models no taller than their maker. Costumed extras sit blithely among technicians, drivers and office staff sipping coffee, a motley spectacle resembling 'leftovers from a carnival' (MOR: 287). For Kracauer, the use of montage as a technique does not explode the dreamworld of modernity as Benjamin would have it. How could it? It is the very *principle* of this surreal, phantasmagoric realm. But herein, *contra* Adorno, might lie some at least of its critical potential – the possibilities of profane illumination, of an enchantment that serves to disenchant.

2 Dreamworld and Dynamite

Cityscape, phantasmagoria and film – as we have seen, this thematic constellation was central to Kracauer's *Offenbach* study and underpinned his 'Motion Picture Treatment'. And, as Anthony Vidler (2000: 115) points out, Benjamin's *Arcades Project*, with its surrealist-inspired notion of Paris as dreamscape, was not lacking cinematic qualities and tendencies. Vidler directs us to Convolute C1,9, where Benjamin muses on the possibilities of filming Parisian 'prehistory' (*Urgeschichte*): 'Could one not shoot a passionate film of the city plan of Paris? Of the development of its different forms [*Gestalten*] in temporal succession? Of the condensation of a century-long movement of streets, boulevards, passages, squares, in the space of half an hour? And what else does the flâneur do?'[5]

Even for the *Passagen-Werk*, this is a puzzling passage. Vidler wonders whether all the textual fragments painstakingly assembled by Benjamin could 'be construed as so many shots, ready to be montaged into the epic movie "Paris, Capital of the Nineteenth Century"; a prehistory of modernity, finally realized by modernity's own special form of mechanical reproduction. While no "film" of this kind was ever made, an attempt to answer the hypothetical question "What would

Benjamin's film of Paris have looked like?" would clarify what we might call Benjamin's "filmic imaginary" ' (2000: 115).

Perhaps 'Arcades: The Movie' would have resembled Kracauer's unrealized Offenbach film. But, as Vidler rightly proceeds to ask rhetorically, while a 'film of the city of Paris is certainly conceivable ... what would a film of "the *plan* of Paris" look like?' (2000: 117). In the absence of any obvious answer to this conundrum, Vidler looks to the 'Work of Art' essay for clues. This study, one should remember, was itself conceived in the constellation of the *Arcades Project* and is, Benjamin claims, methodologically, not thematically, related to the Paris studies.[6] How might this essay bring us to the essence of the cinematic city? In the 'Work of Art', four key notions are relevant for our purposes: the illumination of detail; the detonation of the everyday; the experience of shock; and the concept of distraction.

If Benjamin's critical exploration of Paris, 'capital of the nineteenth century', captured the city as the pre-eminent locus of architectural fantasies, commodity fetishism, illusion and self-deception, then film is able to penetrate and operate upon this dreamworld with surgical precision.[7] Camera techniques – close-up, enlargement, slow motion, time lapse – bring to light that which the human eye sees but cannot discern. A new world appears before us from within the old.[8] Benjamin famously compares this revelation of seen yet unseen things to Freud's pioneering insights: 'It is through the camera', he writes, 'that we first discover the optical unconscious, just as we discover the instinctual unconscious through psychoanalysis' (SW3: 117). If the architecture and objects of the modern city are to be configured as manifestations of its dreaming collectivity, as Benjamin repeatedly suggests, then film's capacity to open up the 'optical unconscious' of the dreamers may have profound consequences: new forms of critical recognition, awakening, the shattering of the dream sleep itself. Film not only dis-covers, it disturbs too. Indeed, for Benjamin, the film-maker is a 'destructive character', a saboteur of the cityscape as dreamscape. The most memorable passage of this much quoted essay reads: 'Our bars and city streets, our offices and furnished rooms, our railroad stations and our factories seemed to close relentlessly around us. Then came film and exploded this prison-world with the dynamite of the split second, so that now we can set off calmly on journeys of adventure among its far-flung debris' (ibid.).[9]

This explosive character of film is also important for understanding its reception. Here Benjamin posits another elective affinity between city and cinema: both are sites of 'shock' experience. Following both Baudelaire and Simmel,[10] Benjamin identifies shock experience (*Chockerlebnis*) as the definitive signature of modern metropolitan experience. The multitude of stimuli continuously assailing the urbanite as part of everyday life find their counterpart in the sensory assault of the cinema.

In *Einbahnstrasse*, Benjamin's prototypical text-as-film, his reflections on contemporary criticism and the medium of advertising extol the violent impact of the commercial:

> It tears down the stage on which contemplation moved, and all but hits us between the eyes with things as a car, growing to gigantic proportions, careens at us out of a film screen. And just as the film does not present furniture and facades in completed forms for critical inspection, their insistent jerky nearness alone being sensational, the genuine advertisement hurls things at us with the tempo of a good film. (SW1: 476)

In the 'Work of Art' essay itself, the provocations of Dada, rather than advertising, provide Benjamin's point of comparison.[11] Dada's assault upon the innocent witness is equally swift, equally lethal:

> the Dadaists turned the artwork into a missile. It jolted the viewer, taking on a tactile [*taktisch*] quality. It thereby fostered the demand for film, since the distracting element in film is also primarily tactile, being based on successive changes of scene and focus which have a percussive effect on the spectator. *Film has freed the physical shock effect – which Dadaism had kept wrapped, as it were, inside the moral shock effect – from this wrapping.* (SW3: 119)

For Benjamin, such shock experiences do not engender mere indifference and forgetfulness, the dulled senses and latent hostility of Simmel's '*blasé* attitude' (Simmel 1972: 329). Rather, the rapid succession of images and sounds 'constitutes the shock effect of film, which like all shock effects, seeks to induce heightened attention' (SW3: 132). The shock of film demands vigilance, warns us, places us on our guard. And it is right to do so. Our very survival is at stake. Benjamin argues:

> *Film is the art form corresponding to the pronounced threat to life in which people live today.* It corresponds to profound changes in the apparatus of apperception – changes that are experienced on the scale of private existence by each passerby in big-city traffic, and on the scale of world history by each fighter against the present social order. (Ibid.)

Film attunes us to modern experience understood as endemic crisis. It alerts us to the permanent 'state of emergency' in which we find ourselves – or would find ourselves if only we could recall where and when we had become lost. And the role of memory is certainly crucial here. For Benjamin, drawing primarily on Freud,[12] traumatic events unassimilated by the conscious mind leave indelible traces in the unconscious. Here they constitute that most enigmatic and inaccessible repository of what once went unnoticed, unprocessed and unreconciled, the Proustian *mémoire involontaire*.[13] The experience of shock is, hence, always potentially twofold: there is the traumatic experience which scars the unconscious mind; and, should it recur one day, there is the shock of sudden, spontaneous recollection as these long-dormant experiences are triggered. Film, in capturing the catastrophic experience of the city and reproducing it in the cinema, corresponds precisely to this dialectics of shock. It not only makes apparent that which otherwise remains hidden in the cityscape (the 'optical unconscious') but also prompts that which is lodged within ourselves *as part of the unconscious*, our memories. Film brings us to our sober senses, alarms and forearms us, wakes us up. Only then can 'we set off calmly on journeys of adventure' among what remains of our destroyed dreaming.

It is hard to reconcile the attentiveness occasioned by film-as-shock and Benjamin's advocacy of that other mode of cinematic reception, distraction (*Zerstreuung*), for which film provides the '*true training ground*' (SW3: 120). But, as we have seen, distraction does not refer to the inability to concentrate, to mere inattention per se, but rather involves attention directed elsewhere, a concern with the peripheral, marginal and neglected. Conceived in this way, distraction signals an openness to contingency and happenstance, a penchant for the diffuse and dispersed. It is a form of accomplishment rather than a failing. Distraction, like losing oneself in a city, is a skill to be learned and honed; it requires time spent on the '*training ground*'. Indeed, as Benjamin stresses, acting in a state of distraction is only possible when the task at hand has already been mastered to such a degree that concentration is unnecessary. Distraction rests on an expertise born of confidence and habitual acquaintance. Film offers us, perhaps, the reproduction, the recognition and mastery of shock, that habitual experience of the city.

Film is not the only aesthetic form which, in opposition to individual, solitary contemplation and immersion, involves collective reception in a state of distraction. Indeed, Benjamin's principal model here is not film but rather architecture, that most ancient of forms, and the very physical fabric of the city itself.[14] This invocation of architecture is certainly curious. While the notion of architecture as a source of collective distraction, of forgetfulness born of familiarity, and of a confidence or expertise grounded in habit is in some ways persuasive, this sits uneasily with shock experience. Speeding cars and flying bullets – these projectiles suggest rapid motion, a sense of dynamism and urgency. Architecture, that most fixed of forms, is familiar precisely because it is established and enduring. Architecture is, surely, the stuff of photography, not film. It is part of the outmoded. Once again, though, oppositions are unhelpful in untangling Benjamin's ideas here. Architecture, as the pre-eminent form of metropolitan phantasmagoria, is far less stable or static. These edifices and streets are highly volatile; they are engines of combustion. Just add film. For Benjamin, for city and film, indeed for elective affinities everywhere, it is all a matter of the right 'chemistry'.

3 Films, Streets and Urban Landscapes

What is so striking – yet it has seemingly struck so few commentators – is the wealth of correspondences between *Theory of Film* and Benjamin's essay written a quarter of a century before.[15] Both are, of course, preoccupied with the elective affinity between film and city. Both conceptualize film as an extension of photography as a medium. Both stress the power of film to penetrate and reveal the 'real', especially urban reality. Indeed, Kracauer makes much of film's ability to capture and record 'things normally unseen' (TOF: 46), the 'blind spots of the mind' (1997: 53), Benjamin's 'optical unconscious', though this term does not appear in *Theory of Film*.[16] And, above all, both texts see in film a radical reconfiguration of our experience of the city. But, in Kracauer's works, the constellation formed by urban architecture, the film medium, and the receptivity and distraction of the metropolitan masses is somewhat different. There are two key aspects here: architecture and the promise of film.

Perhaps the best way to capture the first of these, the position of architecture, is by recalling a key passage in Kracauer's 1931 fragment 'Seen from the Window' ('Berlin Landscape') in which the metropolitan environment as deliberate construction and as unforeseeable improvisation is counterpoised. It is worth quoting this passage again here in full:

> One can distinguish between two types of cityscape: those which are consciously fashioned and those which come about unintentionally. The former spring from the artistic will which is realized in those squares, vistas, building ensembles and perspectives which Baedeker generally sees fit to highlight with a star. In contrast, the latter come into being without prior plan. They are not, like the Pariser Platz or the Place de la Concorde, compositions which owe their existence to some unifying building ethos. Rather, they are creations of chance and as such cannot be called to account. Such a cityscape, itself never the object of any particular interest, occurs wherever masses of stone and streets meet, the elements of which emerge from quite disparate interests. It is as unfashioned as Nature itself, and can be likened to a landscape in that it asserts itself unconsciously. Unconcerned about its visage, it bides its time. (SBA: 40)

The contrast here with Benjamin is pronounced. Architecture here appears as the concrete manifestation of the formative 'artistic will' and the very antithesis of the cinematic rather than, as Benjamin would have it, as 'the prototype of an artwork that is received in a state of distraction and through the collective' (SW4: 268). Moreover, Kracauer's simile here of a *natural landscape* as profusion and confusion is incongruent with Benjamin's invocation of nature in his account of 'aura', the central concept in his 'Work of Art' essay. According to Benjamin, 'aura', the sense of awe and wonder experienced by the onlooker in the presence of the unique, authentic artwork, is precisely that which withers with the advent of photography, film, sound recording and other technologies of mass reproduction. And aura is defined by means of a metaphor involving the perception of a natural landscape. Aura is 'the unique apparition of a distance, however near it may be. To follow with the eye – while resting on a summer afternoon – a mountain range on the horizon or a branch that casts its shadow on the beholder is to breathe the aura of those mountains, of that branch' (SW4: 255).

Kracauer's notion of landscape is very different. He privileges the contingency and spontaneity of the natural vis-à-vis architecture as the monumental 'work of art'. For him, such landscapes connote the fortuitous and momentary, living, restless and ephemeral patternings. For Benjamin, nature is a branch framed by mountains on a clear blue day; for Kracauer it is the rustle of leaves in the wind, the sparkling of sunlight on water, the beating of wings. And such fleeting phenomena are, for Kracauer, the true subject matter of film.

This finds its fullest elaboration in *Theory of Film*. Kracauer's attempt to identify and specify the inherent qualities and possibilities of the film medium takes as its key point of departure the tense balancing of what he sees as two competing cinematic tendencies, impulses which clearly mirror the very distinction between the composed and the coincidental that he observed from his window in Berlin some thirty years previously and, indeed, which inform his 'On Expressionism' essay even earlier. As we have already seen, the 'formative' tendency refers to the film-makers' concern with giving structure, narrative and order to images and sounds so as to fashion a cultural product, a composition, a work of 'art'. All films, of course, involve some degree of this formative process. Without this exertion and imposition of the 'artistic will', films would not exist. But, Kracauer argues, this should not detract from what is most important: film and photography's inherent 'realist tendency'. This refers to the camera's unprecedented and unrivalled capacity for capturing the 'real', for revealing and recording 'physical reality', which Kracauer aptly terms 'camera reality'. Film records the perpetual 'flow of life' (TOF: 71), the infinite flux of contingencies and coincidences as the vital insubstantial substance of modern urban existence. To capture the rapidity and turbulence of metropolitan life once and for all – this, Kracauer insists, is film's unique promise and mission. And one is left in no doubt: this 'flow of life' manifests itself first and foremost on the streets of the city. He writes: 'The affinity of film for haphazard contingencies is most strikingly demonstrated by its un-wavering susceptibility to the "street" – a term designed to cover not only the street, particularly the city street, in the literal sense, but also its various extensions, such as railway stations, dance and assembly halls, bars, hotel lobbies, airports, etc.' (TOF: 62).

Architecture is interesting for Kracauer only in so far as it forms the reservoirs and the conduits of this flow. The ephemeral impressions of the crowd, not the forms and façades of buildings, are the very stuff of cinema:

> The street in the extended sense of the word is not only the arena of fleeting impressions and chance encounters but a place where the flow of life is bound to assert itself. Again one will have to think mainly of the city street with its ever-moving anonymous crowds. The kaleido-scopic sights mingle with unidentified shapes and fragmentary visual complexes and cancel each other out, thereby preventing the onlooker from following up any of the innumerable suggestions they offer. What appears to him are not so much sharp-contoured individuals engaged in this or that definable pursuit as loose throngs of sketchy, completely indeterminate figures. Each has a story, yet the story is not given. Instead, an incessant flow of possibilities and near intangible meanings appears. (TOF: 72)

Wherever his deceptively elegant analysis of film leads us, it returns time and time again to the city street as the channel in which life flows. 'Once again the street' (ibid.) – this is the leitmotif of Kracauer's 'material aesthetics' and of *Theory of Film*.

The streets of Berlin and elsewhere are Kracauer's cinematic inspiration, not the arcades of Paris. Nevertheless, his reference to bars, railway stations and hotel lobbies, to these spaces as the 'extended sense' of the street, inevitably calls to mind Benjamin's vision of these doomed settings in the 'Work of Art' essay. The film-maker, or Benjamin, uses provocative juxtapositions and angles to devastating destructive effect in relation to these structures. Film is a medium of profane illumination and a weapon of explosive political critique. Film will dynamite the dreamworld. And here the second point of difference between Kracauer and Benjamin comes to the fore: this critical promise of the film medium itself. Unlike Benjamin, Kracauer has little time and even less enthusiasm for montage and the revolutionary pretensions of avant-garde experimental film. Such films, he contends, cannot but fail because they privilege the 'formative tendency' over 'camera reality'. However radical or critical their claims and intentions, experimental films inevitably betray the cinematic medium.[17] Clever camerawork and innovative angles do not guarantee radical politics, as the example of Leni Riefenstahl all too clearly demonstrates. Eschewing the gestures of avant-garde film-makers, Kracauer accordingly conceives film's

potential rather differently. In his epilogue 'Film in our Time', his meas-
ured, at times almost pedestrian, analysis of film gives way suddenly
to a critical portrayal of modernity as a world in which the unique and
precious qualities of things go unnoticed. Drawing implicitly on Simmel's notion of indifference as the hallmark of the modern metropolitan
sensibility, and explicitly on his own writings of the Weimar years,
Kracauer conjures up a bleak vision of the contemporary city as a
bureaucratized, rationalized environment marked by instrumentalism,
abstraction and cold calculation. It is a mechanical, monochrome world
of monotonous repetition, of inner loneliness, emptiness and alienation, experiences for which the undemanding products of the culture
industry, mainstream popular film among them, offer insipid consolations. We moderns, we metropolitans, are, let us not forget, 'spiritually
shelterless' (TSM: 88). And, for Kracauer, film points the way home.
Film is our Ariadne guiding us 'no longer on highways leading through
the void' but, instead, 'on paths that wind through the thicket of things'
(TOF: 309). And, on these paths, film opens up unimagined perspectives upon and insights into the heart of things. It brings into focus and
restores to us the colours and the qualities of the things around us. We
see the world anew. The full significance of the optical unconscious for
Kracauer emerges as he writes:

> Film renders visible what we did not, or even could not, see before its
> advent. It effectively assists us in discovering the material world with its
> psychophysical correspondences. We literally redeem this world from
> its dormant state, its state of virtual non-existence, by endeavouring to
> experience it through the camera. ... The cinema can be defined as a
> medium particularly equipped to promote the redemption of physical
> reality. Its imagery permits us for the first time to take away with us the
> objects and occurrences that comprise the flow of material life. (TOF: 300)

This is a particularly rich and evocative passage. What are these
'psychophysical correspondences' exactly? The 'dormant state' of
things – how might this connect with Benjamin's dreamworld of the
nineteenth century from which he seeks to awaken us? Some caution
is needed here. Although the notion of redemption is reminiscent of
Benjamin's work, Kracauer's argument is rather different. Instead of
Benjaminian destruction, sabotage and ruination, Kracauer looks to the
revelation of phenomena and the restoration of human faculties. For
what are these singular, distinctive attributes of things to which our
weary senses are reattuned by film if not their 'aura'? In this sense, film
provides for a new and vivid aestheticization or (re-)enchantment of
the everyday. This should be understood not as some reactionary de-
politicization or spurious mystification but rather as a critical recupera-
tion, rejuvenation and replenishment of human perception, appreciation

and sensitivity. We are touched by things again. We witness 'the radiance of the sunset' (TOF: 296). Film recovers our environment and our place within it as habitat, as 'home'. In exploring the 'texture of everyday life' (TOF: 304), Kracauer contends that films 'help us not only to appreciate our given material environment but to extend it in all directions. They virtually make the world our home' (ibid.). Through the medium of film, our reach will be increased such that we will come to possess the plenitude that surrounds us. Not mere temporary 'shelters', but a genuine and enduring home for the homeless: this is the real promise of film. The city will be ours once more.

4   The Urban Unconscious and Filmic Phantasmagoria

The urban street and its relationship with the unconscious also occupies a central place in Kracauer's *Caligari* book. As we have seen in chapter 7, this study controversially traces and documents how German films produced before 1933 gave form and expression to deep-seated forms of psychological retrogression and irrationalism and how, in its flight from the spectre of democratic freedom, the German psyche moved to embrace National Socialism. As part of this 'secret history' (CAL: 11), Kracauer discusses the development of a popular 'street film' genre during the 'period of stability' in the mid-1920s, films typically portraying the doomed romantic rebellion of youth against the restrictions and cosy comforts of the bourgeois familial home. Kracauer carefully distinguishes early films such as Ufa's 1923 *Die Strasse*[18] from later variations on the theme such as Pabst's *Die Freudlose Gasse* (1925) and Joe May's *Asphalt* (1929). *Die Strasse* presents the street as a site of criminality, violence and corruption, as a chaotic realm from which the unhappy youth is fortunate to escape. 'Instead of acknowledging the values of anarchical life', Kracauer notes, 'the film deprecates this life by marking the street as a region where the law of the jungle rules and happiness is sought in gambling and futile sex affairs' (CAL: 121). In *Die Strasse* and its derivatives, the choice for the would-be rebel is stark: conformity, convention and home, or the street, anarchy and death. The films of Pabst and May, by contrast, offer a far more sympathetic vision of the street: here, amid the social outcasts and misfits, a genuine but doomed love develops between the adolescent rebel and his streetwise protector, the kind-hearted prostitute. The superficialities and insincerities of the conventional bourgeois world are contrasted with and critiqued by the authenticity of the street, here configured as the site of integrity, warmth and honesty. But such well-meaning pathos provides only 'timid heresies', and, far from endorsing revolutionary sentiments, Kracauer insists that even these seemingly more radical street films ultimately 'emphasize desertion of the home, but still in the interests of authoritarian behavior' (CAL: 160).

The street as a site of base instinct and brutality or as a sanctuary for the human spirit, for love and truth – however intriguing such images of the city are, these historical details concerning specific films and genres are not what is most important in the *Caligari* book. It is Kracauer's understanding of the significance of the film medium itself that is crucial.

I will not repeat the arguments presented in chapter 7; suffice to say that, if popular film does indeed constitute a privileged medium for the analysis of a historically specific and ever changing national 'collective mentality' (CAL: 6), providing insight into the fundamental psychological predispositions and the unconscious of both the film producers and popular audiences, then film does not simply redeem physical reality; it redeems *psychological reality*, too. Weimar cinema, for Kracauer, is not a window upon the German soul; it *screens* the German 'Soul at Work' (CAL: 72). Films, then, are like dreams: not individual dreams but rather *collective* ones. The correspondence here with Benjamin's *Arcades Project*, and in particular the idea of an *Arcades film*, is intriguing. In the *Passagenarbeit*, the architecture of the city is the most fundamental manifestation of the dreaming collectivity of the recent past, the collective unconscious of nineteenth-century Paris; in the *Caligari* study, Weimar film is the product of the collective mentality of Germany in the first three decades of the twentieth century. In Kracauer's formulation, then, *film displaces architecture as the key element of the dreamscape of modernity*.

This dreamlike quality of film returns us for the last time to the notion of phantasmagoria. For all his emphasis in *Theory of Film* upon 'camera reality', Kracauer was under no illusions as to the illusory character of film. If film disenchants modernity it does so not because it is inimical to the phantasmagoria of the city but rather because it is part of the enchantment itself. Film *is* phantasmagoric. Film is the ultimate phantasmagoria of modernity – this insight is surely what lies at the heart of Kracauer's fascination with the medium. And could it be that this is why, unconsciously perhaps, he took Wiene's *Caligari* film as the starting point for his 'secret history', not of German film, but of film per se? With its nightmarish Expressionist studio sets and sinister lighting effects,[19] this is a film phantasmagoria whose very subject matter is a ghostly apparition in the marketplace, the murderous sleepwalker Cesare stalking the Holstenwall fair. As a phantasmagoria within a phantasmagoria, does *Caligari* screen the *essence* of film, its very soul? Perhaps. But what of the city? It is evident that, for Kracauer at least, both film and the city are manifestations of the modern unconscious. This is the key to their elective affinity. The contingent patterns and constellations formed out of the crowds, traffic, lights and colours of the city, these unconscious phenomena are what fascinated Kracauer, and film is the medium which brings the content of the unconscious, of the city, of its makers, of its spectators, to light. Film's revelation of the optical unconscious is far more than just the depiction of things unseen. Film presents to us, and redeems, the very soul of the city on screen, the modern metropolitan soul in these most soulless times. Here, amid lost soul shadows and shades, film is not so much our Ariadne as our Orpheus.

Inconclusive: Penultimate Things

1 The Shield of Perseus

In the final pages of 'Film in our Time', the philosophical epilogue to *Theory of Film*,[1] the metaphor of film as a mirror makes an uncanny reappearance, uncanny because this familiar trope from the Weimar years has now taken on an unfamiliar form. Kracauer writes: 'Now of all the existing media the cinema alone holds up a mirror to nature. Hence our dependence on it for the reflection of happenings which would petrify us were we to encounter them in real life. The film screen is Athena's polished shield' (TOF: 305). The mirror has now become a shield, not so much a visual prosthesis as optical armature, enabling us to open our eyes to that which, out of fear, we would otherwise refuse to see, would rather consign to the optical unconscious. The work of reflection performed by such a screen provides the mediation necessary for us bravely to confront and conquer our worst terrors. He continues:

> The mirror reflections of horror are an end in themselves. As such they beckon the spectator to take them in and thus incorporate into his memory the real face of things too dreadful to behold in reality. In experiencing the rows of calves' heads or the litter of tortured human bodies in the films made of Nazi concentration camps, we redeem horror from its invisibility behind the veils of panic and imagination. And this experience is liberating in as much as it removes a most powerful taboo. Perhaps Perseus's greatest achievement was not to cut the head off the Medusa but to overcome his fear and look at its reflection in the shield. And was it not precisely this feat which permitted him to behead the monster? (TOF: 306)

And so it is here that the historical traumas and genocidal atrocities that separate the 'Marseilles notebooks' and *Theory of Film* make their eventual, perhaps long overdue, entrance configured as cinematic reflections. In what might be thought of as an early gambit in the ongoing debate as to the 'representability' or otherwise of the Holocaust, Kracauer points to the necessity of its envisioning – that is to say, the recording as images, the replaying as film of its physical and material manifestations. Piled-up corpses, emaciated bodies, crematoria and mass graves, so-called medical experiments and mutilations – it is to these that film bears witness. Film offers the only way of making visible that which is otherwise unimaginable, unendurable, things which we must also remember and, in some way, overcome.

The Holocaust is not absent from Kracauer's work on the cinematic medium, but its appearance is belated and its treatment almost tangential, as if a kind of self-censorship is at work, as if all this is elided or 'under erasure'.[2] But perhaps we have been made to wait so long for a purpose. And, for me at least, this corresponds to the very experience of reading *Theory of Film* itself: of patiently following Kracauer's own inventory and examination of the various (today doubtless often obsolete) technologies, techniques and devices utilized in camera work, lighting, sound engineering, editing and music; and of dutifully noting his extensive exemplifications by means of scenes, sequences and film. But all this admirably clear and concise iteration and reiteration of topics lacks any climax or crux. It is a circling around in detours of detail, a veritable labyrinth of loose ends. And then, in the epilogue, there is the final disclosure, the denouement. All that has gone before now finds its rightful place as the book's argument crystallizes in a few short paragraphs. Like the apocryphal London buses, two ideas come into view at once, two potentialities for which everything has prepared us. The film medium, as the redeemer of reality, has a twofold mnemonic purpose: on the one hand, to attest to the recent past as catastrophe; and, on the other, to restore our appreciation of the world of things as a 'habitat' for our present shelterlessness. This dual commemoration is both a looking back and a looking forward, of archaeology and anticipation. The medium of film itself is Janus-faced. If the sorrows and sufferings of the twentieth century are indeed hidden below the surface of *Theory of Film*, it is so that they may, in 'Film in our Time', erupt into and out of the text in an afterword that is more epiphany than epilogue.

2   The Historical Approach

As the medium par excellence for the depiction of the past, film is *historio-graphic*. In the light of this, Kracauer's turn following the publication of *Theory of Film* to the subject of history, or, more precisely, of historiography, is less of a surprise than it might first appear. He was to spend the last years of his life on a study that, unfinished at the time of his death, was then to be 'completed'[3] and posthumously published in 1969 under the intriguing title *History: The Last Things Before the Last*.

My intention in what follows is not to provide any detailed examination of this incomplete text. Nor will I be tempted to engage in an exercise of contrast and comparison even if the parallels with Benjamin seem promising – Benjamin's own final work was his enigmatic 'Theses on the Concept of History' (1940), penned as an epistemological preface to the ongoing and ever expanding *Arcades Project*. For, while Benjamin sets in play revolutionary Marxist and Judaic messianic motifs in the delineation of a series of historiographical injunctions and imperatives – denouncing the concept of historical progress and the claims of 'historicism'; insisting on the 'dialectical image' as the redemptive moment of defeated hopes in the past; recovering the discontinuous tradition of the oppressed – Kracauer's work is much more muted in tone and modest in ambition. True, there are some echoes: he shares Benjamin's critique of the teleological notion of historical advance and 'improvement', and 'universal history' is dismissed as 'a mirage, a chimera' (LAST: 134), but he is reluctant to embrace the very historical materialism and theological and mystical speculation that Benjamin foregrounds. And Kracauer also recognizes that history is always and inevitably a product of the present, that the past is constructed only ever in the image of current interests and concerns, but he refuses to concede that the present interest is or should be seen as the weightier consideration, the determining factor.[4] These are *only* echoes. Kracauer's work here is no revolutionary call to arms in the midst of a prevailing 'state of emergency' – though it could have been. Yes, 1930s Europe was not 1960s America, but one should not forget that Marcuse was writing and publishing *One-Dimensional Man* (1964) at much the same time.

Seemingly disengaged from the politics of the moment, Kracauer's book of penultimate things is, then, a much less intense, much less emphatic piece of writing than the tantalizing 'Theses' of 1940. Here the grand themes of history and grandiloquent claims of historical writing – not just teleology and progress, but also Benjaminian visions of revolution and apocalypse – are treated with caution and circumspection. Working with and through the approaches advocated and adopted by European historians and philosophers of history spanning the nineteenth and twentieth centuries – Hegel, Ranke, Dilthey, Rickert, Huizinga, Burckhardt, Croce, Collingwood and Toynbee, among others, by way of Proust – Kracauer produced not a systematic history of history as such but, rather, an idiosyncratic attempt to delineate the very limitations of historiography itself, the impediments to, indeed perhaps the very impossibility of, recapturing and representing the past. And, indeed, if it has something of a melancholy air about it this is no wonder: it is, or rather it becomes, a retrospective study which seeks to make sense of a lifetime's work, to find somewhere in his own disparate writings some subterranean network of connections which will make sense of them all, render them legible as individual pieces of a great mosaic. Kracauer's reflections are no prelude to some *magnum opus* to come but rather are those of an old man aware that this might be his last work.[5]

My goal in this inconclusive conclusion is intended to be in keeping with Kracauer's own unassuming approach: it is to offer some brief reflections upon what I regard as two of his guiding metaphors – the photographic/cinematic and the journey – and adumbrate two of his main themes: the provisional and the improvisional.

a)   *A little photography of history*

The move from *Theory of Film* to the *History* study is a shift of focus, not a new departure. The later book is littered with references to film, photography and the cinematic. In his reiteration of the distinction between, and the imperative to balance, the competing claims of the realistic and formative tendencies, Kracauer explicitly notes the 'exact analogy' (LAST: 56) between the 'photographic approach' of recording and documenting the world and the 'historical approach' of capturing and recovering the past. Indeed, there is a twofold correspondence, since

> Another basic analogy bears on the subject matter peculiar to the two fields of endeavor. Provided the still and motion picture cameras acknowledge the 'basic aesthetic principle', they customarily focus on a world which is certainly not the abstract nature of science. ... Rather, 'camera reality' – the sort of reality on which the photographer, or film maker, opens his lens – has all the earmarks of the *Lebenswelt*. It comprises inanimate objects, faces, crowds, people who intermingle, suffer and hope; its grand theme is life in its fullness, life as we commonly experience it.
>
> Small wonder that camera reality parallels historical reality in terms of its structure, its general constitution. (LAST: 57–8)

And so it is no wonder that Kracauer characterizes the 'historian's fields of vision' as 'full of intrinsic contingencies' (LAST: 45) and 'chance encounters' (LAST: 150); as inherently 'indeterminate as to meaning'; and as 'virtually endless, issuing from a dark which is increasingly receding and extending into an open-ended future' (LAST: 45). Nor that, for him, the gaze of the historian should resemble that of the camera moving deftly between panoramic long-shots and details caught in close-up.[6] Both historian and film-maker must carefully cull fragments from the continuum of the past and configure them

as meaningful elements of a larger picture or sequence through composition and concatenation. And both must always attend to things 'in
flight', capturing that which is on the verge of disappearance.[7] Kracauer
invokes the figure of Orpheus here:

> Like Orpheus, the historian must descend into the nether world to bring
> the dead back to life. How far will they follow his allurements and evoca-
> tions? They are lost to him when, re-emerging in the sunlight of the
> present, he turns for fear of losing them. But does he not for the first time
> take possession of them at this very moment – the moment when they
> forever depart, vanishing in a history of his own making? (LAST: 79)

In this act of Baudelairean 'love at last sight', Kracauer comes very
close to Benjamin's notion of the 'dialectical image' and of 'dialectics
at a standstill', that fleeting moment of historical illumination in the
present of the past, the 'then' recognized in and redeemed by the
'now'.[8] That said, however, it is not so much the monotonous flow of
empty homogeneous time, as Benjamin puts it, and its interruption/
cessation that concerns Kracauer[9] but, rather, the need to render and
resolve 'the inextricable dialectics between the flow of time and the
temporal sequences negating it' (LAST: 158).

Kracauer chooses that seemingly least chronological of writers,
Marcel Proust, to make his point here. Amid all the convolutions of
remembering and forgetting that Proust presents in his 'unique attempt
to grapple with the perplexities of time' (LAST: 160), he 'radically de-
emphasizes chronology' (ibid.) while being 'at pains to keep it intact'
(LAST: 162). Kracauer writes:

> Much as the close-ups with their time-confusing patterns tend to obstruct
> our awareness of a flow of events, they not only point to the situations
> occasioning them but are woven into a narrative which renders Marcel's
> successive selfs in their chronological order. On the whole, the novel
> abides by a strict itinerary. ...
>   Not content with installing it, Proust tries to re-embed the chronologi-
> cally successive worlds – worlds which are spontaneous creations arising
> from nowhere – in the flow of time. The reason is that he wants to make
> that flow an equal partner in the game. (Ibid.)

This sense of continuity punctuated by digressions and deviations
is, for me, highly reminiscent of Kracauer's account of the film musical.
In these movies, one may recall, the storyline is repeatedly interrupted
by characters bursting into song and dance numbers. This formation
and dissolution of the narrative is what gives such musical fantasies
and, similarly, gives the writings of Proust, the ultimate dialectician of
the past if not its historian,[10] the very 'air of cinema'.

b) Historical wanderings

These reflections on Proust's temporal convolutions bring to an end Kracauer's chapter entitled 'Ahasuerus, or the Riddle of Time'. In the figure of Ahasuerus or Ahasver, the legendary 'wandering' or 'eternal Jew',[11] Kracauer invokes his other guiding metaphor of the *History* book: that of the journey. This takes at least three different forms or moments: the entry into or penetration of the unknown; exile and alienation; and the road in retrospect.

The first of these sees the historian adopting the guise of the bold explorer and/or wayfarer venturing into and making accessible distant lands and times, the *terra incognita* and the *tempi incogniti* of the elsewhere and the once upon a time. Kracauer's model here is not so much the venturing of Orpheus into the underworld as Odysseus navigating the perils of his maritime meanderings: 'Modern historiography', he writes, 'would seem to come into its own if it manages to elude not only the Scylla of philosophical speculations with their wholesale meanings but also the Charybdis of the sciences with their nature laws and regularities' (LAST: 45). And one should add to these dangers a couple of others: the Cyclops of theological dogma and the Sirens of revolutionary zeal.

Secondly, one should not forget that Odysseus was, of course, homeward bound. He is a figure en route or in transit because, like Ahasuerus, he has been denied homecoming and must instead endure the experience of 'homelessness' and the homesickness, the nostalgia, which accompanies it. An exile on the oceans, Odysseus becomes a stranger to *terra firma*. The historian is not at home in the past; rather, she/he is never at home at all. Kracauer notes:

> There are great historians who owe much of their greatness to the fact that they were expatriates. ...
> It is only in this state of self-effacement, or homelessness, that the historian can commune with the material of his concern. ... A stranger to the world evoked by the sources, he is faced with the task – the exile's task – of penetrating its outward appearances, so that he may learn to understand that world from within. (LAST: 84)

This is the privileged insight and understanding of the Simmelian stranger, who comes today and stays tomorrow, but always remains an outsider. Or perhaps it is the gaze of the erstwhile exile or itinerant who, having lived elsewhere, finds it impossible to reintegrate into what was once so familiar. Both of these, the stranger and the estranged, share the double optic of the *heimlich–unheimlich* that defines the psychoanalytical uncanny.

Lastly, the historian is concerned less with the way ahead than with the road already taken, with the way-stations along a route that stretches not forwards but winds backwards into the past. This is a journey, a life, a life's work, viewed by the wayfarer in retrospect, at the moment perhaps of homecoming itself, an idea that indeed returns us to Orpheus emerging into the sunlight, or on reaching some destination. Another of Simmel's figures is called to mind here: not the stranger, but the painter, that great master, whose portraits captured every line and blemish in the face of the aged sitter such that the whole of the individual's life could find eloquent expression in that moment. One should recall Simmel's words:

> In the physiognomies of Rembrandt's portraits we feel very clearly that the course of a life, heaping fate on fate, creates this present image. It elevates us, as it were, to a certain height from which we can view the ascending path toward that point, even though none of the content of its past could be naturalistically stated in the way that portraits with a psychological slant might seek to suggest. (REM: 9–10)

The true historian has several incarnations: explorer, exile, itinerant physiognomist of the past. And, of these, the last is perhaps the most significant: the reader of the face marked by the passage of time, by the many faces of the past. And this returns us to Kracaucer's invocation of Ahasuerus. He writes:

> He indeed would know first-hand about the developments and transitions, for he alone in all history has had the unsought opportunity to experience the process of becoming and decaying itself. (How unspeakably terrible he must look! To be sure, his face cannot have suffered from aging, but I imagine it to be many faces, each reflecting one of the periods which he traversed and all of them combining into ever new patterns, as he restlessly, and vainly, tries on his wanderings to reconstruct out of the times that shaped him the one time he is doomed to incarnate.) (LAST: 157)

However nomadic the historian, she/he cannot presume to become his companion in misfortune,[12] but she/he can as faithfully as possible depict and decipher the vestiges of his disintegrating countenance. Such portraits of the ages would, perhaps, be the life's work of a Harmenszoon of history, a true biographer of Ahasuerus. But this art is beyond us. Perhaps, however, we can capture his likeness by means of a photograph.

3 Past Provisional, Future Improvisional

It is true, then, that, in reaching a resting place, a vantage point, and surveying the meandering path trodden, the historian as wayfarer comes to share for a while at least those uplands with Lefebvre's philosopher and those other intellectual alpine aficionados – the theologian, the scientist, the revolutionary – who congregate there. Each of these has engaged in seeking upon the summits, high up in this rarefied atmosphere, the great and fundamental truths of human existence, or at least what they take to be the truth – their own versions of certitude, their own definitions of definitive and ultimate things. The historian is a mere interloper in such exalted company; she/he is neither welcome nor at home on such elevated terrain.[13] And this is as it should be, for the very subject matter of the historian, the past,[14] is always conditional in some measure upon the present, and hence always subject to change, to revision and re-editing in the light of new ideas, investigations and interests. The restless present makes for a restless past. There is no fixed and final version, only ever new director's cuts, so to speak. The historian's work is always, then, contestable and contingent, our understanding of the past always indefinite and uncertain. Hesitant and tentative, the historian's conclusions are only ever *inconclusive*. The past could, and will, be otherwise. *History is only ever provisional.*

This brings us to the final chapter of Kracauer's *History* study and to its curious title. In recognizing and appreciating the limits of the historical enterprise, the boundary which may not be crossed, the terrain not trespassed upon, the historian must be content not with ultimate truths, the last things, so to speak, but with those to hand, ad hoc, the last things *before* the last. And these penultimate things are to be found not at the centre of the labyrinth, not in the magnificent throne room or the secret inner temple where the initiated have exclusive entry – heroes, philosopher-kings, priests, spirits – but always and only in the humble vestibule, the waiting room, the lobby area, those in-between areas that are neither inside nor outside but decidedly *eccentric* and marked by ambiguity. These are the last rooms before the last, 'anterooms', and it is to these that the historian, the sociologist, has access and in which she/he must accommodate her-/himself.[15] Kracauer writes:

> One may define the area of historical reality, like that of photographic reality, as an anteroom area. Both realities are of a kind which does not lend itself to being dealt with in a definite way. The peculiar material in these areas eludes the grasp of systematic thought; nor can it be shaped in the form of a work of art. Like the statements we make about physical reality with the aid of the camera, those which result from our preoccupation with historical reality may certainly attain to a level above mere opinion; but they do not convey, or reach out for, ultimate truths, as do philosophy and art proper. They share their inherently provisional character with the material they record, explore, and penetrate. (LAST: 191)

What does Kracauer find in this anteroom? Not things themselves, even penultimate ones, but a clue, a key to their secret composition and correspondence. Looking back, Kracauer himself is at last, or rather almost at the last, able to name those things that have preoccupied him throughout his life's work. Or, rather, he is able to recognize in them that, as they are still coming into being, they are yet to bear a name. He writes: 'So at long last all my efforts, so incoherent on the surface, fall into line – they have all served, and continue to serve, a single purpose: the rehabilitation of objectives and modes of being which still lack a name and hence are overlooked or misjudged' (LAST: 4). Kracauer has devoted himself to anonymous things for which all manner of epithets has had to suffice: *terra incognita*; the 'extraterritorial'; 'elsewhere'; 'memory images'; spatial hieroglyphs; half-forgotten dreams; the 'air of cinema'; last things before the last.

These are the sad, neglected things of which he has – and we have – as yet only an inkling, some ineffable intimations, faint forebodings and premonitions. They remain unforeseen. And so let us take it upon ourselves here and now provisionally to name these unnamed penultimate things: *the improvisional*.

4 Adieu

Kracauer concludes his historiographical reflections with the image of a pair of adventurers: one, of high birth, educated in all the finest things of life, full of high-flown ideals and aspirations, who fails to see the mundane features of the world or mistakes them for elevated and enchanted objects; the other, humble but clear-sighted, who recognizes things for what they are but who faithfully serves and indulgently ministers to his deluded master on their journeys and adventures together. Or, rather, not so much two companions, but one storyteller: for, in Franz Kafka's reading of the story, Don Quixote and Sancho Panza are one and the same person.[16] Quixote is a projection or avatar, a figment of Panza's imagination, a fictive alter ego whose extraordinary exploits serve as diversion for the stay-at-home servant. Quixote ventures forth on his chivalrous errands, so that the indolent but imaginative Panza does not have to. And so it is that, while we may long for and fantasize about the high ground of mountain paths, with its vistas and panoramas, we should not despise that less elevated terrain which also demands our loyalty: those thorny thickets of things. Citing Kafka, Kracauer's last words before the last[17] are:

'Without making any boast of it Sancho Panza succeeded in the course of years, by devouring a great number of romances of chivalry and adventure in the evening and night hours, in so diverting from him his

demon, whom he later called Don Quixote, that his demon thereupon
set out in perfect freedom on the maddest exploits, which, however, for
the lack of a pre-ordained object, which should have been Sancho Panza
himself, harmed nobody. A free man, Sancho Panza philosophically followed Don Quixote on his crusades, perhaps out of a sense of responsibility, and had of them a great and edifying entertainment to the end ...'
The definition which Kafka here gives of Sancho Panza as a *free man* has
a Utopian character. It points to a Utopia of the in-between – a *terra
incognita* in the hollows between the lands we know. (LAST: 217)

This imaginative roaming and roving, and the opening up of these
unforeseen spaces elsewhere, nestled between the virtual and the actual,
are perhaps the true emancipatory vocation of film. And if these
curious, liminal sites are in some way where freedom resides, then let
us take our leave of Kracauer here and, without fuss, allow him, our
companion, to find some shady spot and rest a while in peace.

Notes

Our Companion Introduced

1 In 'The Curious Realist: On Siegfried Kracauer', his radio broadcast to mark Kracauer's 75th birthday in 1964, Adorno recalls that 'Kracauer made Kant come alive for me' (1991: 160).

2 Kracauer had a sincere appreciation for 'the things that fell through the cracks of high theory', Adorno notes (1991: 172).

3 This is Benjamin's famous description of Kracauer in his review of *Die Angestellten*. See TSM: 114.

4 A critical response to scientific positivism and the Enlightenment's overemphasis upon the faculty of reason and the intellect, and its concomitant undervaluing of intuition, emotional life and empathy, *Lebensphilosophie* is something of an umbrella term covering a number of rather different nineteenth-century German (and other) philosophers and philosophical positions. These share a concern with the central importance of 'life' and the neglected, maligned, non-rational aspects of the human being – such as the 'will', the 'soul', vital energies. In the case of Georg Simmel (1858–1918), Kracauer's erstwhile tutor and key influence, this focused on the conflict between turbulent 'inner life' or 'spirit' (*Geist*) of the individual and the restrictions enforced by modern civilization as 'outer' or 'objective culture'.

5 Of course, Kracauer's antipathy towards obfuscation and erudition did not always impress his friends and colleagues at the Frankfurt Institut für Sozialforschung and elsewhere or endear him among social, cultural and film theorists of various persuasions today.

6 This was certainly Adorno's verdict. He terms the book 'Kracauer's most significant achievement' (1991: 171).

7 Joseph Roth (1894–1939), the Ukrainian-born writer and journalist for the *Frankfurter Zeitung* in Vienna, Berlin and Paris, was the first to make this identification of Ginster with Chaplin. 'Ginster in the War is: Chaplin in the department store', he writes (cited in Belke and Renz 1989: 52). As emerges from Roth's correspondence with the FZ editors, such as Benno Reifenberg (1892–1970), feuilleton editor from 1924, and other journalists, most notably

Bernard von Brentano (1901–64), the paper's Berlin correspondent between 1925 and 1930, Roth had a generally high opinion of Kracauer's literary and intellectual capacities, developed a genuine affection for him, but was not averse to teasing him for his unprepossessing appearance and, most cruelly, for his stammer. See Roth, ed. Hoffmann (2012).

8 Ginster certainly bears more than a passing resemblance to Hašek's eponymous comic figure in *The Good Soldier Schwejk* (1923). In the 1964 radio broadcast, Adorno notes: 'Kracauer called *Ginster* an intellectual *Schwejk*' (1991: 171). Indeed, 'the intellectual Schwejk' (*Der intellektuelle Schwejk*) was Adorno's alternative title for the broadcast and epithet for Kracauer himself. Kracauer though preferred 'the curious realist' (*Der wunderliche Realist*). See their exchange of letters in November 1963 AKB: 619–22.

9 Nothing demonstrates the gulf in sensibilities between Kracauer and Benjamin more than their choice of figures through which to explore Paris, capital of the nineteenth century: Offenbach and the poet Charles Baudelaire, respectively.

10 'There is, as you well know', Kracauer notes in his letter to Adorno (23 December 1963), 'a good part of Sancho Panza in me' (AKB: 633). See also Adorno (1991: 165) and Barnouw (1994: 151).

11 For the most detailed account of Kracauer's life, see Belke and Renz (1989).

12 His *Die Geschichte der Judengasse in Frankfurt am Main* (1906) remains a standard work and is still available today.

13 In Kracauer's letter of 19 April 1920 to the prospective publishers J. C. B. Mohr, cited in Belke and Renz (1989: 33). They declined to publish the study a week later, citing a shortage of paper.

14 The *Zeitschrift für Sozialforschung*.

15 The world of journalism was no less prejudiced in terms of Kracauer's disability. In a letter of 19 December 1925 to Brentano, for example, Roth sarcastically observes that, 'on account of his speech impediment and his un-European appearance', Kracauer is 'never allowed to represent the paper abroad' (Roth, ed. Hoffmann 2012: 60–1).

16 He was a constant correspondent in another sense: the letters collected in the Kracauer archive in Marbach am Neckar are testimony to his industriousness in writing and to the extraordinary range of his contacts. His correspondence constitutes an A–Z of so many leading figures of the European and the American intellectual and cultural scenes of the time: colleagues at and associated with the 'Frankfurt School', of course (including Ernst Bloch), and former tutors such as Georg Simmel; fellow journalists such as Joseph Roth; leading literary figures such as Heinrich Mann; the composer Alban Berg; film-makers, including Fritz Lang and G. W. Pabst; film writers such as Paul Rotha; and American academics such as David Riesman.

17 See Ward (2001: 33).

18 See Belke and Renz (1989: 38).

19 See 'The Bible in German' in MOR: 189–201.

20 *Die Angestellten* appeared in twelve parts in the *FZ* between December 1929 and January 1930, before finally being published as a book in 1930. The book has been translated into English under the title *The Salaried Masses: Duty and Distraction in Weimar Germany*.

21 As Levin points out, Kracauer was certainly a great admirer of Lukács's earlier *Theory of the Novel* (MOR: 13, 15) and much indebted to the notion of 'transcendental homelessness' it presented.

22 Kracauer replaced the writer and journalist Bernard von Brentano. In moving to Berlin, Lili had to give up her post at the Institut.

23 Fortunately, Kracauer did not heed Adorno's advice to return to Germany (letter of 15 April 1933; AKB: 308).

24 Others were not so fortunate. Finding his way into Spain across the Pyrenees blocked, Walter Benjamin committed suicide in September 1940. And, despite Kracauer's efforts in the late 1930s and early 1940s to secure their passage out of Germany, Rosette and Hedwig remained in Frankfurt. They were eventually deported to Theresienstadt and died there in 1942.

25 In his letter of 5 January 1943, Kracauer informs Adorno: 'As for writing in English, I have made great progress; I have a passion for it' (AKB: 431)

26 Adorno writes: 'What is decisive for the likes of us to say, we can say only in German. We could at best write English like the others; as we ourselves, only German' (letter of 1 September 1955; AKB: 482). Acknowledging Adorno's sentiments, Kracauer replied with: 'What you say is certainly true for particular areas of literature … But … certainly doesn't apply to intellectual work, to theory … My own stylistic ideal is that language disappears in the work [*Sache*] as the Chinese painter vanishes in the picture. I am aware that the painter and the picture, the thinker and the work [*Sache*] are one – up to a point' (letter of 5 September 1955; AKB: 484). Kracauer's little joke here is to write 'up to a point' in English. See also Adorno (1991: 172).

27 Adorno notes that Kracauer's 'predilection for lower-order things, things excluded by higher culture … led him to continue to take delight in the annual fair and the hurdy-gurdy even after large-scale industrial planning had swallowed them up' (1991: 168).

28 Adorno observes: 'He thinks with an eye that is astonished almost to helplessness but then suddenly flashes into illumination' (1991: 163).

29 The Adorno–Kracauer correspondence (AKB), for example, was published by Suhrkamp in 2008.

30 See Gemünden and von Moltke (2012), for instance.

31 See von Moltke and Rawson's (2012) edition of Kracauer's American writings (hereafter, KAW).

Chapter 1 Small Mercies

1 Although, at twenty-four years of age, Kracauer was hardly still an adolescent!

2 In his detailed reading of the novella, Dirk Oschmann (1999: 54) notes how, for example, the three female characters (Ilse, an older woman to whom Ludwig makes a disastrously mistaken sexual approach; Barbara, the girlfriend of Ludwig's friend Richard; and the anonymous woman on the bridge) each correspond clearly to a familiar type in turn-of-the-century German literature: the combination of culture–nature (mother); the pure asexual woman (virgin); and the woman as elemental nature (prostitute). The figure of the sculptor Nyström is the embodiment of Nietzsche's Dionysian principle (1999: 51).

3 Oschmann situates the story at the confluence of three intellectual currents: *Lebensphilosophie*, Expressionism and Nietzschean thought (see 1999: 37, 48 and 51, respectively).

4 See, for example, Weber's famous 1918 essay 'Science as a Vocation' ([1948] 1991: 155).

5 Kracauer's archive contains two handwritten letters to Simmel separated by the war years (dated 5 July 1914 and 30 November 1917) (DLA: 72.1793/1 and 72.1793/2).

6 Kracauer's neglected and hitherto untranslated texts range from short sketches of a few pages with suggestive titles, such as 'Of Desire: Study of a Feeling' ('Von der Sehnsucht: Studie über ein Gefühl') (c. 1917, still unpublished) and 'The Typical Self-Reflection of Youth' ('Die typische Selbstbespiegelung des Jünglings') (published 1920), to substantial synthesizing studies (now in WK9) such as 'On the Essence of Personality: A Treatise' ('Über das Wesen der Persönlichkeit: Eine Abhandlung') (1913/14) and 'Suffering under Knowledge and the Desire for the Deed: A Treatise from 1917' ('Das Leiden unter dem Wissen und die Sehnsucht nach der Tat: Eine Abhandlung aus dem Jahre 1917').

7 Although Part 1 of the study, 'Insight' ('Einblick'), appeared separately in the 1963 'Mass Ornament' collection, subsequently translated into English in 1995, the full (German) text was published only in 2004 with the other early writings.

8 Simmel died in September 1918.

9 Kracauer writes: 'If one assumes that every soul forms a living unity that manifests some sort of invariable determinations throughout ... then the expressions of this soul must also be held together, despite extensive internal contradictions, by a tie that links them all and gives objective expression to this unity. A person's essence objectifies itself, for example, in an idea that runs through its work like a red thread' (MOR: 230).

10 For Kracauer: 'Simmel's works on Goethe and Rembrandt are exemplars of just such a topography of being [*Wesenstopographie*], though without their significance lying solely therein' (WK 9.1: 192).

11 Interestingly, Simmel's preoccupation with the concept of 'life' as totality or manifold, the clearest evidence of his attraction to the tenets of *Lebensphilosophie*, is quite a late development, finding fullest expression in the Rembrandt monograph, the last major work published in his own lifetime.

12 'One is struck', Kracauer notes, 'by the essential unity of all of the thinker's works and becomes aware that he solves the most numerous and various problems in the same manner' (MOR: 231).

13 Kracauer observes: 'Simmel liberates a series of phenomena from their isolation by exposing the meaning or the originary ground that they all have in common and from which their individual meanings can be explained' (MOR: 233).

14 Kracauer points out that Simmel's engagement with Kant is 'at the same time a self-revelation, marking an important stage in his development' (WK 9.2: 194).

15 Kracauer states: 'The relationship between the knowing subject and the object known is one of this philosopher's most central problems' MOR: 228).

16 Following Simmel, Kracauer terms the meeting place of the subject and object, this site of intersubjective apprehension and comprehension,

a 'third realm' (*drittes Reich*) (WK 9.2: 207). Simmel's interpretation of Rembrandt becomes intelligible in this context.

17 Kracauer notes: 'Simmel, too, is a relativist. The Absolute has no place in his philosophy and cannot possibly find one here, since no idea is rooted deeply enough in the thinker's being to form the unshakeable foundation of the entire radiation of his spirit' (WK 9.2: 231).

18 For Simmel: 'the philosopher must be a *pluralist*' (WK 9.2: 222).

19 Kracauer notes: 'Simmel lives so exclusively in the small world of individual spiritual [*seelischer*] phenomena that he either totally rejects general statements in the field of ethics or leaves the question of their validity open' (WK 9.2: 191).

20 See WK 9.2: 248.

21 Kracauer writes: 'The historical reality that we call civilization [*Zivilisation*] is in many respects the age of the decline of former cultural togetherness [*Gebundenheit*]. The absolute faith that imbued the souls of the people of a culture [*Kultur*] and which supports their religious and ethical worldview has dwindled. There is no longer any unified worldview whatsoever, spanning the whole of human existence like a heavenly canopy. The complete personality [*Vollpersönlichkeit*], who in an epoch of culture is able to communicate without restraint, lacks in civilization the forms for their expression. People live apart instead of growing together; bridges between them are demolished. Where there once stood a connectedness of being between all members of the community, there now steps the aimless freedom of each individual. Life as a whole loses its meaning; the fixed hierarchy of value-based convictions which distinguishes every true culture yields to a complete anarchy of values' (WK 9.2: 244–5).

22 Kracauer observes of Simmel: 'He can only truly be understood if one has recognized the essence of civilization [*das Wesen der Zivilisation*], that most recent period of our history, the terrible downfall of which it is now our fate to experience' (WK 9.2: 242).

23 Kracauer notes that 'civilization' brings with it 'the victory of individuality over personality' (WK 9.2: 251).

24 The wanderer is permitted some transient pleasures: 'Like the wanderer, he enjoys, now here, now there, an insight and an outlook, and delights in the changing images, their colourfulness and abundance, captivating him, filling him' (WK 9.2: 223).

25 Kracauer notes that while the *Kulturmensch* finds consolation through belief in God, the modern civilized individual experiences 'the loneliness of a soul without a goal or purpose for itself; a soul which dispenses with the forms unifying it with other souls, which is pushed into the void and whose deepest needs lie fallow' (WK 9.2: 261).

26 See also Belke and Renz (1989: 24).

27 More powerful and enduring, indeed, than the ties of many marriages, for instance, Kracauer notes a little mischievously (UFR: 25).

28 Kracauer notes: 'The spirit of camaraderie comes into being wherever people act together. What is decisive for its emergence is first and foremost that the reason for this coming together is not spiritual affinity or special inner force of attraction, but some goal or other introduced from outside' (UFR: 12).

29 'Colleague' is probably the best term to use here, although one could also use 'associate' or the more rudimentary 'fellow employee' or even simply 'co-worker'. Translation is a little tricky given the peculiarities of the German white-collar world, with its complex legal and status distinctions and numerous professional associations. Kracauer actually uses terms such as 'Fachgenossenschaft' or 'Berufsgenossenschaft', but then notes that they themselves refer to each other as 'Kollegen' (UFR: 16).

30 'Impossible to enumerate the occasions that give rise to acquaintance: chance is so decisive here', observes Kracauer (UFR: 19).

31 Hence, Kracauer acknowledges that, although any of the three forms of attachment might lead in time to friendship, and although it may at first sight seem to be the weakest tie of the three, acquaintance is the most likely starting point of friendship precisely because it is chosen freely by the individual her-/himself rather than being the outcome of shared external duress or common employment.

32 Kracauer notes: 'Unlike the relationships of camaraderie, collegiality and acquaintance, sexual love and friendship embrace the whole soul of a person' (UFR: 26).

33 In his 'On Expressionism' essay Kracauer writes: 'The personality [*Persön-lichkeit*] has no home in pure civilization; it is as horribly forsaken as Poe's man of the crowd. Here and there – wherever civilization becomes the end in itself – small cliques of select spiritual community may well arise, but they are only ever exceptions, isolated oases in the desert. The more civilization spreads, the ever more difficult it becomes to build bridges from one personality to another. Civilization separates and divides when, like the civilization of our days, it dominates people who are not spiritually connected instead of being grounded in and held in check from the outset by a strong original culture' (WK 9.2: 69–70).

34 In *Ginster*, Kracauer's friendship with Hainebach finds fictionalized form in the relationship between Ginster and Otto. See WK 7: 35–81.

35 See Belke and Renz (1989: 27).

Chapter 2   Portraits of the Age

1 *Ekphrasis* is the translation of a work of art from one medium into another, in particular, as here, the textual description of a visual representation.

2 The photograph is found in Belke and Renz (1989: 29).

3 See MOR: 54.

4 Kracauer notes: 'It is the fashion details that hold the gaze tight. Photography is bound to time in precisely the same way as fashion' (MOR: 55).

5 Kracauer points out the 'comic quality of the crinoline' – worn until relatively recently, this outfit cannot 'attain the beauty of a ruin' (ibid.).

6 'Historicism', Kracauer notes, 'is concerned with the photography of time' (MOR: 50).

7 Readers of Benjamin might be reminded here of his conception of Charles Baudelaire's sonnet *A une passante* as an instance of 'love at last sight'. See SW4: 24–5.

8 Kracauer concurs on this point: 'What photographs by their sheer accumulation attempt to banish is the recollection of death, which is part and parcel of every memory image. In the illustrated magazines the world has become a photographable present, and the photographed present has been entirely eternalized. Seemingly ripped from the clutch of death, in reality it has succumbed to it' (MOR: 59).

9 Rembrandt's penchant for self-portraiture becomes intelligible here: the painter does not express the inner life of the other as manifest in his/her appearance but vents his own inner life both *in* and *as* appearance. Subject and object are coincident rather than confluent.

10 Simmel writes: 'Each present moment is determined by the entire prior course of life, the culmination of all preceding moments; ... every moment of life is the form in which the whole of the life of the subject is real' (REM: 6).

11 In Rembrandt's works: 'the depicted moment appears to contain the whole living impulse directed toward it; it tells the story of this life course' (REM: 6). 'Miraculously', Simmel adds, 'Rembrandt transposes into the fixed uniqueness of the gaze all the movements of the life that led up to it: the formal rhythm, mood and colouring of fate, as it were, of the vital process' (REM: 10).

12 Simmel observes: 'The older we get, the more the multicoloured experiences, sensations, and fates that populate our path through the world mutually paralyze themselves, as it were. All this forms our "appearance" in the widest sense in which each line is a result of our actual self and of the things and events around us' (REM: 96). Hence: 'the richest and most moving portraits of Rembrandt are those of old people, since in them we can see a maximum of lived life' (REM: 11).

13 A Rembrandt portrait 'never is, it is always becoming' (REM: 11).

14 For Rembrandt: 'the starting point or foundation of the depiction is not the image of a moment as viewed from the outside, as it were, in which the motion has reached its portrayable zenith, a self-contained cross-section of its temporal course. Rather, it contains from the outset the dynamic of the whole act concentrated into a unity. The entire expressive meaning of the movement, therefore, lies already in the very first stroke' (REM: 7).

15 Simmel captures this sense of life as flow and passage with the metaphor of the wanderer looking back upon the sweeping course of a long journey: 'In the physiognomies of Rembrandt's portraits we feel very clearly that the course of a life, heaping fate upon fate, creates this present image. It elevates us, as it were, to a certain height from which we can view the ascending path toward that point' (REM: 9–10).

16 Simmel notes: 'Rembrandt's faces actually display little of that which one calls the 'character' of a human being; of that which is continuously effective and given to the human being once and for all'. Instead, 'this solid, continuous, relatively atemporal feature of the personality is dissolved into the flow of its total fates' (REM: 79).

17 Simmel observes: 'Out of his portraits shines above all essentially that which we know about a person at first sight, as something completely inexpressible, as the unity of his existence. For only the totality of the human being (that which Rembrandt makes visible as the total course of his fate) is unique' (REM: 67).

18 See REM: 89.

19 Simmel writes: 'Death is within us from our first day on, not as an abstract possibility that at some point will realize itself, but as the simple concrete fact [*So-Sein*] of life, even if its form and its measure are highly changeable, and if only in the last moment it permits no deception. We are not "under the spell of death". ... Rather, our life and its whole appearance would be totally different from the onset if it would not be pervaded by that which we call (according to its definition) death' (REM: 72).

20 Simmel points out: 'That perceptibility of death in the greatest Rembrandt portraits corresponds to the extent to which they adopt the absolute individuality of the person as their object. And this is understandable from within. The type ... does not die but the individual does. And the more individual, therefore, a person is, the more "mortal" he is, because the unique is simply irreplaceable, and its disappearance is therefore all the more the more unique it is' (REM: 77).

21 Simmel observes: 'the religious as he presents it is not the objective relationship between human and God but rather that innermost being of a person in which, or out of which, the relationship to his God is established in the first place' (REM: 118).

22 One might be tempted to say that Rembrandt's portraits capture what Max Weber (1930) famously terms the 'Protestant ethic', that unwavering individual faith in God and in one's own salvation that is, at the same time, an intense inner loneliness occasioned by the absence of the mediation of church, priestly intercession and religious community. Simmel, though, is at pains to distance Rembrandt from Calvinism. The doctrines of calling and predestination, and the concomitant denigration of this-worldliness as insignificant compared with the realm of God, run counter to Rembrandt's own intense preoccupation with the unplanned, contingent flow of individual life and the central importance for him of mundane human experience (see REM: 128–9). Accordingly, Rembrandt's images are anything but doctrinaire. Simmel writes: 'Not what a person believes, not the specific content of the religious life, but the particularity of the life insofar as it is religious constitutes his problem' (REM: 121).

23 Rembrandt's depictions of Jesus, for instance, emphasize his human qualities.

24 For example, one might fruitfully explore the historical and/or biographical circumstances of Simmel's study. It might be read as a recovery of *Kultur* in the context of the ongoing Great War – Simmel certainly makes a number of references to what he esteems as the specifically 'Germanic' qualities of Rembrandtian vis-à-vis Latin art. Alternatively, the themes identified in these portraits – old age, death, the soul – might be interpreted in terms of Simmel's own advanced years.

25 See REM: 51.

26 It would not be stretching the point to say: as the 'aura' of such paintings disappears. Indeed, Kracauer anticipates Benjamin's famous 1935–6 essay 'The Work of Art in the Age of its Technological Reproducibility' when he notes how photography obliterates the 'crucial traits' of a person, a thing, a moment, which memory retains: 'Artworks suffer this fate through their reproductions. The phrase "lie together, die together" applies to the

multiply reproduced original; rather than coming into view through the reproductions, it tends to disappear in its multiplicity and to live on as art photography' (MOR: 58). Kracauer shares Benjamin's contempt for the pretensions of 'art photography' (see Benjamin's 1931 'Small History of Photography', especially SW2: 523 and 526).

27 See his 1961 essay 'The Photographic Message' (Barthes 1984: 17).

28 See Barthes 1993: 76. He later notes: 'nothing can prevent the Photograph from being analogical; but at the same time, Photography's *noeme* has nothing to do with analogy .... The realists, of whom I am one and of whom I was already one when I asserted that the Photograph was an image without code ... the realists do not take the photograph for a "copy" of reality, but for an emanation of *past reality*: a *magic*, not an art' (ibid.: 88). Barthes here is surely as curious a realist as Kracauer.

29 Writing at almost the same moment, Benjamin, too, was to use this trope of a snowstorm in his 'One-Way Street' collection (*Einbahnstrasse*) to character-ize the surfeit of information spawned by contemporary journalism, a superabundance in inverse proportion to the actual communication of meaning and acquisition of knowledge. See SW1: 456.

30 One is reminded here once again of Simmel's vision of the overstimulation of the human senses in the modern metropolitan environment, excitations leading only to the dulling of the senses and a blasé attitude. For Kracauer, the deluge of modern media, rather than the cityscape, leads to this de-sensitization and withdrawal.

31 Kracauer writes: 'Since nature changes in exact correspondence with the particular state of consciousness of a period, the foundation of nature devoid of meaning arises with modern photography. No different from earlier modes of representation, photography, too, is assigned to a particu-lar developmental stage of practical and material life. It is a secretion of the capitalist mode of production' (MOR: 61).

32 Frisby's excellent discussion of Kracauer's Expressionism study in his chapter 'The City Dissolved' also takes Simmel as the key point of access, drawing not so much on the Rembrandt study as on essays such as 'Philosophy of Landscape' (1910), 'Rodin' (1910) and 'The Conflict in Modern Culture' (1914). See Frisby (2001: 236–63).

33 Kracauer acknowledges that these works are met by most with 'a feeling of deep discomfiture [*Befremdung*]' (WK 9.2: 11).

34 Kracauer rightly recognizes that Expressionism embraces a number of dif-ferent artistic media: 'the achievements of the youngest generation in the fields of the fine arts and poetry stem from the same state of the soul [*See-lenverfassung*]. There exists between the creations of a Franz Marc and those of a [Franz] Werfel or Georg Kaiser an immanent spiritual connection already given to immediate sensation' (WK 9.2: 11).

35 Kracauer notes: 'More precise recognition of the principal features shared by Expressionist artistic creations eventually leads to the insight that these are the works of the youngest according to content and direction and are somehow determined by the total situation of our time' (WK 9.2: 12).

36 As the subtitle for *Die Angestellten*, his 1929 study of Berlin's white-collar workers discussed in the next chapter.

37 See WK 9.2: 19.

38 Kracauer notes that, in such cases, 'to the artist, his "self" and the "object" do not present themselves as two separate entities. Simply the material spreads itself in him requiring artistic composition' (WK 9.2: 17).

39 This 'artistic type wishes to entirely erase the person in the work. Whatever he creates should – at least this should be the intention – be free of any reference to the self. The endeavour culminates in disappearing completely behind the creation' (WK 9.2: 14).

40 Such an artist 'can keep to the representation of the "real" where "real" to him/her is that which has substance independent of personal feelings' or, 'in order to achieve impersonality, she/he can conform to the requirements and rules of a form which, as a consequence of its rigid determination, renders impossible any free outflowing from the artist' (WK 9.2: 15).

41 The much later works of Abstract Expression take this rejection of the external world to a new degree perhaps.

42 'The core endeavour' of the Expressionist artist, Kracauer notes, 'is to lay himself bare' (WK 9.2: 32).

43 Kracauer notes: 'The single great artist is relatively independent of his time. He fashions the ideas that unfathomable mercy has bestowed. ... He does not live in and with the time but far removed from his contemporaries, often lighting their way as leader, also often as if banished to an island, there to witness the current of events surging by. ... Solitude is his destiny' (WK 9.2: 12). Rembrandt was extraordinary and inimitable and therefore his masterpieces are, *pace* Simmel, an unreliable guide to the prevailing conditions and sentiments.

44 Sociologically speaking, rather than aesthetically, the most significant portraits of an age are those not of its greatest masters or radical innovators but of its more numerous and hence more representative artisans working to meet the conventional tastes of (bourgeois) buyers and critics. Here we see an early instance of Kracauer's abiding concern with the more humble and humdrum aspects of (mundane popular) culture as the surface manifestations of everyday life, as the most important clues to deciphering modernity. Mention of the studio in this context is deliberate: as a reference not only to the artist, of course, but to its now more familiar usage in designating the site of film production. As Kracauer makes clear in the first part of his 1927 series 'Little Shop Girls Go to the Movies' (MOR: 291–4), and then again in his *Caligari* book, film is the collaboratively produced cultural artefact par excellence. On the one hand collectively realized, on the other appealing to the tastes of the collective, films, rather than paintings, become the 'mirror of the prevailing society' (MOR: 291).

45 Kracauer ponders: 'What is the nature of elemental being which is to be expressed? It is not a nature full of gentle idyllic contemplation and self-sufficient harmony but a self trembling with outrage and passion, boundless and opaque. Everything that Expressionist art embodies has the effect of a single scream; the foundation of our being that it reveals proves to be in restless motion and shot through with currents of Dionysian ardour. Not without reason does the Expressionist painter revel in garish and blazing colours; they seem to him the only appropriate expression of what is felt inside' (WK 9.2: 46).

46 To borrow Norbert Elias's term (Elias 2000).

47 Kracauer notes that 'Expressionism, namely, is essentially nothing other than indignation, a cry of desperation from the personality which is enslaved and condemned to impotence in the present' (WK 9.2: 70). The Norwegian painter Edvard Munch's famous set of paintings *The Scream* (*Der Schrei der Natur*) (1893–1910) would seem the exemplary instances of Expressionist agonistics here.

48 Kracauer points out that 'The pure intellect is deeply despised as the creator of convention, as the oppressor of the unconscious creative sources in humans, as the denier of the soul and the self. Its burgeoning has contributed considerably to the elimination of the personality from community life, the decay of the human essence, and the petrification of the world' (WK 9.2: 71).

49 'To my knowledge', he notes in parentheses, 'we are not indebted to Expressionism for any works of superior humour; it would be alien to its very nature' (WK 9.2: 48).

50 In Expressionism 'the will for the deed, for action, is emphasized' (WK 9.2: 49).

Chapter 3 On the Surface

1 He is later drafted into the reserves and then stood down once more owing to 'general physical weakness' (WK 7: 199).

2 Military training, Kracauer notes, brings to the fore 'the thing-like character of the human being' (WK 7: 156).

3 Ginster later muses: 'Perhaps we did indeed design it too small' (WK 7: 229).

4 Ginster recalls: 'The mother did not so much walk, she rolled like an automaton' (WK 7: 83).

5 Ginster tries to feel sorrow, but 'He was unsuccessful; instead a sense of joy crept into him which he wanted to expel, so mean did he feel it to be, but it stayed and swelled up in him. The joy that he, Ginster, had not been in Otto's place, but lived on. He wanted to live long' (WK 7: 81). He continues: 'But he was not sad, only ever happy to be here, even if he were alone. That is to say, happy was overstating it, since the fear that he himself might perhaps have to go to war smothered the joy immediately' (ibid.).

6 In his review, Joseph Roth emphasizes this connection: 'Ginster in the war, that is: Chaplin in the department store. ... In the face of department stores, wars, clothing, fatherlands, Chaplin and Ginster are equally clueless and cowardly, odd and awkward, laughable and tragicomic. At last we have the literary Chaplin' (cited in Belke and Renz 1989: 52).

7 Roth's review is significantly entitled 'Who is Ginster?' (*Wer ist Ginster?*). He muses: 'Anonymous: in this case that means: revelatory, sincere – not dissembling! Anonymous! ... there is no author's name under a book like 'Ginster'. Ginster describes himself just as Chaplin plays himself' (cited ibid.: 52–3).

8 Christian Rogowski describes this as 'an elaborate game of hide-and-seek' between writer and reader 'in which the transformation of experience into fiction emerges as a kind of self-fashioning, an authoring of an alternate

self' (Gemünden and von Moltke 2012: 199, 200). He adds: 'From this perspective, the novel's subtitle, "written by himself," attains a particular significance: the entire novel can be read as an effort on the part of the subject, Ginster (i.e. Kracauer) to control the narrative of his own life, to "write" the story "himself" rather than having a story and an identity ascribed to him by others' (ibid.: 206). This is not entirely convincing: use of the first-person singular ('I') would surely have solved such a problem. The point is rather that Kracauer is *staging the problem of identity and authorship* by means of this narrative device.

9 See his letter to Kracauer of 4 September 1962 (AKB: 538–9). The volume is dedicated to Adorno.

10 The essay appeared in two instalments, on 9 and 10 June 1927.

11 In a letter to Jeanette Baldes of 6 October 1959, Kracauer notes of the essay: 'I loved working on it and even today it remains close to my heart' (DLA: 72.1157).

12 Given the lack of psychological depth Kracauer provides with respect to his character, Ginster himself might be seen to serve as such a 'surface-level expression'.

13 Their arrival in Berlin from a highly successful US tour is doubtless the source of Kracauer's misidentification.

14 The Tiller Girls troupe (obviously not the original members!) gave their final performance as recently as 2008.

15 Even in the 1920s these were 'an established form', having gained 'an international stature' and prompting considerable 'aesthetic interest' (MOR: 76). The features of the mass ornament became staple components of the propaganda spectacles of totalitarian regimes: the Soviet sporting rallies of the Spartakiads first staged in Moscow in 1928 and then, of course, the Nuremberg rallies of the National Socialists in the 1930s.

16 The opening and closing ceremonies of the Olympic Games are the most obvious example here. For a critical examination of these media mega-events, see Kellner (2002).

17 Kracauer notes that 'The mass movements of the girls ... take place in a vacuum; they are a linear system that no longer has any erotic meaning but at best points to the locus of the erotic' (MOR: 77). Interestingly, this view of mechanization as de-sexualization perfectly reverses what occurs in Fritz Lang's 1926 film *Metropolis*: here a robot created by the sinister inventor Rotwang takes on the physical form of the angelic Maria and performs an erotic jazz dance number.

18 Indeed, this is even more the case today, in *our* times, when the performance, display or sporting action itself is so intimately and exhaustively covered by television.

19 Commonly, this is done by spectators holding up differently coloured pieces of card and perhaps turning them at particular moments prompted by the stadium announcer.

20 Such aerial shots were a standard part of the Busby Berkeley musicals. The mass ornament was choreographed as a cinematic object.

21 In his 1936 exposé 'Mass and Propaganda' ('Masse und Propaganda'), Kracauer observes that, under fascism, 'The masses are obliged to look at themselves everywhere (mass gatherings, mass marches, etc.). Thus, the

masses are ever-present to themselves and often in the aesthetically seductive form of an ornament or an effective image' (cited in Belke and Renz
1989: 88).

22 With regard to Debord, the mass ornament prefigures many of the key
features of what Situationism termed 'the Spectacle', a central yet enigmatic
category intended to capture the transformation of capitalism, commodity
culture and human alienation into the realm of images. Both mass ornament
and Debord's spectacle are ways of seeing in the world, forms of *Weltanschauung*. As for Foucault, he famously juxtaposes a rather different version
of spectacle, as the violent demonstration of sovereign power, with its
modern successor 'discipline', as the routinization of punishment. In Kracuaer's example of the mass ornament, *discipline itself has become the spectacle*,
but of a distinctive kind: this is neither the many watching the few (Foucault's
sovereign spectacle) nor the few keeping watch over the many (disciplinary
surveillance). Rather, it is the many indulging in the (mediated) spectacle
of themselves. This actually comes closest to Foucault's formulation of
panopticism – the inmate becomes the subject/object of the gaze – but here
in Kracauer's conception this is understood in terms of a collective narcissism and as entertainment. One might say that Kracauer leapfrogs Foucault
into our world today not only with its Olympic mega-events but also with
Big Brother, 'reality TV' and 'fly on the wall' police shows parading panopticism for pleasure.

23 In her Introduction to *The Salaried Masses*, Inka Mülder-Bach astutely notes:
'It was with good reason that Adorno assured Kracauer in 1933 that "he
had been the first of us to tackle afresh the problem of the Enlightenment."
In retrospect "The Mass Ornament" reads like a nucleus of *The Dialectic of
Enlightenment*' (TSM: 12). Adorno's comments are an aside made in a letter
of 12 January 1933 in which he asks Kracauer to review Ernst Cassirer's
1932 book *Die Philosophie der Aufklärung*. See AKB: 298. Little wonder then
that Adorno suggested the 'strange essay' as the title of the first collection
of Kracauer's feuilletons (AKB: 539).

24 Kracauer notes: 'Determinations of meaning rendered as abstract generalities – such as determinations in the economic, social, political or moral
domain – do not give reason what rightfully belongs to reason' (MOR:
81–2). Instead of being made by active human beings, the social world is
governed by mysterious forces and immutable laws such as 'the market',
'progress' and 'development'.

25 Perhaps this is primarily a matter of different historical moments and contexts. In 1927 Kracauer could not have envisaged what was to transpire in
Germany over the next two decades. Adorno and Horkheimer are penning
their utterly pessimistic vision in the aftermath of war, as the full horrors
of the Holocaust emerge.

26 Curiously, Kracauer's formulation bypasses Adorno and Horkheimer's
irredeemably bleak vision of the 'eclipse of reason' and anticipates the
revisionist attempts of second-generation critical theorists, most notably
Jürgen Habermas, to reconfigure and reassert the still unfulfilled promise
of Enlightenment. Reason has not failed as such; it has yet to be fully
realized. For Habermas, this involves a continuing hope in the possibility
of undistorted communication in the 'ideal speech situation' as the

fundamental premise governing a lifeworld de-colonized by systemic imperatives and logics. Kracauer's insistence on *more* rather than *less* rationalization ironically strikes a chord with *our* contemporaries even as it fails to do so with his own.

27 For an extended discussion of Kracauer's writings on this employee culture, see Band (1999) and Hofmann in Kessler and Levin (1990: 87–104).

28 Following their marriage (5 March 1930), the Kracauers relocated to Berlin from Frankfurt in May 1930. Kracauer assumed the position of feuilleton editor for the Berlin city edition of the *FZ*.

29 See Belke and Renz (1989: 57–8). In a postcard of 3 January 1930, Ernst Bloch notes of the 'Asyl für Obdachlose' instalment: 'It is the most important and instructive view of our being I have read in a long time' (1985, Vol. 1: 330). The Belgian social psychologist Hendrik de Man writes: 'My delight with your "Angestellten" has grown with each instalment. I consider your work by far the best sociological monograph of a social stratum that exists to date' (in a letter of 10 January 1930; see also DLA: 72.2679/1). In addition, Karl Mannheim comments positively in a letter of 2 April 1930 (DLA: 72.2682/2).

30 Kracauer writes: 'Hundreds of thousands of salaried employees throng the streets of Berlin daily, yet their life is more unknown than that of the primitive tribes at whose habits those same employees marvel in films ... Even radical intellectuals do not easily get behind the exoticism of a commonplace existence' (TSM: 29).

31 Kracauer compares the situation of this class with that of the purloined letter in Edgar Allan Poe's famous story, a missive that eludes detection because, rather than being hidden, it remains in full view among other letters casually left on a writing desk (ibid.).

32 Kracauer gives 3.5 million as the national figure (ibid.).

33 Women have 'flooded into salaried jobs', Kracauer notes, such that they now form a third of all such employees. Band (1999: 135) confirms that, in 1925, 1.2 million of these workers were female.

34 In the section 'Short Break for Ventilation', Kracauer tours a firm in the company of its commercial director and is shown the new machinery of bureaucracy: not just typewriters, but machines for punching and sorting cards of various kinds, tabulating and accounting machines dealing with pre-printed forms and such like (see TSM: 41–2). Just as, according to Marx, industrial workers become mere appendages of the machinery they serve in factories, so here, in the offices, employees must work to the routines and tempi set by technological systems.

35 This tone of 'refined informality' is imitative of the very language and social ambience of the white-collar world with its deceptively 'friendly face' (see TSM: 74). One should bear in mind that the salaried masses were, of course, the readership of the metropolitan newspapers for whom Kracauer is writing here. In short: his account of the salaried masses is penned *for* the salaried masses.

36 Benjamin observes 'the author's distaste for all that has to do with reportage and *die neue Sachlichkeit*' (TSM: 113).

37 And, of course, the woman, too. Indeed, appearances appear even more important with respect to the recruitment and work of female employees.

38 As Janet Ward (2001) stresses in her panoramic study of the many urban surfaces of Weimar culture.

39 Indeed, Kracauer seems somewhat taken aback by her disarming candour: sitting opposite a stranger on the train, a little 'tipsy' perhaps, she blithely recounts her assignations and flirtations with her boss, wholly instrumental relations which, she emphasizes, in no way interfere with or compromise her real affections for her fiancé.

40 The dismal reception given to the works of Kafka is exemplary – sales of fewer than a thousand copies, Kracauer notes.

41 Adorno's later accusation that Kracauer's Offenbach book was an attempt to write a bestseller, even though it was nothing of the sort, should be understood in the light of such an account. See chapter 5.

42 Kracauer observes: 'The middle class and the impoverished masses in general demand heart, which costs nothing. When people lack all else, *feeling* is everything' (MOR: 96).

43 Kracauer writes: 'In the recent past, people have been forced to experience their own insignificance – as well as that of others – all too persistently for them to still believe in the sovereign power of any one individual. It is precisely this sovereign power, however, which is the premise of the bourgeois literature produced during the years preceding the war' (MOR: 102).

44 'History', Kracauer notes, 'is condensed in the lives of its highly visible heroes' (MOR: 103).

45 'If there is a confirmation of the end of individualism', Kracauer declares, 'it can be glimpsed in the museum of great individuals that today's literature puts on a pedestal' (MOR: 105). Indeed, this museum was soon to be occupied by new exhibits. As Löwenthal observes a decade later in his study of the 'Mass Idols', biographies of such world historical figures no longer excited the imaginations of the masses: now 'personalities' have come to the fore – sportsmen and women, media figures, popular entertainers, film stars and celebrities of the moment, the new 'heroes of consumption', as he terms them, rather than, as previously, the 'heroes of production' (industrialists, politicians, inventors, scientists). See Löwenthal (1961: 109–36).

46 Interestingly, in presenting them as subjects of sociological study to themselves as newspaper readers, Kracauer himself might be seen as promoting some self-recognition of this employee class.

47 Kracauer writes: 'The average worker, upon whom so many lowly salaried employees like to look down, often enjoys not merely a material but also an existential superiority over them. His life as a class-conscious proletarian is roofed over with vulgar-Marxist concepts that do at least tell him what his intended role is. Admittedly, the whole roof is nowadays riddled with holes' (TSM: 88).

48 In this sense, one might say that the employee is the very antithesis of the critical theorist who is both/and – that is to say, educated in true bourgeois style and versed in *Kultur*, yet at the same time insistent upon solidarity and staunch comradeship with the proletariat.

49 Or, better, 'spiritually shelterless'. It is important to note a shift in Kracauer's thinking here: the *Lebensphilosophie* version of existential spiritlessness as the modern condition is given a Marxist inflection as a *class-specific and historically bound* situation.

50 See Lukács's (1971) *Theory of the Novel*, first published in 1920.
51 The French social anthropologist Marc Augé (1995) coined the term 'non-places' (*non-lieux*) to designate those sites and settings of everyday metropolitan life bereft of meaning and memory: fast food outlets, supermarkets and shopping malls, motorway service stations, car parks, airport lounges, bus stations, all kinds of foyers, vestibules and atria. Kracauer's discussion of the hotel lobby as part of his treatise on the detective novel could be considered a pioneering study of a non-place. See MOR: 173–85.

Chapter 4   Berlin Impromptus

1 *Das Ornament der Masse* appeared the previous year. It, too, contains a plethora of the feuilleton pieces along with a number of more substantial writings. There is some overlap in terms of content between the two collections.
2 In a letter to Adorno of 22 July 1930, Kracauer observes: 'I ... sacrifice my strength for articles and essays which for the most part have no life beyond the newspaper. And I never succeed in polishing them off on the side but rather write them with the same loving care as my novel, etc.' (AKB: 232).
3 Kracauer states: 'Spatial images are the dreams of society. Wherever the hieroglyph of a spatial image is deciphered, the basis of social reality presents itself' (SBA: 52). This apparent conflation of a 'hieroglyphics of space' with the interpretation of dream images leads to a fascinating little spat with Adorno. On 25 July 1930, Adorno writes: 'Your essay on labour exchanges ... struck me as excellent. It was with astonishment and agreement that I noticed you had accepted the Benjaminian formula of buildings as the dreams of the collective – without using the word collective, which I cannot stand either. The thing is really very aggressive and striking. One of your best things; pursues certain intentions from the 'Mass Ornament' but is more radical. I am in complete agreement' (AKB: 236). On 1 August 1930, Kracauer replies with a correction: his formulation is neither accepting of nor indebted to Benjamin's 'dreaming collective' thesis: 'I addressed certain spatial images as dreams of the society because they represent the being of this society, which is veiled by its consciousness. I therefore encounter Benjamin, who by the way shares this view, only in the word dream. That is as if one were to meet at a crossroads and go on according to different directions. The conception of the city as a dream of the collective still appears to me as romantic' (AKB: 240–1).
4 Ward (2001: 81) rightly describes Kracauer as 'the archanalyst of Weimar surface culture'. For a discussion of Kracauer's technique of critical decipherment, see Stalder in Volk (1996: 131–55).
5 See DLA: 72.3496a.
6 All of these miniatures, along with many of Kracauer's other feuilleton writings, have subsequently been published in the three volumes of his SCH 5 and in two further collections: BEN and *Frankfurter Turmhäuser*. Many of the film reviews have also appeared in Kracauer's 1974 *Kino* collection and, most recently, in the three volumes of WK 6, *Kleine Schriften zum Film*.

7 Indeed, how do they speak to us *now*, another fifty years later? Given that they provide snapshots of a society of mass unemployment amid economic turmoil, perhaps they have even more significance for today's readers than those in the middle of the German 'economic miracle' (*Wirtschaftswunder*) of the 1960s.

8 Perhaps he hoped Adorno's retrospective essay 'The Curious Realist' ('Der wunderliche Realist'), written to mark Kracauer's seventy-fifth birthday in 1964, would perform this task. Of course, it did no such thing and served only to provoke another acrimonious exchange between the two.

9 Fifteen if one includes the extract from *Ginster*, published in the *FZ* in 1931.

10 See 'Seen from Berlin' ('Von Berlin aus gesehen'), the first part of Kracauer's 1931 'Parisian Observations' ('Pariser Beobachtungen') (SCH 5.2: 25–6).

11 SBA: 56.

12 See 'On Labour Exchanges' ('Über Arbeitsnachweise') (17 June 1930) (SBA: 52–9).

13 See 'Warming Rooms' ('Wärmehallen') (18 January 1931) (SBA: 59–63).

14 See 'Critical Day' ('Kritischer Tag') (15 July 1931) (BEN: 54–6).

15 See 'Cinema in Münzstrasse' ('Kino in der Münzstrasse') (2 April 1932) (SBA: 69–71).

16 See 'Girls and Crisis' ('Girls und Krise') (1931) (SCH 5.2: 320–1).

17 See Kracauer's description of the Christmas market in 'Weihnachtlicher Budenzauber' (24 December 1932) (SBA: 30–2).

18 The enigmatic piece 'Screams on the Street' ('Schreie auf der Strasse') is a good example of this all-encompassing urban anguish: the terrifying scream which pierces the tense atmosphere and which sends a shiver down Kracauer's spine emanates neither from political disturbances on the street nor from the unfortunate victims of everyday violence, but seemingly from the very streets themselves (see SBA: 21–3). Is this perhaps the 'desperate scream' (*Verzweiflungsschrei*) (WK 9.2: 70) of his 'On Expressionism' essay?

19 See SBA: 108.

20 In 'Organized Happiness: On the Reopening of the Lunapark' ('Organisiertes Glück: Zur Wiedereröffnung des Lunaparks') (7 May 1930) (BEN: 73–5), Kracauer writes: 'unseen organization ensures that pleasure assails the masses in a prescribed order. Perhaps people want it that way; after all, during the day they are guided by signals, party manifestos and associations' (BEN: 73).

21 See 'Sunday Outing' ('Sonntagsausflug') (BEN: 43–5). Perhaps they have all gone to the office wedding.

22 The term *Mittelgebirge* means a low mountain range. Kracauer uses the term to describe an urban hinterland, the site of weekend excursions. He plays on the notion of the *Mittelstand* (the middle classes), who turn the *Mittelgebirge* into a leisure setting. See SBA: 90–1.

23 See BEN: 29–30.

24 Kracauer notes: 'The places in which there is laughter are indicative of the audience' (SBA: 70).

25 See BEN: 31.

26 See Kracauer's 1924 'Boredom' ('Langeweile') (MOR: 331–4). Interestingly, when the pianist takes a break, radio music is broadcast to fill the void: 'Even in the café, where one wants to roll up into a ball like a porcupine

and become aware of one's insignificance, an imposing loudspeaker effaces every trace of private existence. The announcements it blares forth dominate the space of the concert intermissions, and the waiters (who are listening to it themselves) indignantly refuse the unreasonable requests to get rid of this gramophonic mimicry' (MOR: 333).

27 See, for example, Adorno's 'on the Fetish character of Music and the Regression of Listening' (in Arato and Gebhavdt, 1994) and 'Perennial Fashion – fazz' (in Bronner and Kellner, 1990).

28 Kracauer's enthusiasm for the performance of the Andreu–Rivel clowns at the Scala Variety Theatre is the clearest example of this here. See 'Akrobat – Schöön' (SBA: 101–4).

29 See Benjamin SW4: 264 and 268–9.

30 See Benjamin SW4: 268.

31 See Benjamin SW1: 487. Kracauer's pianist is an exemplary instance of such mastery amid distraction. Our musician plays fluently and flawlessly, demonstrating a professional expertise developed through many years of practice. He exhibits a technical, tactile control of the keyboard and pedals born of familiarity and habit. His work no longer requires his attention. His complete proficiency enables him to be both here and elsewhere in the same moment.

32 See Benjamin SW4: 266. Compare Kracauer TOF: 46.

33 In *Die Angestellten*, cinema is also understood to play an ideological role: obscuring and legitimizing existing social reality; drugging its audiences with 'pseudo-glamour'; providing images of emotional compensation and consolation; serving as temporary refuges for the 'shelterless' (TSM: 94).

34 As Hansen (2012) suggests, following Heide Schlüpmann (1998), a new kind of public and public sphere is intimated here. She writes: 'The cinema is the signature of modernity for Kracauer not simply because it attracts and represents the masses but because it is the most advanced cultural institution in which the masses, as a relatively heterogeneous, undefined and as yet little understood form of collectivity, constitute a new form of public' (2012: 54). She continues: 'Kracauer sees in the cinema the blueprint for an alternative public sphere that can realize itself only through the destruction of the dominant, bourgeois public sphere that draws legitimation from institutions of high art, education and culture no longer in touch with reality' (ibid.: 55). Hansen overlooks or at least underestimates the obverse of this: Kracauer's negative portrayal in the 1930s of the 'mass' as the homogeneous recipient of fascistic propaganda.

35 Kracauer observes that distraction 'is meaningful only as improvisation' (MOR: 327). As we will see, 'improvisation' is central not only to his valorization of slapstick comedy (chapter 9) but also to his vision of the elective affinity between film and cityscape (chapter 10).

36 For a discussion of architecture in Kracauer's journalistic writings, see Hess in Volk (1996: 111–29).

37 See Hessel (1999, Vol. III: 340–1).

38 Indeed, the *Strassenbuch* may even be seen as a counterpoint and corrective to the abstract and contrived use of montage in Ruttmann's 1927 *Berlin – Symphony of a Great City*, a film Kracauer condemned as portentous, contrived and vacuous. See Kracauer's review of 17 November 1927 in Kracauer, 1974: 404–5. See also CAL: 182–8 and TOF: 207.

39 Ward (2001: 160) astutely notes this cinematic quality of Kracauer's texts in the *Strassen in Berlin* collection.

40 The Lindenpassage was built in 1873, but the fashionable period of the arcade was already over by 1888. See Levin's editorial notes (MOR: 388–9).

41 This moment of recognition and redemption, in which an object or edifice appears to us for the first and only time, becoming memorable in the very instant in which it is about to vanish irrevocably, lies at the heart of Benjamin's *Arcades Project*. It corresponds to the notion of the 'dialectical image', that conjuncture and mutual illumination of past and present which constitutes Benjamin's decisive historiographical category. Kracauer's observations on the railway bridge over Friedrichstrasse, offering at one and the same moment a first and a final image of Berlin, serve an allegorical function in this regard. See SBA: 33–4.

42 See SBA: 113–14.

43 As Kracauer suggests, the images that arise before him are 'without doubt memories, which would like to hold on to him. Paralysed he confronts the past and his child-like face shows only too clearly that he has never come to terms with it' (SBA: 107).

44 See TOF: 137–8.

45 See 'Braces: A Historical Study' ('Die Hosenträger: Eine historische Studie') (30 October 1926) (SBA: 86–8).

46 See 'False Demise of Umbrellas' ('Falscher Untergang der Regenschirme') (7 April 1926) (SBA: 88–90).

47 See 'The Piano' ('Das Klavier') (23 February 1926) (SBA: 77–81).

48 See Benjamin SW1: 463.

Chapter 5   Offenbach in Paris

1 Published in England in 1937 as *Offenbach and the Paris of his Time* and in 1938 in the USA under the title *Orpheus in Paris: Offenbach and the Paris of his Time*. This translation was reissued by Zone Books (New York, 2002) under the full title *Jacques Offenbach and the Paris of his Time*. This version includes a translation of Kracauer's original 'preface', unaccountably absent from the 1937 translation. All references here are to the 2002 edition.

2 In fact, published simultaneously in French, German and English.

3 The longest of the folders or convolutes of the *Arcades Project*, Convolute J, took Baudelaire as its title and theme.

4 For a discussion of the origins of the Baudelaire studies in relation to the *Arcades Project* and the changing form they were to take, see Gilloch (1996: 98–9; 2002: 201–7).

5 Such animosity was not universal. In a letter to the writer Ferdinand Lion, Kracauer notes: 'A letter from Thomas Mann was a particular delight. He wrote soon after receiving the book and expressed himself in the most positive way. You can imagine that such signs of a response brighten the horizon for us' (DLA: 72.1561/2). Among the numerous letters from Walter Landauer, editor at Allert de Lange, Kracauer's Amsterdam-based publishers, one dated 30 June 1937 notes: 'Hermann Hesse sent us a letter about it

completely unsolicited. I enclose a copy for you' (DLA: 72.2589/31). Another, dated 12 August 1937, refers to 'a very good review from Max Brod' (DLA: 72.2589/34). There is a certain bitter irony pervading Landauer's correspondence with Kracauer: while the editor is tirelessly reassuring as to the critical merits and enthusiastic reception of the book in literary circles, the impoverished author only ever asks about sales, rights and revenues.

6 'He has simply made an example of the thing' (ABC: 186), Benjamin decides.

7 In this epistle, Adorno patronizingly couches his otherwise vehement critique in terms of a difficult but dutiful act to sustain a vital, meaningful friendship. 'I am attacking you', he writes, 'to defend you from yourself' (AKB: 359). Kracauer robustly defended his study in his reply of 25 May 1937, refuting Adorno's critique as so 'foolish' (*töricht*) and misplaced that 'your supposed complete panning of my work results in only one thing, the total neglect of its actual worth' (AKB: 364). Two days later Adorno responded to this rebuttal with a disingenuous disappointment born not of Kracauer's defence but of his supposed refusal to engage with his critique: 'What saddens me more is that you do not engage with my criticism at all' (AKB: 365).

8 Benjamin should have been far more wary of this high-handed view of supposedly misdirected intellectual endeavours. The next couple of years would see Adorno instructing him as to his own best interests with regard to the Baudelaire studies.

9 Published in vol. 6, no. 3, 1937, pp. 697–8. Adorno congratulated himself on his 'dance on eggshells [*Eiertanz*]' (letter to Löwenthal of 1 October, in LLA, Mappe A7: 208).

10 In a letter to Adorno of 21 September 1937, Löwenthal writes: 'Under the circumstances, the review of Kracauer's book seems to me to be very good. Whoever reads it carefully will be left in no doubt as to your condemnation; admittedly, you do have to read it carefully. All the same, the review does the book much credit simply by virtue of its being reviewed by us at all' (LLA Mappe A7: 205).

11 The most notable exception being Frisby (1988). See also Kari Grimstad, in Kessler and Levin (1990: 59–76), and Gertrud Koch (JOF: 11–21).

12 Benjamin explains the plan of this book in his letters to Horkheimer (16 April 1938) and Adorno (28 August 1938). See COR: 555–8 and ABC: 273.

13 See, in particular, Adorno's lengthy letter of 10 November 1938 and Benjamin's reply a month later (9 December), in ABC: 280–96.

14 The word 'parallel' is not chosen lightly: although there was, of course, contact between the two men during their Paris years, Benjamin observes that Kracauer was always at pains 'to isolate his work from all our discussions during the years in which he was preparing this book' (ABC: 185).

15 Frisby (1988) once more is the exception.

16 Kracauer observes: 'It was no accident that Offenbach and the Boulevards were contemporary. They were related by their very nature. ... On the Boulevards he found his fellows, and the atmosphere of liberty that he required, and consequently felt at home, just because the Boulevards were no home in the ordinary sense. There he found the spirit that attracted him and the kind of society in which he flourished' (JOF: 106).

17 Kracauer notes: 'in the midst of the social hum he was in his element, and without a buzz of conversation all around him he lacked the air to breathe and to soar in' (JOF: 78).

18 Kracauer uses this formulation when he writes of Edouard Plouvier, librettist for Offenbach's comic duet *Le Moine bourru*: 'So fertile was the atmosphere of the Boulevards that many who ordinarily would never have seen a sentence of their own in print discovered a talent for writing. The truth was not that they wrote but that the Boulevards used them as a medium for self-expression' (JOF: 111).

19 Kracauer notes: 'Few have been so dependent on environment as Offenbach' (JOF: 119).

20 'By disclosing the connections between the operetta and society', Kracauer claims, 'the book demonstrates through an exemplary case the dependence of every genre of art on specific social conditions' (JOF: 24).

21 Jay observes, *pace* Kracauer: 'Although clearly indebted to Marx's *Eighteenth Brumaire*, *Offenbach* was no real landmark in Marxist cultural criticism' (1986: 166).

22 Their exchange is found in SW4: 99–115.

23 His example is Benjamin's supposed reading of *Le Vin des chiffonniers* ('The Ragpickers' Wine') as a response to the imposition of taxes on wine. See SW4: 7–8.

24 See Benjamin (1985).

25 Benjamin writes: 'Baudelaire's genius, which is nourished on melancholy, is an allegorical genius. For the first time, with Baudelaire, Paris becomes the subject of lyrical poetry. This poetry is no hymn to the homeland; rather, the gaze of the allegorist, as it falls on the city, is the gaze of the alienated man' (SW3: 39).

26 With Baudelaire: 'The crowd is a new subject in lyric poetry' (SW4: 35).

27 Benjamin notes: 'The masses had become so much a part of Baudelaire that it is rare to find a description of them in his works. His most important subjects are hardly ever encountered in descriptive form. ... Baudelaire describes neither the Parisians nor their city. Avoiding such descriptions enables him to invoke the former in the figure of the latter' (SW4: 322).

28 Kracauer writes of Offenbach: 'No one was more drawn than he toward the surface things of life or so receptive to the impressions that crowded in on every side' (JOF: 47).

29 Benjamin notes: 'In a time of dire need, Kracauer believed that he had to establish some positive access to the book market' (ABC: 185).

30 According to Landauer's letter of 2 February 1938, the Offenbach book sales account showed just sixty-six copies sold in the period 1 July – 31 December 1938. The publishers were still Fl. 75.25 to the good on Kracauer's initial advance (DLA: 72.2589).

31 Following the triumph of *La Belle Hélène* at the end of 1864, and with performances in Vienna and Berlin, Kracauer notes, 'Europe was at Offenbach's feet' (JOF: 280).

32 In this sense, Kracauer notes, his study could be understood as 'a biography of a city' (JOF: 24).

33 Kracauer later adds: 'All the ingredients of Offenbach's operettas existed in reality' (JOF: 299).

34 According to Benjamin at least. See especially Convolute K, ARC: 388–404.

35 The beginnings of the culture industry are very much in evidence here. Regarding the 'commercial vaudeville writers' with whom Offenbach had dealings, Kracauer notes that they 'produced almost on a mass-production scale, generally in collaboration, employing methods as rationalized as those of Hollywood scenario writers at the present day. Their work was a branch of industry rather than a profession' (JOF: 83).

36 Kracauer notes: 'His extensive contacts with journalists, singers and librettists kept him in touch with public tastes and tendencies' (JOF: 110).

37 'Les Fleurs du mal is the first book of poetry to use not only words of ordinary provenance but words of urban origin as well' (SW4: 62), Benjamin notes.

38 See Baudelaire's letter of 23 December 1865 cited in ARC: 313 and SW4: 5.

39 See SW4: 40.

40 Baudelaire earned some 15,000 francs from his entire work, Benjamin observes (SW4: 17).

41 See ibid.

42 The poet 'goes to the marketplace as a flâneur, supposedly to take a look at it but in reality to find a buyer' (ibid.).

43 Baudelaire may have lacked money, 'But this did not mean that he lacked insight into the true situation of a man of letters. He often confronted the writer, first and foremost himself, with the figure of the whore' (ibid.).

44 Such a profane vision of the poet is to be found in Baudelaire's prose piece 'Loss of a Halo'. See SW4: 342.

45 Benjamin writes: 'The poets find the refuse of society on their streets and derive their heroic subject from this very refuse' (SW4: 48).

46 The painter of modern life, Baudelaire insists, 'makes it his business to extract from fashion whatever element it may contain of poetry within history, to distil the eternal from the transitory' (1986: 12).

47 Baudelaire's deepest wish was eventually 'to be read like a classical poet' (SW4: 55).

48 A 'peculiarly Parisian product' (JOF: 216).

49 Nevertheless, Benjamin still bemoaned Kracauer's idea of a utopian moment in the operetta as an unconvincing 'apologia' (ABC: 186). Benjamin notes, in an early draft of the Arcades Project, 'Offenbach sets the rhythm of Parisian life. The operetta is the ironic utopia of an enduring reign of capital' (SW3: 38).

50 Kracauer writes, for instance: 'Joy and glamour was also the motto of Louis Napoleon. In his zeal for it he instituted a ruthless regime of terror directed against all who might disturb it. Immediately after the coup d'état tens of thousands of Socialists, republicans, and members of secret societies were summarily arrested, sent into exile or deported like common criminals' (JOF: 151). If this were not explicit enough for contemporary readers, Kracauer later states plainly: Louis Napoleon was 'the first modern dictator' (JOF: 155).

Chapter 6   Orpheus in Hollywood

1 In his brief correspondence with the Los Angeles-based film producer Max Laemmle in 1939, Kracauer asks Laemmle to speak with William Wyler,

whose dance scenes in *Jezabel* had impressed Kracauer, and with the director of *The Great Ziegfeld*, Robert Z. Leonhard, in connection with the proposed Offenbach film (DLA: 72.1531/1).

2 Letter to Horkheimer of 16 September 1941 (MHA, Mappe I 14, letter 161).

3 In the early autumn of 1941, Kracauer's hopes for the Offenbach film were briefly rekindled in New York. He wrote to Laemmle (24 September 1941) to ask for the return of his copy of the 'Motion Picture Treatment', having left his own in Paris in the chaos of departure. With Horkheimer's encouragement, Kracauer made contact with the European Film Foundation. The film director and writer William Dieterle and his wife, the actress Charlotte Dieterle, expressed their enthusiasm. Kracauer realized, however, that there was no genuine interest in an Offenbach film any more and the subject was dropped (see MHA, Mappe I 14, letters 161–3).

4 See WK 6.3: 523–5. Discussed in chapter 9.

5 Discussed in chapter 8. See DLA: 72.3620 and MHA, Mappe IX.

6 Letter to Laemmle, DLA: 72.1531/3.

7 See TOF: 151 and 200.

8 Letter to Horkheimer of 16 September 1941 (MHA, Mappe I 14, letter 161).

9 See TOF: 52.

10 See chapter 10 and, for example, TOF: 19, 31–2, 50, 62, and 72.

11 See TOF: 72 and 170.

12 Kracauer notes how, 'In the midst of a crowded social gathering, Offenbach would suddenly become absorbed and begin to cover sheets of paper with innumerable little flies' feet. Others might have required deep peace, but the concentration and poise necessary for composition would come to him in the midst of a buzz of conversation' (JOF: 195–6).

13 See M19,2 in ARC: 451.

14 A particularly fashionable café after 1856 and the frequent setting for wild revelries and excesses. See JOF: 284–5.

15 The Duc apparently had a fondness for throwing the café's crockery out of the windows. See JOF: 284.

16 Kracauer notes how those who chose 'to plunge headlong into a life of pleasure' were required to undergo 'the most extraordinary fatigues for its sake' (JOF: 80). Boredom also appears as the greatest of horrors in the opening of Baudelaire's *Les Fleurs dul mal*.

17 As we will see in chapter 9, Kracauer emphasizes how the cinematic medium, with its possibilities of intercutting narratives and/or of shifting vantage point to reveal something previously hidden or obscured, is particularly adept at comic debunking. See TOF: 306–8.

18 Such mockery of classical antiquity is also found in Baudelaire's advocacy of the satirical images of the lithographer Honoré Daumier: 'Daumier pounced brutally upon antiquity and mythology and spit on them. The hot-headed Achilles, the prudent Ulysses, the wise Penelope, and that great ninny Telemachus, the beautiful Helen who ruined Troy, the ardent Sappho, patroness of hysterical women – all were portrayed with a farcical homeliness that recalled those old carcasses of classical actors who take a pinch of snuff in the wings' (ARC: 743).

19 See JOF: 271–2.

20 See MPT: 4–5.

21 See MPT: 15 and JOF: 314. Kracauer notes that, for Schneider, 'the differences between operetta and real life were visibly obliterated' (JOF: 313).
22 See MPT: 16.
23 Interestingly, Kracauer's example of this is Michael Powell and Emeric Pressburger's 1951 film version of Offenbach's *Tales of Hoffmann* starring Moira Shearer (TOF: 155).
24 Kracauer's model here is Duvivier's *The Great Waltz*.
25 See JOF: 273.
26 As Kracauer observes, the success of this operetta was such that 'Europe was at Offenbach's feet' (JOF: 280).
27 For example, panoramic images of the 1867 World Exhibition and of Schneider's mischievous visit merge into the gala of Offenbach's *La Grande-Duchesse de Gerolstein*.
28 As when Paris burns to the accompaniment of Zimmer's waltz tune.
29 Consider the following: A republican insurrection is taking place on the boulevards; from the side streets, mounted dragoons ride out to disperse the crowds; a street battle ensues; a woman screams. 'Finally', Kracauer notes, 'this scene of terror is seen from a bird's-eye perspective: from the balcony of the Théâtre des Variétés on which Halévy is standing with two ballet dancers' (MPT: 15).
30 Marx in *The Communist Manifesto* (1977: 224).
31 In his letter of 13 May 1937, Adorno complains that the Offenbach book 'contains not a single trenchant criticism of him' and continues with: 'You take Offenbach as representative of society or at least half-way so – and then you agree with him? Are you not then in agreement with the society? With ours, in the phantasmagorical mirror of his?' (AKB: 357). This is the final straw for Kracauer: 'That you believe you can conclude from my method (consciously residing in the immanence of bourgeois society) that I am in agreement with the society in question completely manifests your foolishness and discredits your criticism once again' (letter of 25 May 1937, AKB: 364).

Chapter 7   The Caligari Complex

1 This is certainly the case for Anglophone readers, as Gemünden and von Moltke (2012: 8) among others note. According to Miriam Bratu Hansen, as Kracauer's first book written in English, the *Caligari* study 'established his American reputation' (2012: 258) – she might have added, for good or ill.
2 As the Italian film historian Leonardo Quaresima points out in his introduction to the 2004 edition, 'Rereading Kracauer', its reception among film scholars at the time was mixed, to say the least, ranging from the enthusiastic adoption of its principles to some caustic reviews. See CAL: xl–xlii.
3 Quaresima attributes this recent neglect by scholars ironically to its earlier fame and relative familiarity. The renewal of interest in Kracauer's work has tended to focus on the recovery of his unpublished early works and myriad feuilleton pieces. Drawing upon these, contemporary film scholars have engaged in some recontextualization of *Theory of Film* but surprisingly, for example, neither Heide Schlüpmann (1998) nor Miriam Bratu Hansen

(2012) offers more than a scattering of comments on the *Caligari* study. Quaresima writes of *Caligari*: 'Rightly or wrongly it is the work most closely associated with Kracauer's name over the years. Yet it has also received the least critical attention and reinterpretation during this latest phase' (CAL: xvii).

4 This was initiated at Horkheimer's suggestion in May 1937.

5 Kracauer's research was initially funded by a one-year Rockefeller grant which was then extended to 1943. Thereafter, support came from the Guggenheim Foundation through to 1945.

6 For Kracauer's account of the experience of arrival in New York, see his essay 'Why France Liked our Films' (1942). in KAW: 39–40. and also cited by Inka Mülder-Bach in Gemünden and von Moltke (2012: 277).

7 This is key to Koch's (2000) reading of the Offenbach book. She makes much of the Jewish elements in Offenbach's musical apprenticeship.

8 As we will see, such an approach is first sketched in the innocuously, if patronizingly, entitled series of eight sketches of cinema-going audiences from 1927, 'The Little Shopgirls Go to the Movies' (see MOR: 291–304).

9 Such a methodological, as opposed to thematic, connection actually recalls Benjamin's own rather puzzling verdict on his 1935–6 'Work of Art' essay.

10 In this regard, Quaresima rightly makes the connection between the *Offenbach* and *Caligari* books in relation to Kracauer's initial 'Sketch of Ideas' ('Ideenskizze zu meinen Buch über den Film') from 1938–9 which he sent to, and which so impressed, John Abbott. This 'is modelled upon Kracauer's study of Jacques Offenbach ... in which he devoted to operetta the same place that cinema would occupy in his later work' (CAL: xxiii).

11 In these writings, now helpfully collected into volume 6 of the *Werke*, Kracauer was frequently concerned with what constituted the 'cinematic' – i.e., how these films attended to what he saw as the proper subject matter of the film medium. In this regard, they anticipate the *Theory of Film* book more than the *Caligari* study.

12 Quaresima notes that Kracauer retained his antipathy towards Ruttmann's 1927 *Berlin, Symphony of a Great City* and Slatan Dudow's Brecht-scripted 1932 film *Kuhle Wampe*, even though his dismissal of the latter had led to a breakdown in relations with Ernst Bloch. Interestingly, Ruttmann's film was scripted by Carl Mayer, co-author of the original *Caligari* story.

13 Quaresima gives the example of Kracauer's reassessment of Arnold Fanke's mountain films of the mid-1920s: 'Kracauer the film critic ultimately praised Fanke's cloud motifs for their expressive technique and visual appeal .... Kracauer the historian, however, saw the same motifs as related to the canons of Nazi cinema and culture – even precursors of them' (CAL: xxii).

14 'There are few instances', Quaresima writes, 'in which his judgment as a historian enriched his original critique' (CAL: xxi).

15 This 'double fault' – of selectivity in choosing the films, on the one hand, and the shoehorning of material as 'evidence' of and into a pre-established argument, on the other – remains central to the reservations of otherwise sympathetic scholars such as Dagmar Barnouw (1994) (see CAL: xxxii–xxxiii). She finds this Kracauer's 'least satisfying work' and one which 'exhibits some of the more important fallacies that can trap the historian' (1994: 94).

16 While he is certainly appreciative of Kracauer's project, Quaresima is forced to conclude that the 'anticipationist stance' adopted 'does not mark a real interpretive or methodological contribution' (CAL: xxxix–xl).

17 Kracauer was paid the sum of 6,000 francs for this undertaking. See Belke and Renz (1989: 84).

18 See ibid.: 93.

19 He writes: 'behind the overt history of economic shifts, social exigencies and political machinations runs a secret history involving the inner dispositions of the German people. The disclosure of these dispositions through the medium of the German screen may help in the understanding of Hitler's ascent and ascendency' (CAL: 11). Kracauer was dismayed when the German-language version of the *Caligari* book was finally published in 1958. The word 'to' in the title was translated as 'until' (*bis*), suggesting only a temporal precedence instead of a definite connection between Weimar film and the National Socialist mentality.

20 This characterization is, of course, from Daniel Goldhagen's controversial 1997 study.

21 Kracauer writes: 'Since one always runs the danger, when picturing current events, of turning easily excitable masses against powerful institutions that are in fact often not appealing, one prefers to direct the camera toward a Middle Ages that the audience will find harmlessly edifying. The further back the story is situated historically, the more audacious filmmakers become. They will risk depicting a successful revolution in historical costumes in order to induce people to forget modern revolutions, and they are happy to satisfy the theoretical sense of justice by filming struggles for freedom that are long past. … The courage of these films declines in direct proportion to their proximity to the present' (MOR: 293).

22 Kracauer asserts: 'Stupid and unreal film fantasies are the *daydreams of society*, in which its actual reality comes to the fore and otherwise repressed wishes take on form' (MOR: 292).

23 See Quaresima, CAL: xxvii and xxxv. Kracauer began what proved to be a lifelong correspondence with Panofsky almost immediately upon arrival in the USA (Kracauer's first letter is dated 14 May 1941). Panofsky was based at the Institute for Advanced Study in the School of Humanistic Studies at Princeton University and was an enthusiastic reader of Kracauer's drafts and essays. His intercession was crucial in bringing Kracauer's manuscript to the attention of Princeton University Press, the eventual publishers. In a letter of 29 April 1947, Panofsky tells Kracauer how, being familiar with many of the German films analysed, he read the *Caligari* book with a 'peculiar feeling – "nostalgic is too much, "retrospective" too little' (KPB: 46). He wittily suggests a 'parallel study' exploring American film in the same period under the title 'From Shirley Temple to Truman' (ibid.).

24 Panofsky's study of the life and art of Albrecht Dürer was published in 1944. In foregrounding the connection with Panofsky, Quaresima supports Volker Breidecker's claim that Kracauer's work might constitute a vital bridge between the Frankfurt Institut für Sozialforschung and the London-based Warburg Institute, in which Panofsky played such a key role. Quaresima contends: '*From Caligari to Hitler* is the most advanced document of this convergence' (CAL: xxvii).

25 See CAL: 74. Kracauer reiterates this point in his discussion of *Dr Mabuse, Der Spieler* from 1922 (CAL: 83).

26 See CAL: 73–4 and then again CAL: 84.

27 See CAL: 3.

28 For example, we later encounter the following evocative albeit ungrammatical passage: 'The German soul, haunted by the alternative images of tyrannic rule and instinct-governed chaos, threatened by doom on either side, tossed about in gloomy space like the phantom ship in NOSFERATU' (CAL: 107). This absence of a safe haven recalls the condition of the salaried masses, so it is perhaps not surprising that Kracauer proceeds to note 'the craving for a spiritual shelter which possessed the young, the intellectuals' (ibid.).

29 Quaresima notes: 'Rather than construct a specific model, he prefers a free, mobile system of relations made more complex by his psychoanalytic and phenomenological influences' (CAL: xxxi).

30 Remarkably, he makes no specific mention of anti-Semitism.

31 For a discussion of this film in relation to Kracauer's reading, see Hunt, in Elsaesser (1990: 389–401), and Gilloch (2010).

32 Kracauer notes 'the profound aversion of all German middle-class strata to relating their mental dilemma to their ambiguous social plight. They shrank from tracing ideas or psychological experiences to economic and social causes after the fashion of the socialists. Founded upon the idealist concept of the autonomous individual, their attitude was in perfect harmony with their practical interests. ... This led them to conceive outer duplicities as inner dualities, but they preferred such psychological complications to issues involving a loss of their privileges' (CAL: 30–1).

33 In some intriguing early remarks, Kracauer attributes the absence of German detective fiction and films after the model of Sherlock Holmes to such insecurities of the middle classes and the failure to establish robust legal-rational democratic structures (see CAL: 19–20). Interesting, too, are his asides here on slapstick comedy, which, though popular with German audiences, does not become a major feature of its own film industry. Kracauer attributes this to the German preoccupation with gloomy fate as opposed to slapstick's celebration of serendipity and benign happenstance (CAL: 21). See chapter 9 below.

34 Cesare, Kracauer claims, is not a brutal murderer as such but rather is himself a victim of control and domination. Like a soldier, he is 'drilled to kill and to be killed' (CAL: 65). He is, therefore, like the eponymous figures of the Golem and the Homunculus, the very embodiment of the German condition.

35 This phrase is, of course, from the penultimate line of Benjamin's 'Work of Art' essay (see SW3: 122).

36 Such vast staging and mass choreography was also a feature of Lang's notorious *Metropolis* (1927), a film fantasy of *faux* class reconciliation shot through with Christian iconography which Kracauer also considers proto-fascistic in orientation: 'In fact, Maria's demand that the heart mediate between hand and brain could well have been formulated by Goebbels' (CAL: 163–4).

37 Tellingly, Fanck's 1931 *The White Frenzy (Der weisse Rausch)* featured none other than Leni Riefenstahl in an early role. She branched out on her own the following year to both direct and star in *The Blue Light (Das blaue Licht)*,

a sensational and sentimental folk-tale set in the Italian Dolomites. Riefenstahl played the free-spirited Junta, 'a sort of gypsy girl' (CAL: 258) and a 'true incarnation of elemental powers' (CAL: 259).

38 Kracauer states unequivocally: 'New Objectivity marks a state of paralysis. Cynicism, resignation, disillusionment: these tendencies point to a mentality disinclined to commit itself in any direction' (CAL: 165).

39 Kracauer critically compares Ruttmann's film with Dziga Vertov's *Man with a Movie Camera* (1929): 'Had Ruttmann been prompted by Vertov's revolutionary convictions, he would have had to indict the inherent anarchy of Berlin life. He would have been forced to emphasize content rather than rhythm. His penchant for rhythmic "montage" reveals that he actually tends to avoid any critical comment on the reality with which he is faced. Vertov implies content; Ruttmann shuns it. ... BERLIN is the product of the paralysis itself' (CAL: 187).

40 Kracauer notes of this film: 'In it, the paralyzed collective mind seemed to be talking with unusual clarity in its sleep' (CAL: 162).

41 'The street films', Kracauer notes, 'emphasize desertion of the home but still in the interest of authoritarian behavior' (CAL: 160). Indeed, such 'youth films affirm fixation to authoritarian behavior precisely by stressing rebellion against it' (CAL: 162). In presenting Freder's rebellion against, and then eventual reconciliation with, his father, Lang's *Metropolis* too partakes of some of the conventions of this genre. Such films were perhaps not so far from screening the Ludwig Loos complex.

42 These cinematic paeans to Frederick the Great began with the 1922 film *Fridericus Rex*, 'an opulent, if cinematically trivial, Ufa product' in which the young heir to the throne baulks under his father's harsh discipline, seeks to run away from his destiny and duty as monarch, and then, when the time comes, learns to become 'the father of his people' and 'the national hero who, through several successful wars, elevates little Prussia to the rank of a great power' (CAL: 115–16).

43 'The whole series', Kracauer notes, 'was a thorough attempt to familiarize the masses with the idea of a *Führer*' (CAL: 268).

44 There are numerous inconsistencies and some dubious interpretations. For example, while downplaying the critical significance of Lang's 1933 *Das Testament des Dr Mabuse* because 'it is hard to believe that average German audiences would have grasped the analogy between the gang of screen criminals and the Hitler gang' (CAL: 249), Kracauer later emphasizes the importance of precisely such 'unnoticed' parallels in his discussion of Kurt Bernhardt's 1931 *Der Mann der den Mord beging* (CAL: 255). Even *Caligari*, he concedes, was 'too high-brow to become popular in Germany', before insisting nonetheless that 'its basic theme – the soul being faced with the seemingly unavoidable alternative of tyranny or chaos – exerted extraordinary fascination' (CAL: 77).

45 The curious figure of the sinister inventor Rotwang in *Metropolis* is called to mind here: like a medieval alchemist in terms of appearance and residence, he is also of course the technician who fashions the robot Maria.

46 And also like the figure in Paul Klee's *Angelus Novus*, which Benjamin famously reconfigures as the 'angel of history' (see Benjamin SW4: 392). Cesare is an angel of death.

Chapter 8   Re-Surfacing Work

1 This chapter substantially reproduces an earlier published paper written with Dr Jaeho Kang. I am grateful to my co-author for permission to include our paper with minor revisions in this book.

2 The screenplay itself, detailing the action and dialogue of the drama, and numerous accompanying memoranda, specifying the underlying principles and objectives of the project, are to be found today in the Max Horkheimer Nachlaß (MHA) of the Archivzentrum of the Stadt- und Universitätsbibliothek, Frankfurt am Main (Mappe IX 150–152), and in the Kracauer Nachlaß in the DLA (Inventar Nr. 72.3620, microfiches 005603 and 005604, with a note from Thomas Levin dated 12 August 1987 and a further reference to Attachment VIII of Attachments II-IX, Inventar Nr. 72.3710/4).

3 In an interview from July 1966, Friedrich Pollock recalls the test film project in this context: 'Yes, at one point ... there was a talk about and consideration given to making a film in which the ... results of *The Authoritarian Personality* and such like could be shown in a story, but it was then dropped relatively soon' (MHA XIV 15, X 132b: 199).

4 Who today, one might ask, reads Leo Löwenthal and Norbert Gutermann's 1949 *Prophets of Deceit: A Study of the Techniques of the American Agitator*, or Nathan Ackermann and Marie Jahoda's 1950 *Anti-Semitism and Emotional Disorder: A Psychoanalytic Interpretation*?

5 As Benjamin once observed in his *Trauerspiel* study (1985: 27–30), lesser works should be treated no differently from major ones: indeed, minor pieces often manifest the fundamental structures and motifs of the particular literary idea with far greater clarity and precision.

6 From the mid- to late 1930s on, both Kracauer and Löwenthal were preoccupied with developing empirical and historical social research on popular culture, mass media and communication in relation to the rise of fascism and National Socialism. While Löwenthal's essay 'Knut Hamsun: Zur Vorgeschichte der autoritären Ideologie' appeared in the 1937 edition of the *Zeitschrift für Sozialforschung*, Kracauer's 'Exposé: Masse und Propaganda' (MHA I 14: 251–9) of December 1936, intended for the same issue, and his subsequent 'Zur Theorie der autoritären Propaganda' (MHA XIII 82) were sidelined. See also Kracauer's 1943 study 'The Conquest of Europe on the Screen: The Nazi Newsreel 1939–1940' (MHA V 105: 148b).

7 On a page dated March 1945 some examples of possible questions are given: 'Which were the leading characters? Describe each one of them'; 'List each of these characters according to whom you liked best, next-best, a.s.o. until the one whom you disliked most, and give reason (*sic*) why' (MHA, Mappe IX 150-2, document 10).

8 Wiggershaus ([1995] 2010: 356).

9 In a letter to Horkheimer of 30 March 1945 (MHA I 14 137).

10 DLA Attachment VIII, Inventar Nr. 72.3710.

11 In the Kracauer archive there are two versions of this text with minor textual differences. Both of these early drafts have handwritten corrections by Kracauer – indicative of his editorial responsibility at this stage at least – but are without any of the variants Kracauer later developed at Horkheimer's suggestion. Kracauer's letter to Horkheimer of 29 December 1944 notes:

'Here is the completely rewritten script. You will see how I tried to realize your idea of two variants – one with the gentile being guilty, the other with the Jew as the guilty one' (MHA I 14 140).

12 MHA I 14 137.

13 MHA Mappe IX 150, document 9.

14 Ibid., document 17.

15 Or, as in the Kracauer archive at the DLA, the misleading title: *Below the Surface Final Version*.

16 MHA Mappe IX 150-2, document 8.

17 Ibid., document 4.

18 Ibid., document 16.

19 Ibid., documents 3 and 2 respectively.

20 The 'Notes' of 25 April 1946 contain the following: 'There will also be two or three groups according to how many versions we are going to show. Individuals of the members of these groups will be divided under some very neutral motivation and will possibly be invited by a local university or college where the picture will be shown. After each group has seen one version there will be questionnaires, possibly followed by interviews' (MHA IX 150-2, document 2).

21 Ibid., document 10.

22 The use of voice-over techniques to reveal their thoughts at the very beginning of the test film (and at its conclusion in later versions) is the clearest example of this, but this device actually discloses only the most banal and commonplace themes. It is, rather, by presenting contradictory utterances and clear-cut discrepancies between words and deeds that the film really allows us to penetrate below the surface of its characters. For example, the musings of one character read as follows: WOMAN IN FUR COAT: 'I'm no snob. I like people all – like this – mixed together. Even colored people.... No gratitude Negroes ... no loyalty. The minute you treat them like equals – you just can't do it' (MHA 1a: 2. NB: in the following discussion, the version of the script discussed is MHA IX 150-2, document 1a (MHA 1a).

23 MHA IX 150-2, document 10 ('Notes').

24 Ibid., document 3: 2.

25 'Audience reactions are significant', he points out, 'only if they are expressed spontaneously, involuntarily. The purpose of this test film must be veiled' (ibid., document 11a/b).

26 TSM: 88.

27 Kracauer writes: 'What films reflect are not so much explicit credos as psychological dispositions – those deep layers of collective mentality which extend more or less below the dimension of consciousness. Of course, popular magazines and broadcasts, bestsellers, ads, fashions in language and other sedimentary products of a people's cultural life also yield valuable information about predominant attitudes, widespread inner tendencies. But the medium of the screen exceeds these sources in inclusiveness' (CAL: 6).

28 MHA 1a: 7.

29 The WOMAN IN FUR COAT 'much enjoying her lack of enjoyment' is exemplary (MHA 1a: 2).

30 MHA 1a: 3.

31 MHA 1a: 13.
32 See Adorno (1994). Tellingly, none of Adorno's four essays in this collection, three of them from the 1940s and all focusing on the relationship between irrationalism and anti-Semitism, mention Kracauer or his 'test film' project.
33 MHA 1a: 11.
34 MHA 1a: 13.
35 He is 'a small-time peddler of discontent' (Löwenthal and Guterman 1970: 4).
36 MHA 1a: 8.
37 MHA 1a: 17. The sense of being 'pushed' is key to the feelings of impotence and manipulation the fascist agitator invokes and articulates. See Löwenthal and Guterman (1970: 24).
38 MHA 1a: 8.
39 MHA 1a: 18.
40 The events portrayed in *Below the Surface* also mirror an incident in Joseph Roth's novella *Rebellion* (1924), in which the central character, the wounded war veteran Andreas Pum, reduced to eking out a living as a street musician and pedlar, becomes embroiled in a bitter argument with a well-heeled bourgeois figure, Herr Arnold, as they try to board a crowded tram-car at the same time, a dispute which escalates until Pum is eventually arrested and jailed. Perhaps Kracauer had this episode in mind when first sketching the plot for the 'test film'.
41 MHA 1a: 5.
42 Ibid.
43 MHA 1a: 4.
44 MHA 1a: 21.
45 As Kracauer notes, this was to be a key part of the test film: in Hypothesis 11 we read: 'anti-Semitism is connected with anti-intellectualism in the sense of "sophistication"' (MHA IX 150-2, document 10).
46 MHA 1a: 19.
47 International Public Opinion Research Inc.
48 In his article 'The Challenge of Qualitative Content Analysis', published in a special issue of *Public Opinion Quarterly* in 1952, Kracauer critically assesses the limitations of quantitative analysis in communication research and explicates the significance of a new qualitative paradigm. He specifies work on the 'Satellite Mentality' study as an exemplary case of the latter. This issue (16) was a special one on international communications research, edited by Löwenthal, and included articles by pioneering figures in American communications research such as Paul Lazarsfeld and Harold Lasswell.
49 These were concerned principally with evaluating the Voice of America radio service as a propaganda instrument, not only in Soviet 'satellites' and along its peripheries but also in other countries deemed unenthusiastic towards American interests and/or susceptible to communist communications. Kracauer wrote reports on Bulgaria, Greece, Spain and Austria (December 1950 – January 1951); the Near and Middle East (February–April 1952); and Greece (June 1952).
50 Kracauer's reticence regarding his reports is also perhaps partially due to another factor: their classified status. Their actual level of confidentiality is

not easy to assess. For example, in a letter to David Riesman of 15 September 1957 accompanying copies of 'Appeals to the Near East', 'Challenges of Qualitative Analysis' and *Satellite Mentality*, Kracauer writes: 'Regarding the first item, this report to the State Department is still classified, and fairly high at that. May I therefore ask you to treat it as completely confidential and return it as soon as possible' (DLA: 72.1726/4). How much of this is posturing is open to debate: after all, Kracauer still felt able to post Riesman the documents.

51 For example, Kracauer received a one-year award from the Bollingen Foundation in February 1949.

52 For a time, Löwenthal was both head of the Bureau and chief of the Evaluation Division of the International Broadcasting Service, a section of the US State Department. In early 1955 he took up a professorial post at Stanford and then the following year at Berkeley.

53 See Kracauer's letter to Löwenthal of 5 August 1951 (LKB: 141).

54 See Belke and Renz (1989: 111).

55 This notion of 'extraterritoriality' as a perennial sense of marginality, dislocation and estrangement is the leitmotif of Martin Jay's famous, and in many ways still unsurpassed, essay on Kracauer from 1975–6 (republished in Jay 1986: 152–97).

56 As a threshold of waiting and boredom, of anonymity and indifference, the transit camp resembles a kind of Spartan hotel lobby.

57 Between November 1948 and May 1950, Lili worked for the United Service for New Americans (USNA), an organization helping Jewish displaced persons and emigrants from Europe. Its successor, the New York Association of New Americans (NYANA), was eventually to become the beneficiary of the Kracauer estate after her death. See Belke and Renz (1989: 107–8).

58 Returning from a summer trip to Europe in 1956, coincidentally just as *Satellite Mentality* was published, Kracauer tells Löwenthal (letter of 28 October 1956) that 'we are happy to be home again, for it is home for us now that we have definitely ceased to be immigrants' (LKB: 183). Two years later, though, again arriving home from their European travels, Kracauer writes the following in a letter to David Riesman of 1 October 1958: 'At home, we first felt like strangers. Is it really a natural kind of existence to have a home and be there? All genuine scholars or artists are, or should be, vagrants' (DLA: 72.1726/16).

59 This is not to say 'representative' in any statistical sense: the authors recognize that 'the sample may not be complete but it comprises a colourful variety of Satellite people' (SAT: 6).

60 One might even be tempted to say Weberian ideal-type here.

61 The authors note: 'Among the workers this feeling of economic insecurity originates with the inadequacy of their wages and their experience that under the Satellite piecework and quota system no one can be sure of his daily earnings' (SAT: 17). See also SAT: 26.

62 Interestingly, as Jay points out, many years earlier, in 1926, Kracauer utterly rejected Georg Lukács's 'advocacy of personal realization through submission to the will of the party' (Jay 1986: 163), insisting instead on individual autonomy.

63 One is reminded here of Erving Goffman's account of the 'total institution' in his famous 1961 study *Asylums*. Goffman, too, explores the destruction and reconstruction of the self and, importantly, the numerous coping strategies of the inmates, the so-called underlife of the institution. In their account of forms of active and passive resistance in satellite societies, Kracauer and Berkman are interested in the 'underlife' of communist regimes.

64 In his various studies of fascist propaganda in the 1930s, Kracauer stresses the dissolution of the individual into the mass as the key precondition for totalitarian misinformation. As is clear from his Weimar writings, this is to be understood as the intensification, not reorientation, of tendencies in capitalist modernity.

65 See SAT: 58–9.

66 The authors observe: 'There are people whose indignation at opportunists exceeds their hatred of genuine Communists' (SAT: 75).

67 The authors write: 'The effects of much Western propaganda broadcast to the Satellites converge with those produced by Communist propaganda itself', with the result that, 'Instead of accepting the content of one and rejecting the other, they assimilate elements of both, transforming them into mutually supporting evidence of what they want to believe' (SAT: 169).

Chapter 9   Film, Improvisation and 'the Flow of Life'

1 Most notably of course, the Offenbach 'Motion Picture Treatment' discussed in chapter 6, but also at least three other proposals from the 1930s as Kracauer explored every avenue for much needed income.

2 His film reviews eventually number over 800, more than 700 of which were for the *FZ*. His final review for the paper (7 April 1933) includes a Paris showing of Pabst's *Don Quichotte* (1933).

3 Hansen singles out the same review and quotation in her discussion (2012: 13).

4 In the *FZ* on 17 November 1923.

5 See Hansen's mention of these films (2012: 8–9).

6 In his review essay 'Artistisches und Amerikanisches' from early 1926, Kracauer emphasizes film's radical capacity for overturning conventions when he writes of a scene in *Eine Minute vor Zwölf* (Nunzio Malasomma, 1925): 'The Lunapark, itself already filled with spinning things, is turned upside down more than it already is by its very nature. Things happen as they are meant to happen in film: the continuous topsy-turvy of the external world, the deranged disarrangement of its objects' (WK 6.1: 198).

7 Kracauer notes: 'The mythical world needs the word for its form, for the word alone entirely exhausts the reality which the spirit defines' (WK 6.1: 80).

8 Published in the *FZ* on 7 May 1924.

9 Observing film production at first hand in the Ufa studios in 1926, Kracauer notes: 'Life is constructed in a pointillist manner. It is a speckling of images that stem from numerous locations and initially remain unconnected. Their sequence does not follow the order of the represented events. A person's fate may already have been filmed even before the events leading up to it

are determined; a reconciliation may be filmed earlier than the conflict it resolves. The meaning of the plot emerges only in the finished film; during the gestation, it remains unfathomable' (MOR: 287).

10 As Ruttmann's 1927 Berlin film demonstrates.

11 Review in the *FZ* of 23 October 1926.

12 Indeed, even after the publication of *Theory of Film*, these axioms are still at work: in a set of notes dated 5 May 1961, Kracauer reproaches *The Connection* (Shirley Clark, USA, 1961) in terms that seem essentially unchanged from those of forty years earlier: 'The whole film suffers from its dependence on techniques of the theatre' (WK 6.3: 472). The film was based on a stage play of the same name.

13 We will return to the issue of whether film is dependent on storyline at all. Kracauer is sometimes seen, as Hansen rightly notes, as 'one of the major theorists of the nonnarrative aspects of cinema' (2012: 274).

14 The second volume of a trilogy of picaresque novels involving the hapless hero Tartarin: *Tartarin de Tarascon* (1872) and *Ponte-Tarascon* (1890) being the others.

15 Here, Kracauer notes, 'Nature … has been put out to pasture. Its landscapes are surpassed by those that are freely conceived and whose painterly appeal is no longer subject to chance' (MOR: 285).

16 Quaresima questions this kind of designation for both of Kracauer's film books and suggests that it may have done their reception more harm than good.

17 In point of fact, *longer* and *more* complex.

18 See Hansen (2012: 256–7). In her emphasis upon the key formative work of the three 'Marseilles notebooks' in 1940–1, Hansen's response to such views is to 'restore this dimension of history in and to the book' through grounding the work in the very experience of catastrophe itself (see ibid.: 257–8). My response here is to foreground the fundamental significance of the book's controversial epilogue, 'Film in our Time', which explicitly engages with both of these disasters.

19 See ibid.: 254.

20 Even though he returned to work on his film aesthetics project as early as November 1948, with a draft of nearly 200 typed pages completed by 1954, the labour of revision and theoretical elaboration was subject to continual interruption by all those Voice of America and UNESCO projects mentioned in chapter 8 as well as bouts of ill health.

21 Hansen gives three reasons why the significance of slapstick diminishes: firstly, the technological development of cinema meant that the comedies themselves now seemed more like curios from a bygone age rather than defining instances of the medium; secondly, and compounding this, the advent of sound 'killed' the genre (as Kracauer admits in his 1951 essay; see KAW: 216); and, thirdly, his thoughts took a more sombre, even morbid, turn, with death, not laughter, imbuing the book's pages (see Hansen 2012: 265).

22 These 'inherent affinities' are set out explicitly in TOF: 60–71.

23 For Kracauer, 'cinema is conceivably animated by a desire to picture transient material life, life at its most ephemeral' (TOF: xlix).

24 In its penchant for 'the refuse' of everyday life, the film camera takes on the role of 'ragpicker' (TOF: 54).

25 Of the photographer, Kracauer writes: 'He resembles perhaps most of all the imaginative reader intent on studying and deciphering an elusive text. Like a reader the photographer is steeped in the book of nature' (TOF: 16).

26 The very selectivity of the camera operator ensures that, in all images, photographic and cinematic, there is a formative element. Kracauer hence rejects both any notion of the 'objectivity' of the image and any equation of the 'objective' and the 'realistic'. See TOF: 13–15.

27 See in particular TOF: 148–9. Kracauer's reasoning here has already been outlined in connection with his Offenbach 'Motion Picture Treatment' in chapter 6.

28 Hansen rightly recognizes the deft dialectics at work here: 'While clearly invested in having the balance tipped toward the pole of realism, what interests Kracauer is how narrative films engage with the dialectical tension generated by its antinomies, how they seek to resolve a "dilemma" that is by definition irresoluble' (2012: 275). Perhaps all those screen doubles and doppelgängers Kracauer identifies in early Weimar cinema are nothing other than an early envisioning of film's own schizophrenic character.

29 Benjamin notes: 'For the first time – and this is the effect of film – the human being is placed in a position where he must operate with his whole living person, while forgoing its aura. For the aura is bound to his presence in the here and now. There is no facsimile of the aura. The aura that surrounds Macbeth on stage cannot be divorced from the aura which, for the living spectators, surrounds the actor who plays him. What distinguishes the shot in the film studio, however, is that the camera is substituted for the audience. As a result, the aura surrounding the actor is dispelled – and, with it, the aura of the figure he portrays' (Benjamin SW3: 112).

30 See also 'The Photographic Approach' (1951), 'Silent Film Comedy' (1951) and 'The Found Story and the Episode' (1956) in KAW: 204–13, 213–17 and 217–25, respectively. In the first, echoing Benjamin in his 'Little History of Photography' (see especially SW2: 514–15), Kracauer is critical of the attempts of early photographers who, instead of exploring the unique potential of the camera, sought to create (for commercial reasons above all) 'artistic' photographs' by imitating the effects found in paintings. Kracauer notes how one, Antony Samuel Adam-Salomon, specialized in photographic portraits with a distinctive 'Rembrandt lighting' (KAW: 206).

31 Here the film itself is only an exemplary episode which 'emerges from and again dissolves into the ' "flow of life" ' (KAW: 221–2).

32 See TOF: 151–2 and the discussion of Clair's 1931 musical comedy *Le Million* in chapter 6 above.

33 Tara Forrest's 2007 study is the most notable and honourable exception here.

34 First published in *Sight and Sound* in 1951 (see KAW 213–17). Translated into German in WK 6.3: 459–65.

35 See 'Chaplin' (1928/9) and 'Chaplin in Retrospect' (1929) in Benjamin SW2: 199–200 and 222–4. See also (in SW2: 792–3) the remarkably prescient 1934 fragment 'Hitler's Diminished Masculinity', written before Chaplin's *The Great Dictator* (1940).

36 He notes: 'Children's play is everywhere permeated by mimetic modes of behavior, and its realm is by no means limited to what one person can

imitate in another. The child plays at being not only a shopkeeper or a teacher, but also a windmill and a train' (SW2: 720).

37 Imitation is also a kind of bodily practice in which the human *physis* becomes something else, playfully taking on the form and properties of another being or thing. Such copying relies for success in the first instance on the acute observation of this other and then consummate physical transformation and performance. This is the ludic basis of all acting.

38 Imitation also involves a non-instrumental relationship with objects and the non-human realm: one becomes an object through a process of self-reification. Objects as accessories are adopted as (often deceptive) signs, as markers and modes of disguise; simple sets of objects are resources drawn upon through improvisation to create alternative characters and personas.

39 Kracauer observes that distraction 'is meaningful only as improvisation' (MOR: 327).

40 'Akrobat – Schöön' immediately precedes 'The Piano Player'. The tale of the inebriated musician providing accompaniment at the cinema reappears virtually verbatim in *Theory of Film* in the chapter on film music under this title (see TOF: 137–8).

41 Chaplin's presumptuous sampling of the goods on offer in the department store in *The Floorwalker* (1916), for example, suggests anything but reverence for the exchange mechanisms and values of capitalist commerce.

42 'Crafty' as in cunning, not craft. If craft is understood as a form of *poeisis*, as the authentic bringing forth from the material itself that which in some sense resides within it, then improvisation is a wholly different mode of clever adaptation and 'making do'.

43 Hansen curiously underplays Kracauer's preoccupation with the world of things when she writes 'Compared to Benjamin's, Kracauer's interest in Chaplin and slapstick comedy – as in cinema in general – was less focused on the question of technology, either in the Marxist sense as a productive force or as a Heideggerian enframing or *Gestell*' (2012: 49). Human–object relations are central to both Kracauer's key categories of improvisation and redemption.

44 Kracauer is not uncritical of slapstick routines. On occasions, he finds himself bored by the repetition of gags and the Chaplin formula: 'There is no denying that the two-hour American lesson proves somewhat monotonous' (WK 6.1: 65). In a 1924 review of Chaplin's *Laughing Gas* (1914) he writes: 'for the principle of the Chaplinesque is always the same: … The same old game is replayed such that the joke loses its piquancy and one unwillingly senses the rawness of this whole Chaplin world, which lacks any trace of the soul' (WK 6.1: 69).

45 For a more recent cinematic example, see my discussion of the intrepid toys crossing the road in *Toy Story 2* (Gilloch 2007).

Chapter 10   Film, Phantasmagoria and the Street

1 See Strathausen in Shiel and Fitzmaurice, 2003: 25. See also Helmut Weihsmann's discussion of 'city films' between 1900 and 1930 in Penz and Thomas, 1997: 8–27.

2 While Benjamin does not specifically refer to Dziga Vertov's (1929) *Man with a Movie Camera* as exemplary in this context, this film does seem to be a model of so many of these techniques and principles. For a discussion of this film and Ruttmann's 1927 *Berlin – die Sinfonie der Großstadt* in relation to Benjamin, see Strathausen in Shiel and Fitzmaurice, 2003: 15–40. Kracauer was, as we have seen, far less enthusiastic about avant-garde film.

3 This aside is intended to substantiate Adorno's fundamental complaint: Benjamin both overestimates the radical, technologically progressive aspects of the film medium and production process and underplays the 'technical complexity' (*Technizität*) and critical experimentation of 'autonomous art' (*autonomen Kunst*), especially the pioneering works of high modernism.

4 As we have already seen in chapter 9, this encounter with the 'calico-world' is surely the inspiration for 'Switzerland' in the Tartarin film proposal.

5 This is Vidler's own translation; cf. ARC: 83.

6 See Benjamin's letter to Werner Kraft of 27 December 1935 in COR: 516–17.

7 In an extended essay Benjamin explicitly compares the camera operator to the surgeon (SW3: 115–16).

8 Benjamin emphasizes this prosthetic character of film technology: '*The most important social function of film is to establish equilibrium between human beings and the apparatus.* Film achieves this goal not only in terms of man's presentation of himself to the camera but also in terms of his representation of his environment by means of this apparatus. On the one hand, film furthers insight into the necessities governing our lives by its use of close-ups, by its accentuation of hidden details in familiar objects, and by its exploration of commonplace milieux through the ingenious guidance of the camera; on the other hand, it manages to assure us of a vast and unsuspected field of action [*Spielraum*]' (SW3: 117).

9 This startling passage recalls another explosive urban encounter. In *Einbahnstrasse*, under the title 'Ordnance', Benjamin recalls an impromptu visit to his beloved Asja Lacis in Riga. A stranger to the Latvian capital, Benjamin wanders its streets in a state of electrifying anticipation: 'From every gate a flame darted; each cornerstone sprayed sparks, and every streetcar came toward me like a fire engine. For she might have stepped out of the gateway, around the corner, been sitting in the streetcar. But of the two of us, I had to be, at any price, the first to see the other. For had she touched me with the match of her eyes, I would have gone up like a powder keg' (SW1: 461). For both the unexpected and expectant lover and the film-maker, the cityscape becomes a charged environment laden with tensions, dangers and desires – perhaps this is why, to answer one of Vidler's questions, Benjamin envisaged his Parisian movie as 'a passionate film'. If it was to detonate this dreamworld so that we may awaken from it, then how could such a film *not* be imbued with love, longing and hope?

10 See SW3: 119.

11 He notes: '*Dadaism attempted to produce with the means of painting (or literature) the effects which the public today seeks in film*' (SW3: 118).

12 For Benjamin's discussion of Freud's 1921 *Beyond the Pleasure Principle* with respect to shock and memory, see SW4: 316–18.

13 A reservoir of images of past times and things that we have certainly witnessed but which we cannot consciously recall having seen or, conversely, whose sight we have repressed: is not film here both a prompt for, and a technological counterpart to, the *mémoire involontaire*?

14 Benjamin notes that: 'Architecture has always offered the prototype of an artwork that is received in a state of distraction and through the collective' (SW3: 119–20 or SW4: 268).

15 Of course, the actual time difference is less than this might suggest. One should not forget that Kracauer's book began life in 1940 at the latest.

16 Interestingly, Kracauer here includes 'the familiar' among such phenomena (TOF: 54).

17 See TOF: 175–92.

18 This assessment of the film is an interesting example of Kracauer's dubious revisionary work in the *Caligari* book. His original review (5 May 1925) commends the film for portraying the very spiritlessness of modern metropolitan existence: 'These people of the city street have no connection to that which is above us; they are only an exterior, like the street itself, where there is a lot going on without anything happening. The hurly-burly of the figures is like the whirl of atoms: they never actually meet but bounce off each other; they move apart but remain together' (WK 6.1: 138). He concludes: 'A silent soulless togetherness of driven vehicles and unsteered drives, a swarm on the asphalt and in the bars that exhausts itself in simple vital manifestations in so far as it does not adhere to the purposes set by the displaced Ratio. Anyone, wakeful and full of longing, who strays into this lost reality seems to be a dreamer; for reality becomes dream whenever emptiness simulates the real' (ibid.).

19 Kracauer notes in regard to the film that 'The architect's facades and rooms were not merely backgrounds, but hieroglyphs. They expressed the structure of the soul in terms of space' (CAL: 75).

Inconclusive

1 In a letter dated 7 February 1963 to one Edward Shoben, editor of *Teachers College Record*, Kracauer suggests the possibility of republishing this separately: 'this chapter deals with the role of film in our time; indeed it is a philosophy of our time' (DLA: 72.1788).

2 See Hansen (2012: 257).

3 At Lili's request, by Kracauer's friend at Columbia University, Paul Oskar Kristeller. As Kristeller points out in his preface, the book was substantially written, albeit in draft form. Of its planned eight chapters, the first four and chapter 7 were largely complete. Chapter 5 was half written; the remainder of chapter 5 and chapters 6 and 8 existed in draft sketches 'that were quite readable but in need of careful editing' (LAST: vii).

4 As should become clear, to stress the present would be to give undue emphasis to the 'formative tendency'.

5 Kracauer cites Robert Graves: 'History is an old man's game' (LAST: 96).

6 'As I see it', Kracauer notes, 'the vast knowledge we possess should challenge us not to indulge in inadequate syntheses but to concentrate on

close-ups and from them casually to range over the whole, assessing it in the form of aperçus. The whole may yield to such light-weight skirmishes more easily than to heavy frontal attack' (LAST: 134–5).

7 Kracauer writes: 'The photographic media make it much easier for us to incorporate the transient phenomena of the outer world, thereby redeeming them from oblivion. Something of this kind will also have to be said of history' (LAST: 192).

8 Kracauer observes: 'Historical ideas appear to be of lasting significance because they connect the particular with the general in an articulate and truly unique way. Any such connection being an uncertain venture, they resemble flashes illumining the night. This is why their emergence in the historian's mind has been termed a "historical sensation" and said to "communicate a shock to the entire system ... the shock ... of recognition." ... Whenever this happens, the flow of indeterminate historical events is suddenly arrested and all that is then exposed to view is seen in the light of an image or conception which takes it out of the transient flow to relate it to one or another of the momentous problems and questions that are forever staring at us' (LAST: 101). Remarkably, Kracauer does not mention Benjamin here: the citation is from Isaiah Berlin.

9 Indeed, in the book's one and only explicit reference to Benjamin, Kracauer takes him to task for his overemphasis on discontinuity. Kracauer writes: 'Benjamin on his part indulges in an undialectical approach; he drives home the nonentity of chronological time without manifesting the slightest concern over the other side of the picture. That there are two sides to it has rarely been recognized' (LAST: 155).

10 If, at this point, Kracauer's earlier distinction between photographs and 'memory images' (see chapter 2) finally seems to collapse, a word of caution is needed. Proust is no historian: the ultimate reconciliation of time's antinomies is the privilege of the artist and not of the historian, for whom such a resolution remains 'unthinkable' or utopian (LAST: 163).

11 Not surprisingly, there are numerous conflicting stories concerning the name, origins and supposed sightings of this figure across medieval Christendom. Condemned to roam the world without rest until the Second Coming, the wandering Jew's transgression may derive from the Old Testament story of Cain or from claims that this was a person who insulted or struck Christ as he paused momentarily under the weight of the cross on his last ascent to Calvary.

12 Kracauer duly notes, but does not wholeheartedly endorse, Marc Bloch's warning of the fruitlessness of 'wandering perpetually at random' (LAST: 85).

13 Adorno captures this perfectly in his radio broadcast: 'Kracauer's experiential stance remains that of the foreigner, transposed to the realm of spirit. He thinks as though he had transformed the childhood trauma of problematic membership into a mode of vision for which everything appears as it would on a journey and even what is gray and familiar becomes a colourful object of amazement' (1991: 169).

14 Kracauer contrasts history and philosophy thus: 'Instead of proceeding from, or climaxing in, statements about the meaning, or, for that matter, the meaninglessness, of history as such, it is a distinctly empirical science which explores and interprets given historical reality in exactly the same manner

as the photographic media render and penetrate the physical world about us. History is much closer to the practically endless, fortuitous, and indeterminate *Lebenswelt* ... than philosophy' (LAST: 194).

15 Kracauer writes: 'As viewed from the lofty regions of philosophy, the historian devotes himself to the last things before the last, settling in an area which has the character of an anteroom. (Yet it is this 'anteroom' in which we breathe, move, and live.)' (LAST: 195).

16 One might say that these are the last in a whole procession of doubles and doppelgänger.

17 Three lines and another Kafka quote are designated as 'In Lieu of Epilogue' (LAST: 219).

References and Bibliography

Abbreviations used in the text are given in bold

1 Principal Works by Siegfried Kracauer

Siegfried Kracauer Nachlaß, Deutsches Literaturarchiv, Marbach am Neckar; **DLA**

Schriften, ed. Inka Mülder-Bach. Frankfurt am Main: Suhrkamp; **SCH**

> Vol. 1: *Soziologie als Wissenschaft / Der Detektiv-Roman / Die Angestellten* (1978)
> Vols 5.1, 5.2 and 5.3: *Aufsätze* (1990)

Werke, ed. Inka Mülder-Bach and Ingrid Belke. Frankfurt am Main: Suhrkamp; **WK**

> Vol. 2.2: *Studien zu Massenmedien und Propaganda* (2012)
> Vols 6.1, 6.2 and 6.3: *Kleine Schriften zum Film* (2004)
> Vol. 7: *Romane und Erzählungen* (2004)
> Vols 9.1 and 9.2: *Frühe Schriften aus dem Nachlaβ* (2004)

Jacques Offenbach and the Paris of his Time, trans. Gwenda David and Eric Mosbacher. New York: Zone Books ([1937] 2002); **JOF**

'Jacques Offenbach: Motion Picture Treatment', unpublished typescript, DLA Inventar Nr. 72.3529; **MPT**

From Caligari to Hitler: A Psychological History of the German Film. Princeton, NJ: Princeton University Press ([1947] 2004); **CAL**

Satellite Mentality: Political Attitudes and Propaganda Susceptibilities of Non-Communists in Hungary, Poland and Czechoslovakia (with Paul L. Berkman). New York: F. A. Praeger (1956); **SAT**

Theory of Film: The Redemption of Physical Reality. Princeton, NJ: Princeton University Press ([1960] 1997); **TOF**

The Mass Ornament: Weimer Essays, ed. and trans. Thomas Y. Levin. Cambridge, MA: Harvard University Press ([1963] 1995); **MOR**

Straßen in Berlin und anderswo. Berlin: Das Arsenal ([1964] 1987); **SBA**

History: The Last Things Before the Last (completed by Paul Oskar Kritsteller). New York: Oxford University Press (1969); repr. Princeton, NJ: Markus Wiener (1995); **LAST**

Über die Freundschaft. Frankfurt am Main: Suhrkamp (1971); **UFR**

Kino: Essays, Studien, Glossen zum Film. Frankfurt am Main: Suhrkamp (1974)

Berliner Nebeneinander: Ausgewählte Feuilletons 1930–33, ed. Andreas Volk. Zurich: Epoca (1996); **BEN**

Frankfurter Turmhäuser: Ausgewählte Feuilletons 1906–30, ed. Andreas Volk. Zurich: Epoca (1997)

The Salaried Masses: Duty and Distraction in Weimar Germany, trans. Quintin Hoare. London: Verso (1998); **TSM**

Siegfried Kracauer's American Writings, ed. Johannes von Moltke and Kristy Rawson. Berkeley: University of California Press (2012); **KAW**

2 Correspondence

Theodor Adorno and Walter Benjamin: The Complete Correspondence 1928–1940, ed. Henri Lonitz, trans. Nicholas Walker. Cambridge: Polity (1999); **ABC**

Theodor W. Adorno–Siegfried Kracauer: Briefwechsel, 1923–1966, ed. Wolfgang Schopf. Frankfurt am Main: Suhrkamp (2008); **AKB**

Walter Benjamin, *The Correspondence 1910–1940*, ed. Gershom Scholem and Theodor W. Adorno, trans. Manfred R. Jacobson and Evelyn M. Jacobson. Chicago: University of Chicago Press (1994).

Ernst Bloch: Briefe, 1903–1975, ed. Karola Bloch et al. Frankfurt am Main: Suhrkamp (1985).

Siegfried Kracauer–Erwin Panofksy Briefwechsel, 1941–66, ed. Volker Breidecker. Berlin: Akademie (1996); **KPB**

In Steter Freundschaft: Leo Löwenthal–Siegfried Kracauer, Briefwechsel 1921–1966, ed. Peter-Erwin Jansen and Christian Schmidt. Springe: Zu Klampen (2003); **LKB**

Joseph Roth: A Life in Letters, ed. Michael Hoffmann. London: Granta (2012).

3 Other Key Primary Sources

Archivzentrum of the Stadt- und Universitätsbibliothek of the Johann Wolfgang Goethe University, Frankfurt am Main, materials in the Max Horkheimer (**MHA**) and Leo Löwenthal (**LLA**) archives.

Arato, Andrew, and Gebhardt, Eike (eds) (1994) *The Essential Frankfurt School Reader*. New York: Continuum.

Adorno, Theodor W. (1991) 'The Curious Realist: On Siegfried Kracauer', *New German Critique*, 54: 159–77 [special issue on Siegfried Kracauer].

— (1994) *The Stars Down to Earth and Other Essays*. London: Routledge.

Adorno, Theodor W., and Horkheimer, Max ([1947] 1997) *Dialectic of Enlightenment*. London: Verso.

Benjamin, Walter (1973) *Understanding Brecht*. London: NLB.

— (1985) *The Origin of German Tragic Drama*. London: Verso.

— (1999) *The Arcades Project*. Cambridge, MA: Harvard University Press; **ARC**

— (1996) *Selected Writings*, Vol. 1: *1913–26*. Cambridge, MA: Harvard University Press; **SW1**

— (1999) *Selected Writings*, Vol. 2: *1927–34*. Cambridge, MA: Harvard University Press; **SW2**

— (2002) *Selected Writings*, Vol. 3: *1935–38*. Cambridge, MA: Harvard University Press; **SW3**

— (2002) *Selected Writings*, Vol. 4: *1938–40*. Cambridge, MA: Harvard University Press; **SW4**

Bronner, Eric, and Kellner, Douglas (eds) (1990) *Critical Theory and Society*. London: Routledge.

Horkheimer, Max (ed.) (1937) *Zeitschrift für Sozialforschung*, Vol. 6. Munich: DTV [contains T. W. Adorno's review of Kracauer's *Jacques Offenbach und der Paris seiner Zeit*, pp. 697–8].

Simmel, Georg (1972) *On Individuality and Social Forms: Selected Writings*, ed. Donald Levine. Chicago: University of Chicago Press.

— (2005) *Rembrandt: An Essay in the Philosophy of Art*, trans. and ed. Alan Scott and Helmut Staubmann. London: Routledge; **REM**.

4 Secondary Sources

Band, Henri (1999) *Mittelschichten und Massenkultur: Siegfried Kracauers publizistische Auseinandersetzung mit der populären Kultur und der Kultur der Mittelschichten in der Weimarer Republik*. Berlin: Lukas.

Barnouw, Dagmar (1994) *Critical Realism: History, Photography and the Work of Siegfried Kracauer*. Baltimore and London: Johns Hopkins University Press.

Belke, Ingrid, and Renz, Irina (eds) (1989) *Siegfried Kracauer*. Marbach am Neckar: Deutsche Schillergesellschaft.

Brodersen, Momme (2001) *Siegfried Kracauer*. Hamburg: Rowohlt.

Busch, Annira (2007) *Siegfried Kracauer: sein Leben und sein Werk*. Munich: GRIN.

Forrest, Tara (2007) *Politics of Imagination: Benjamin, Kracauer, Kluge.* Bielefeld: Transcript.

Friebe, Doreen (2004) *Der Leser und Literaturkritiker Siegfried Kracauer.* Munich: GRIN.

Frisby, David (1988) *Fragments of Modernity: Theories of Modernity in the Work of Simmel, Kracauer and Benjamin.* Cambridge, MA: MIT Press.

— (2001) *Cityscapes of Modernity.* Cambridge: Polity.

Gemünden, Gerd, and von Moltke, Johannes (eds) (2012) *Culture in the Anteroom: The Legacies of Siegfried Kracauer.* Ann Arbor: University of Michigan Press.

— (2010) 'Mirror, Mirror: *The Student of Prague* in Baudrillard, Kracauer and Kittler', in *Jean Baudrillard: Fatal Theories,* ed. David Clarke et al. London: Routledge.

Hansen, Miriam Bratu (2012) *Cinema and Experience: Siegfried Kracauer, Walter Benjamin and Theodor W. Adorno.* Berkeley: University of California Press.

Jay, Martin (1973) *The Dialectical Imagination: A History of the Frankfurt School and the Institute of Social Research 1923–1950.* Boston and London: Little, Brown.

— (1986) *Permanent Exiles: Essays on the Intellectual Migration from Germany to America.* New York: Columbia University Press.

Kessler, Michael, and Levin, Thomas (eds) (1990) *Siegfried Kracauer: Neue Interpretationen.* Tübingen: Stauffenburg.

Koch, Gertrud (2000) *Siegfried Kracauer: An Introduction.* Princeton, NJ: Princeton University Press.

Levin, Thomas Y. (1989) *Siegfried Kracauer: Eine Bibliographie seiner Schriften.* Marbach am Neckar: Deutsche Schillergesellschaft.

Mehlman, Jeffrey (1993) *Walter Benjamin for Children: An Essay on his Radio Years.* Chicago: University of Chicago Press.

Mülder, Inka (1985) *Siegfried Kracauer: Grenzgänger zwischen Theorie und Literatur: Seine frühen Schriften 1913–33.* Stuttgart: J. B. Metzler.

Oschmann, Dirk (1999) *Auszug aus der Innerlichkeit: Das literarische Werk Siegfried Kracauers.* Heidelberg: Winter.

Reeh, Henrik (2004) *Ornaments of the Metropolis: Siegfried Kracauer and Modern Urban Culture.* Cambridge, MA: MIT Press.

Schlüpmann, Heide (1998) *Ein Detektiv des Kinos: Studien zu Siegfried Kracauers Filmtheorie.* Basel: Stroemfeld.

Stalder, Helmut (2003) *Siegfried Kracauer: Das Journalistische Werk in der 'Frankfurter Zeitung' 1921–1933.* Würzburg: Könighausen & Neumann.

Volk, Andreas (ed.) (1996) *Siegfried Kracauer: Zum Werk des Romanciers, Feuilletonisten, Architekten, Filmwissenschaftlers und Soziologen.* Zurich: Seismo.

Ward, Janet (2001) *Weimar Surfaces: Urban Visual Culture in 1920s Germany.* Berkeley: University of California Press.

Wheatland, Thomas (2009) *The Frankfurt School in Exile*. Minneapolis: University of Minnesota Press.
Wiggershaus, Rolf ([1995] 2010) *The Frankfurt School*. Cambridge: Polity.

5 Special Issues of Journals

Text+Kritik, no. 68 (1980).
New German Critique, no. 54 (1991) [special issue on Kracauer].
New Formations, no. 61 (2007) [special issue on Kracauer].

6 Other References

Ackermann, Nathan W., and Jahoda, Marie (1950) *Anti-Semitism and Emotional Disorder: A Psychoanalytic Interpretation*. New York: Harper.
Adorno, Theodor W., et al. ([1950] 1980) *The Authoritarian Personality*. New York: W. W. Norton.
Augé, Marc (1995) *Non-Places: Introduction to an Anthropology of Super-modernity*. London: Verso.
Barthes, Roland (1984) *Image–Music–Text*, trans. Stephen Heath. London: Fontana.
— (1993) *Camera Lucida*. London: Vintage.
Baudelaire, Charles (1986) *The Painter of Modern Life and Other Essays*. London: Phaidon Press.
Elias, Norbert (1994) *Mozart: Portrait of a Genius*. Cambridge: Polity.
— (2000) *The Civilizing Process*. Oxford: Blackwell.
Elsaesser, Thomas (ed.) (1990) *Early Cinema: Space, Frame, Narrative*. London: BFI.
— (2000) *Weimar Cinema and After: Germany's Historical Imaginary*. London: Routledge.
Gilloch, Graeme (1996) *Myth and Metropolis: Walter Benjamin and the City*. Cambridge: Polity.
— (2002) *Walter Benjamin: Critical Constellations*. Cambridge: Polity.
— (2007) 'The Life and Times of Sheriff Woody: Benjamin, Baudrillard and some Theoretical Toys', *InterCulture*, 4(2): 1–18 [special issue: 'Reproducing Art: Walter Benjamin's "Work of Art" Essay Reconsidered'].
Goffman, Erving (1961) *Asylums: Essays on the Social Situation of Mental Patients and Other Inmates*. Harmondsworth: Penguin.
Goldhagen, Daniel (1997) *Hitler's Willing Executioners: Ordinary Germans and the Holocaust*. London: Abacus.
Hessel, Franz (1999) *Sämtliche Werke*, Vol. III. Paderborn: Igel.

Kellner, Douglas (2002) *Media Spectacle*. London: Routledge.

Kracauer, Isidor (1906) *Die Geschichte der Judengasse in Frankfurt am Main*. Frankfurt am Main: Kauffmann; repr. UCLAN Press.

Lefebvre, Henri (2000) *Everyday Life in the Modern World*, trans. Sacha Rabinovitch. London: Continuum.

Löwenthal, Leo (1961) *Literature, Popular Culture and Society*. Englewood Cliffs, NJ: Prentice Hall.

Löwenthal, Leo, and Guterman, Norbert ([1949] 1970) *Prophets of Deceit: A Study of the Techniques of the American Agitator*. Palo Alto, CA: Pacific Books.

Lukács, Georg (1971a) *Theory of the Novel*. London: Merlin Press.

— (1971b) *History and Class Consciousness*. London: Merlin Press.

Marcuse, Herbert (1958) *Soviet Marxism: A Critical Analysis*. New York: Columbia University Press.

Marx, Karl (1977) *Selected Writings*, ed. David McLellan. Oxford: Oxford University Press.

Penz, François, and Thomas, Maureen (eds) (1997) *Cinema and Architecture*. London: BFI.

Poe, Edgar Allan (1986) *The Fall of the House of Usher and Other Writings*. Harmondsworth: Penguin.

Roth, Joseph ([1924] 1999) *Rebellion*. London: Granta Books.

Shiel, Mark, and Fitzmaurice, Tony (eds) (2003) *Cinema and the City: Film and Urban Studies in a Global Context*. Oxford: Wiley/Blackwell.

Tönnies, Ferdinand ([1887] 1974) *Community and Association (Gemeinschaft und Gesellschaft)*. London: Routledge & Kegan Paul.

Vidler, Anthony (2000) *Warped Space: Art, Architecture and Anxiety in Modern Culture*. Cambridge, MA: MIT Press.

Weber, Max (1930) *The Protestant Ethic and the Spirit of Capitalism*. London: Allen & Unwin.

— ([1948] 1991) *From Max Weber: Essays in Sociology*, ed. H. H. Gerth and C. Wright Mills. London: Routledge.

Index